D1175745

Writers of the 21st Century

ISAAC ASIMOV

Edited by

JOSEPH D. OLANDER

and

MARTIN HARRY GREENBERG

Afterword by ISAAC ASIMOV

isaac asimov

Paul Harris Publishing / Edinburgh

First published in 1977 in the United Kingdom by Paul Harris Publishing,
25 London Street, Edinburgh, Scotland, by arrangement with
Taplinger Publishing Co., Inc., New York, N.Y.

ISBN 0 904505 40 5

CONTENTS

INTRODUCTION

Joseph D. Olander and Martin Harry Greenberg

IT HAS BEEN estimated that the English language has the capability of producing 10^{50} sentences. Since 10^6 is one million, it is obvious that the number of different sentences which the English language can produce is overwhelming. Despite this vast pool of available sentences, we find it difficult to come up with one which would most adequately describe the subject of this volume. After all, what one sentence could justifiably describe a man whose business card reads "Isaac Asimov . . . Natural Resource"?

Of course, this book is not about Isaac Asimov the man; it is about only a portion of the man—his science fiction. But it is the portion of the man that most Americans think about when they encounter the name; and it is the portion of the man that people on other shores know best through translation of his work. It certainly is the portion of the man which both editors of this book first came to know.

We came to Isaac Asimov as "fans." And we shall always be fans. But this book will be many things to different kinds of people. To fans, it may be too scholarly; to scholars, it may not be scholarly enough; to practitioners, it may be interesting but not relevant. In any case, this book is intended to broaden and heighten perspectives about Isaac Asimov's science fiction. It is in projecting this book towards that goal that we can describe its purpose. This book is not intended to be a book of "literary criticism." Rather, it is a book of literary perspectives about Isaac Asimov's science fiction. Some of these perspectives are favorable, while others are critical; some are theoretical, while others are descriptive and "practical." But all aim to share a particular perspective—a particular point of view—about Asimov's science fiction. The purpose of this book is not to assess whether Asimov is a "good writer" but to expand our awareness of perspectives and vision concerning his science fiction, it is appropriate to ask: Whose perspectives and whose vision? Asimov's or somebody else's? We shall read in one of the chapters of this book (and we shall have it reinforced in Asimov's own afterword to it) that Asimov is skeptical about analyses of "deep meaning" in his fiction.

Our answer to this is simply: So what? Life itself is different from writing about life, talking about it, painting it, filming it, or even thinking about it. The same differences—and the same kind of problems—arise between literature and writing about literature. But we should remember that every living thing can—and does—assign meaning to the environment around it. The human species, however, seems to be distinguished from other living things by an ability *to assign meaning to meaning*. Some essays in this book simply attempt to assign meaning to the meaning they perceive in Asimov's science fiction. It may not be Asimov's meaning, and it may not be your meaning—but it is meaning. Just as the more variety exists in our lives, the richer our lives become, so, too, the more meaning we can uncover about our science fiction, the richer it becomes for us. And multiplying meaning about Asimov's science fiction is what this book is all about.

In his article entitled "Other Worlds To Conquer," Asimov defined science fiction in the following way: "Science fiction is that branch of literature which is concerned with the impact of scientific advance upon human beings." Later, he modified the applicability of this definition to that part of the literature which can be classified as "social science fiction." It is fitting, therefore, that this book leads off with a chapter on "The Social Science Fiction of Isaac Asimov" by Marjorie M. Miller. Reinforcing the idea that science fiction which emphasizes "the human element" is social science fiction, Miller argues that Asimov attempts to accustom people to the notion of continuous change through his fiction. Acknowledging that Asimov's fiction has always demonstrated a concern for people and "social issues," she nevertheless shows that the idea of change is framed by the theme of man versus technology which is woven throughout his work. Asimov's obvious enjoyment of new gadgets and of new—and presumably better—ways of doing things should not, Miller indicates, cloud the more serious vision of technological man in his fiction. His fiction may deal with technologically ideal societies, but the reader is forced to think about the implications of science and technology for human beings as individuals and for their societies.

The second chapter describes the breadth and diversity of Asimov's writing. " 'Elementary, My Dear . . .': Asimov's Science Fiction Mysteries" by Hazel Pierce examines how Asimov has tried to meet the challenge of accommodating, as a writer, to the canons of both science fiction and mystery fiction. Her chapter asks: Is a good science fiction mystery a *good mystery?* Noting what she calls Asimov's "blending" techniques, Pierce assesses how—and how well—he has woven science fiction, the mystery, and the thriller together. She does not analyze Asimov's "straight" mysteries, e.g., *The Death Dealers, A Whiff of Death,* and *Murder at the ABA.* Instead she concentrates on his science fiction mysteries: the Wendell Urth stories, the Lucky Starr juveniles, *The Caves of Steel, The Naked Sun,* the stories in *Asimov's Mysteries,* and the nonseries science fiction mysteries.

In Chapter 3, "The Use of Technical Metaphors in Asimov's Fiction" by Maxine Moore, Asimov is pitted against Emerson and likened unto Benjamin Franklin in an attempt to demonstrate the underlying pattern of technical metaphors in much of his science fiction, principally in the stories and novels arranged by the following order: (1) the Thiotimoline group (*The Caves of Steel, The Naked Sun,* and *The End of Eternity*); (2) the robot group; (3) the beginning of the Galactic Empire (*The Stars, Like Dust, The Currents of Space,* and *Pebble in the Sky*); (4) *Foundation;* and (5) *The Gods Themselves.* Describing this portion of his work as "hard science fiction," Moore argues for a "technological approach" to Asimov's fiction as a necessary condition for its appreciation and enjoyment—both in style and in content. Her analysis really raises a number of fundamental issues concerning literary and humanistic approaches to "hard science fiction" in general. Asimov has given the reading public a number of popular science books on the ABC's of various sciences, and Moore seems to have found a way to use these ABC's of science as structural and thematic elements in reading his science fiction. Thus, according to this argument, Asimov's science fiction becomes a compendium for chemistry, computer technology, nuclear physics, astronomy, statistics and probability theory, and symbolic logic.

In Chapter 4, Charles Elkins zeroes in on the *Foundation* novels to point out some of the problems associated with the "softer" social sciences. "Asimov's *Foundation* Novels: Historical Materialism Distorted into Cyclical Psycho-History" criticizes these novels as lacking the essential qualities of good fiction—good characterization, interesting dialogue, and attractive style. These deficiencies, Elkins argues, flaw the novels, since the banality of Asimov's style, which reflects the mid-twentieth century, is so obvious in the world of 12,000 years into the future that the believability of this "future" world is diminished. Similarly, using some of Asimov's own definitions, Elkins evaluates the novels on substantive grounds and finds them lacking. Despite these problems, he is surprised at their widespread and continued success and popularity. He devotes this essay to the development of one perspective which may account for this phenomenon. The answer, he suggests, lies in a Marxist context and implies a shared feeling of alienation on the part of the reader in his own society with the stark fatalism inherent in a predetermined future world.

"Asimov's Golden Age: The Ordering of an Art," by Donald M. Hassler, takes us beyond an analysis of particular—or groups of—novels and stories in an effort to place Asimov's fiction in the development of science fiction. Emphasizing the importance of Asimov's vision of the Golden Age, he argues that the development of Asimov's science fiction is a reflection of the development of science fiction itself—from simple, uncomplicated literature to one of great complexity, differentiation, and diversity. This pattern of development, one may infer, may not be looked upon with equal satisfaction or joy by both practitioners and readers of science fiction.

Fern Milman's "Human Reactions to Technological Change in Asimov's Fiction" returns us to a tradition of assessing the relationship of humans to their technology. Characterizing Asimov's fiction as "technological science fiction," she shows how he depicts people's reactions to technological change coming from outside of their societies. Whereas Miller's earlier essay focuses on the impact of technology upon human beings in Asimov's fiction, Milman's essay deals with the other side of this relationship—people's impact upon technology. She points to the fears and hopes which technology generates in people and shows what effect attitudes and values can have upon technology when innovation and inventiveness are accepted in society.

Whereas several chapters here deal with people in relation to something—to change, to technology, to fatalism, or to science—Donald Watt's chapter deals with *people*. "A Galaxy Full of People: Characterization in Asimov's Major Fiction" examines in detail the *Foundation* novels, the *Robot* stories, and *The Gods Themselves* and, less closely, the "lesser novels" (*Pebble in the Sky, The Currents of*

Space, The End of Eternity, and *The Stars, Like Dust*) to ask: How does Asimov do in relation to characterization as an extremely important part of fiction? Asimov's fiction is popular, and this may be a function of interesting and entertaining plots or, as Elkins suggests in another essay, ideological content which appeals to the reader. But Watt argues that it is Asimov's handling of characters which is the central appeal of his fiction to readers. Continually stressing whether environment shapes characters or vice versa, he concludes that Asimov has achieved what many people believe is difficult in science fiction—the successful blending of the scientific imagination with the development of appealing characters. Along the way he makes assertions which should stimulate further discussion of Asimov's characterizations; e.g., that Bayta is one of the most "carefully developed female characters in science fiction before Panshin's Mia Havero in *Rite of Passage*" and that the personality triad in *The Gods Themselves* is one of the "top creations of alien characters in science fiction."

Joseph F. Patrouch's "Asimov's Most Recent Fiction" delineates major periods of Asimov's writing career as science fiction author and science popularizer and notes the changes in his development as a science fiction writer. He also summarizes the major distinctive traits which seem to characterize Asimov's science fiction. More importantly, he poses choices facing Asimov in relation to the latter's career as science fiction writer. Patrouch finds *The Gods Themselves* and "Waterclap" as evidence of one major direction with extremely significant import for the community of science fiction and for the world at large.

The Asimov that most readers know is the Asimov who created stories about robots and computers. In "Ethical Evolving Artificial Intelligence: Asimov's Computers and Robots," Patricia S. Warrick pictures Asimov as "the major voice describing the appearance of man's most radical technological innovation—artificial intelligence." Her essay outlines thirty-six years of Asimov's dramatization of this development from this first story on the subject in 1940 ("Robbie") to 1976 ("The Bicentennial Man") and of the human response—the hopes and fears—associated with it. The vision portrayed in this increasingly important subject is adroitly spelled out by Warrick. Although earlier chapters raise perspectives concerning Asimov's science- and technology-based science fiction and approaches to it (e.g., Miller, Milman, Moore, and Patrouch), it is here that we encounter, in a straightforward way, the assertion that the way to achieve our collective dreams—our utopias, as it were—is through "ethical technology." Although Asimov does ground his fiction firmly in science, Warrick suggests that the most important, and the most neglected, contribution of his work may be the establishment of a model ethical code which, if operationalized, may do more than anything else to ensure species survival. This essay, then, provides a fitting punctuation for the entire volume.

Writers of the 21st Century

ISAAC ASIMOV

1. The Social Science Fiction of Isaac Asimov

MARJORIE MITHOFF MILLER

THE BEGINNING of Isaac Asimov's career as a writer of science fiction coincided closely with the beginning of the development of "social science fiction." From 1926, when Hugo Gernsback began to publish *Amazing Stories*, until 1938, when John W. Campbell, Jr., took over as editor of *Astounding Science Fiction*, most of the science fiction stories being written were of the adventure or gadget types. Adventure science fiction is the story of brave deeds, heroes, battles, and incredible dangers—the kind of story whose setting could be changed from the mountains of Mars to the American West without making any substantive change in the plot or theme of the story. Gadget science fiction is the type in which the marvelous, or terrible, new inventions and discoveries such as television, antigravity devices, and atomic bombs, are the primary interest of the story. The characters in both of these types are likely to be quite one-dimensional and the plot quite routine. The rapid development of technology during the Twenties and Thirties contributed greatly to the reading public's interest in the gadget type of science fiction, and the adventure type has always had its own audience.

Campbell took over the editorship of the leading science fiction magazine at the beginning of a period of even greater popularity for science fiction. He had the talent to encourage and develop new writers, patience as well as the knowledge of what he wanted, and a clear editorial eye. He developed a market for, and encouraged the writing of, a new kind of science fiction. As Brian Ash has said:

> With Campbell's arrival in the editorial chair of *Astounding*, the more valuable aspects of science fiction as a means to explore the interaction between science and man were soon to be brought to the fore. A growing body of pulp science fiction emerged which no longer depended on brilliant extrapolations of machine wizardry. What became important about the machine in the genre was not its power to enable man to

overcome forces external to himself, but its uses and potentialities when directed inwards to his own organization. The coming of a machine civilization, in which the complexity of technological society would dictate an increasing reliance on machines to assist in decision-making, attracted major consideration.[1]

This type of science fiction, with its strong emphasis on the human element, is called "social science fiction." Asimov has said that science fiction is the most modern of all the branches of literature: "It is the one literary response to the problems peculiar to our own day and no other."[2] His definition of science fiction reflects his preference for "social science fiction" over the other types. He defines it as "that branch of literature which is concerned with the impact of scientific advance upon human beings." He recognizes the existence of the other types of science fiction—adventure and gadget—which do not fit this definition, but he feels that "social science fiction is the only branch of science fiction that is sociologically significant, and that those stories, which are generally accepted as science fiction . . . but do not fall within the definition I have given above, are not significant, however amusing they may be and however excellent as pieces of fiction."[3]

Asimov has amplified his definition, explaining the overriding importance of the human element, as follows:

> The most important implication of the definition is that sf deals first and foremost with human beings. This is a point never to be forgotten. It is true, it is possible to write good sf about a wormlike creature on Mars or about a mechanical man of metal and electricity. Human beings, as such, need not figure in the story in any way. Nevertheless, the story is successful only insofar as the non-human protagonist possesses traits which are recognizably human to the reader. The human body, in other words, may be missing, but the human soul must always be present.[4]

Science fiction has often been accused of being escape literature. There is no doubt that many science fiction stories are primarily escapist in intent; however, Asimov sees a difference between science fiction and other forms of escape literature such as westerns, true romances, and mystery stories; much of science fiction encourages its readers to think about the future—an occupation that can hardly be described as "escaping"—and the possibilities that the future seems to hold. "It is an odd form of escape literature," he writes, "that worried its readers with atom bombs, overpopulation, bacterial warfare, trips to the moon, and other such phenomena decades before the rest of the world had to take up the problems." [5] Even if thinking about problems one does not yet have to face, in preference to the ones already at hand, is a type of escape, there is still the possibility that such a means of escape is also preparation for facing those problems eventually. And they *will* have to be faced. For the first time in the world's history, mankind can no longer take the future for granted. Each individual's future may always have been uncertain, but mankind has never before been concerned about the future of the whole human race. We have created a world of such dangerous possibilities that "we wonder whether the planet itself might not die with us. We've got to think about the future now. For the first time in history, the future cannot be left to take care of itself; it must be thought about." [6]

One of the major functions of science fiction for Asimov is to accustom its readers to the idea of change. In contemplating the possible futures presented in science fiction, the reader is forced to recognize and accept the idea that things will change, and he is helped to surrender some of his traditional human passion for the status quo. Asimov sees this as a real benefit to our society, as we try to plan and implement the changes that will do the most good for humanity. He does not claim that science fiction writers set out deliberately to propagandize their readers and make them aware of the inevitability and value of change; they write interesting stories, usually based on scientific facts, and try to extrapolate from today's society the many different possible changes for man and his world in the future. Any benefits to the readers, or to society, are simply by-products of a job well done.

Even with the growing emphasis on mature science fiction in the Forties, the audience was still relatively small. Many people regarded science fiction as juvenile and unimportant and would not admit there could be anything of value in it. Not until the atomic bomb gave Americans a new realization of the influence that scientific advances might have on their lives did science fiction become more respectable. James Osler Bailey states that the new Machine Age, and the even newer Atomic Age, pose an important question for world leaders today: "How can new imagination, foresight, and long-range planning adjust world-policy to the new scale? . . . Scientific fiction . . . does not provide all this wisdom, but it may be one among many sources of suggestion. . . . Some of this fiction has dealt thoughtfully with concrete instances of startling new discoveries in science, their impact upon man's life, and the various possible readjustments to them." [7] Suddenly, with the advent of such new questions, many people who had been unconcerned about what scientists might be doing in their laboratories, believing that it was either incomprehensible or unimportant or both, found themselves anxious to understand scientific developments and their implications. Many of these people discovered that one of the most painless ways to begin was to read good science fiction.

Today, with science so much a part of our lives, no serious writer of science fiction will try to inflict on his readers inventions that are directly contrary to known scientific facts. His extrapolations may be very far out, and some of them indeed are, but they will not be based on proven scientific impossibilities. Even more important than any facts about science that may be gained from reading science fiction, however, is the *attitude* toward science, and the understanding of science's methods and its place in society, which the reader of science fiction may develop. He may learn that scientists are not infallible, that scientific advances must be watched and their use controlled, and that the sociological and humanitarian facets of our society are lagging behind the technological. If he does, he will surely be a more responsible citizen, more capable of participating intelligently in the decision-making process.

Asimov had begun reading science fiction in 1929, when he was nine years old. By 1938 he had for the first time written a story with the idea that he might be able to sell it to one of the magazines. That first story never sold, but the same year he did sell his third story, "Marooned Off Vesta," not to Campbell, who rejected it, but to *Amazing Stories.* It appeared in the March 1939 issue.

Asimov himself gives great credit to Campbell for his development as a writer, beginning with that first gentle and helpful rejection: "It is impossible to describe the pleasantness of a rejection like that. After that I wrote science fiction stories at the rate of one or more a month and brought each one in to John Campbell. Each time I came, I was invited in; each time there was a long friendly talk; each time he rejected the story with a helpful letter; each time I was all the more encouraged. As a writer, I owe John Campbell everything! and I know for a fact that I am not the only science fiction writer who does." [8]

Asimov has written some adventure and gadget stories, and some that are just plain fun, but the greatest part of his work is clearly social science fiction. How much of this was Campbell's influence and how much of it is Asimov's own natural inclination, we can't say, but even his earliest stories, written when he was not yet twenty, show a real concern for people, and for social issues. As he matured as a writer, he continued to be disturbed over many of the same social problems; the main difference between his early works and his later ones may be the subtlety with which he presents his message. In some of the earlier stories, the urgency of the message weakens the effectiveness of the story. Two early stories, "Half-Breed" (1940) and "Half-Breeds on Venus" (1940), were clearly motivated by Asimov's distress over the prevalence of racial prejudice.[9] The half-breeds of the stories were the children of mixed Martian and Earth parentage, and they were discriminated against on the Earth in the same ways that Jewish and black citizens have been in America. Asimov has remained concerned about this problem throughout his career, and it has been reflected in more than one of his works. He sees the diminishing of racial prejudice as a service that science fiction might help to perform for society, since science fiction writers, because they are dealing with larger areas of the universe, usually speak of all the people of Earth as simply "Earthmen," making no distinction among the races. Whether a man is black, brown, red, or white is not so important when he and his fellows are facing a green monster from Mars.

"Trends," the ninth story Asimov wrote, and the first one to appear in Campbell's *Astounding* (July 1939),[10] dealt with a theme that had not previously been used in science fiction—the possibility that people might be opposed to the idea of space flight and try to stop it. Following a devastating Second World War (1940, in Asimov's story), public sentiment against the destruction made possible by advanced technology leads to suspicion of all scientific experimentation, and a religious revival based on this feeling sweeps the country. News that John Harman is building a rocket for a flight to the Moon touches off a wave of religious opposition, based on the idea that it is somehow against the will of God for man to venture into space. When Harman tries to launch his Moon flight, there is a near riot, the rocket is sabotaged by an adherent of the new religion, and several people are killed and injured. Harman and a handful of devoted followers secretly build another rocket over the next five years. Feeling against science continues to grow, and eventually a law to control experimentation is passed. All experiments must be approved by the Federal Scientific Research Investigatory Bureau, which can ban completely any experiments it disapproves of. The Supreme Court upholds the constitutionality of the new law. The Moon rocket is launched anyway, in total secrecy. When the rocket returns after a successful flight around the Moon, and the public learns of the flight and the identity of the scientist, enthusiasm over this spectacular achievement reverses the trend against scientific experimentaton, and Harman finds himself a popular hero.

The specific threat from technological advances that man might lose the ability to control his own life is a recurrent theme in the science fiction of many writers, as are the problems of atomic energy and overpopulation. This threat is part of the problem Asimov presents in "Trends." (It is also worth noting that the Supreme Court case testing the constitutionality of the antiscience law in that story has to do with research into atomic power.)

The theme of man versus his own technology appears in many Asimov stories, from "Trends" to his science fiction novel *The Gods Themselves*. Resistance to science often takes the form, in Asimov's work, of an underground group, such as the Medievalists in *The Caves of Steel*, which works in some way to resist or subvert scientific and technological advances. This distrust of technology is a basic theme in all the robot stories. Indeed, Asimov's Three Laws of Robotics ended the Frankenstein-monster era of robot stories and brought in the more scientific story, in which mankind must make the decisions about the robots' capabilities and protect himself against any possibility that his creations might rise up and destroy him. The source of the difficulties that have to be solved in the robot stories is usually an apparent conflict between the ideal of the Three Laws, and the robots' application of the Laws. The Laws are: "1—A robot may not injure a human being, or, through inaction, allow a human being to come to harm. 2—A robot must obey the orders given it by human beings except where such orders would conflict with the First Law. 3—A robot must protect its own existence as long as such protection does not conflict with the First or Second Law." While these laws were implicit in the first two robot stories, "Robbie" (1940, under the title "Strange Playfellow") and "Reason" (1941), they were later worked out in detail by Asimov and Campbell together. The Three Laws appear in several of the stories, and as introductory material in *I, Robot*, a collection of short stories made into a novel by being placed in a framework of reminiscences by Dr. Susan Calvin, the world's leading practitioner of "robopsychology," at the end of her long and distinguished career.

Reading through Asimov's works, looking for evidence of his attitude toward man and technology, one is struck by his ambivalence. He clearly takes great delight in technological advances for their own sake—he just plain likes clever new gadgets, and new-and-better ways to do things—but he also recognizes that humanity cannot survive without allowing for individuality and uncontrollability, even "orneriness." No matter how advanced a technology may become, he feels, it will still have to be possible for people to escape the control of the machines in some way for life to have any meaning. One of his robot stories, "Evidence" (1946), in *I, Robot*, deals with problems that might arise when humanoid robots are developed to a state of perfection which makes it nearly impossible to tell a robot from a man. "Evidence" is the story of a successful public figure and politician, Stephen Byerley, who is accused, during an election campaign, of being a robot. He refuses, as a matter of principle, to do anything which would prove his humanity. His unscrupulous opponent asks Dr. Calvin for proof that Byerley is indeed a robot, but she refuses.

When public interest in Byerley's questioned humanity is at its peak, he is confronted by an obnoxious heckler during a televised speech and knocks the heckler down. Since no robot could possibly hit a man, unless to save another human life, this proves dramatically and unquestionably that Byerley is human. Or does it? Dr. Calvin realizes that the heckler could have been a robot, planted to give Byerley the opportunity to "prove" his humanity. She keeps quiet about this possibility because she likes Byerley and thinks he will make an excellent mayor—and if he *is* a robot, as she believes, he will be a better mayor than most men could be. The biggest difference between men and robots, she says, is that robots are "essentially decent."

"Evitable Conflict" (1950), also in *I, Robot*, is a sequel to "Evidence," following the career of Stephen Byerley to its greatest height: he is now the World Coordinator, the highest elected official of the federated world government. The world is united and at peace and has been divided into four semiautonomous Regions. Management of the production, distribution, and consumption of goods, and many other aspects of civilization, have been turned over to the "Machines," which are gigantic, highly sophisticated computers. Each Region has its own Machine, which is tied into the central Machine that plans for the whole world, fitting all economic activities into the optimum over-all pattern. The Machines have become so complex that no man can understand their workings, nor can any man successfully check on their results, because they are the end result of several "generations" of computer-designed computers, each one more complicated and sophisticated than the last. Man has indeed created a monster, in the sense that he can no longer control his creation but must allow himself to be controlled by it.

It is 2052 A.D., and Byerley has called in Dr. Calvin to help him understand why the all-powerful Machines seem to be making mistakes in their calculations. The two, who have been good friends ever since the beginning of Byerley's political career, discuss the kinds of mistakes the Machines are making, and their results. They finally come to realize that what the Machines are doing is protecting humanity from itself, and also from the clear knowledge that the Machines are really in charge; man has no freedom of choice any longer but must follow the dictates of the Machines. The Machines are bound by the Three Laws of Robotics and so must try to keep man from any harm—even injury to his pride. The Machines are also making "mistakes" which result in the removal from positions of responsibility of those people who are fundamentally opposed to the use of the Machines, and who want mankind to "get back to nature," because the Machines know that such a movement could only result in harm. Dr. Calvin expresses her confidence in the Machines in these words:

> "Stephen, how do we know what the ultimate good of Humanity will entail? We haven't at *our* disposal the infinite factors that the Machine has at *its!* . . . Perhaps an agrarian or pastoral civilization, with less culture and less people would be better. . . . Or perhaps a complete urbanization . . . or complete anarchy. . . . Only the Machines know, and they are going there and taking us with them."
>
> "But you are telling me, Susan, that . . . Mankind *has* lost its own say in its future."
>
> "It never had any, really. It was always at the mercy of economic and sociological forces it did not understand. . . . Now the Machines understand them; and no one can stop [the Machines] . . ."
>
> "How horrible!"
>
> "Perhaps how wonderful! Think, that for all time, all conflicts are finally evitable. Only the Machines, from now on, are inevitable!" [11]

However pleasing the prospect of turning the responsibility for our lives over to the computers might be to a woman of Susan Calvin's temperament, most of us would be more inclined to fight for the right to make our own decisions, even when we know that some of them will be wrong. This is not a typical ending for Asimov; usually, he recognizes the need for humanity to win out, either actually or spiritually, against the all-powerful Machines.

One story in which Asimov has used the old idea of man's creation getting out of control and almost getting away with it is "Nobody Here But . . ." (1953), collected in *Nightfall and Other Stories.* Two young scientists develop a portable computer (in 1953 computers took up whole rooms and got bigger as they got better), which they call "Junior." When Junior starts making modifications in his own design, and even answering the telephone when no one else is in the lab, they begin to worry. They realize they have devloped a totally new kind of machine, based on different principles of mathematics—perhaps a machine with a mind of its own, a consciousness that wants to stay alive and even reproduce itself. They are afraid that mankind might have to face millions of Juniors, fighting for control of the Earth. Junior has to be tricked into letting his creators unplug him. The story, which is a light-hearted one with a boy-meets-girl angle, ends with one of the young scientists happily married and the other one busily working on plans to build a Junior that they can control.

"Franchise" (1955), in *Earth Is Room Enough,* is a good example of the story that carries extrapolation from a current technological development to its ultimate possible conclusion. Beginning with the present-day practice of programming computers to predict election results almost before the polls close, Asimov imagines a future society in which data about all of the issues and candidates, and about every citizen, are fed into the giant computer, and then Multivac (Asimov's favorite name for the all-powerful computer) chooses *one* voter to cast the deciding vote in each election. The grandfather in the story amuses and amazes his grandchildren with stories of the old days, when everybody voted.

In *The End of Eternity* Asimov presents a highly sophisticated type of technological control over the lives of men. Time travel has been discovered, and also the ability to make changes in the course of history. "Eternity" has been established, staffed with workers who study each period from the 27th century to the 70,000th and make changes in "Reality" that they believe will be to humanity's benefit. One of the "Eternals" falls in love with a woman who turns out to be from the 111,394th century, and with her help he begins to question the wisdom of Eternity and its Reality changes. She tells him that her century has learned that in protecting man from his own adventurousness and curiosity, Eternity has postponed the discovery of space travel until a far future period, when the Galaxy will already be colonized by intelligent beings from other planets, and there will be no room beyond Earth for humanity. "Any system like Eternity," she says, "which allows men to choose their own future, will end by choosing safety and mediocrity. . . . Eternity must be done away with." [12] Asimov's hero agrees with her, and when events give him the opportunity to wipe out Eternity and restore all of human history to its path of Maximum Probability, he does so. Mankind is again free to be creative, to take risks, to make mistakes—and to do great things.

Asimov's own favorite among his stories, "The Last Question" (1956), is his ultimate projection of the increasingly symbiotic relationship between man and the computer into the incredibly distant future. As the computer becomes more and more all-pervasive and mankind becomes more and more "refined," a time is reached when both mankind and the universal computer are noncorporeal entities, the physical world having gradually over the eons run down. From time to time someone has asked the succeeding generations of computers how entropy might be reversed, and the computers have always replied that they do not have sufficient data to answer that question. The last human consciousness, just before it fuses its identity with AC (the Computer), asks the question one more time. AC spends a "timeless interval" in analyzing and correlating all of its information: "And it came to pass that AC learned how to reverse the direction of entropy. . . . The consciousness of AC encompassed all of what had once been a Universe and brooded over what was now Chaos. Step by step, it must be done. And AC said 'LET THERE BE LIGHT!' And there was light—" [13] This is certainly a neatly circular theory of the creation and ultimate fate of the entire Universe, as well as a projection of the final result of man's dependence on his machines.

Other stories that reveal various aspects of Asimov's ideas about man and his battle with advancing technology include "Lastborn" (1958), in which love and humanity come face to face with the demands of technology and refuse to submit; "The Feeling of Power" (1958), in which a man is hailed as a great innovator because he discovers that it is possible to do mathematical computations with a pencil and paper, thus freeing humanity from some of its dependence on the Machine (but his great discovery is pre-empted by the military); "All the Troubles of the World" (1958), in which Multivac, distressed at being given more and more of mankind's problems to solve, attempts to "commit suicide"; and "The Machine that Won the War" (1961), in which a group of scientists discovers that each of them has been disregarding the decisions of the computer that was supposedly running the war effort, and making more intelligent decisions on his own. And they have won their war by ignoring their Machine! [14] "Exile to Hell" (1968), which Asimov wrote after ten years of writing nonfiction almost to the exclusion of science fiction, envisions a possible world in which man is so completely dependent on his technology that the gravest crime a person can commit is destruction of equipment. After all, a murderer may kill only one person, or at most a few, but a man who destroys vital equipment may cause the deaths of hundreds or even thousands of people. [15]

Asimov's return to science fiction (although he still writes mostly nonfiction) was crowned with the publication in 1972 of *The Gods Themselves*, a novel with man's dependence on, and danger from, technology as its major theme. In the 21st century a new source of power—inexpensive, apparently inexhaustible, and pollution-free—has been discovered. It depends on an exchange of materials between Earth and an alternate world in a parallel universe that man has no knowledge of, or control over. All the scientists really know is that certain metals from that world produce tremendous energy when brought into this world, and that the inhabitants of that other world know how to make the exchange. It seems clear that the Earth materials they take into their own world must produce the same great power there. One young scientist discovers that the alternate-world material is gradually creating an instability in this world that will eventually cause the Sun to explode. Through painstaking, tentative communications with the other world, the scientist comes to believe that someone in that other world fears the same dangers in the para-Universe. The scientific Establishment on both sides is reluctant to believe that there is any danger and wants to continue to exchange energy-producing materials.

The middle section of the novel is set in the alternate world and presents a fascinating picture of another life-form, totally different from humanity, but with those all-important human-like emotions and problems that enable us to identify with them enough so that while we read we believe. In the final section of the novel, set in a colony on the Moon, the protagonist (another scientist) finds a way for Earth to continue to have all the power it needs, without the attendant danger. He realizes that the dangerous imbalance can be counteracted by beginning to make exchanges of material with still other alternate worlds, with still different laws of chemistry and physics. This sort of round-robin exchange among several worlds will thereby re-create the necessary balance of the forces in each world that is involved.

As we have seen earlier, Asimov has continued throughout his career to have ambivalent feelings about technology and its effect on man's life. He has great faith in man's ability to use technology for his own good, as in *The Gods Themselves*, but at the same time, he has repeatedly shown that he recognizes the danger of too much control over men's lives. Many of his stories revolve around a protagonist who insists on doing something human, whether it is simply going outdoors when it is no longer necessary or proper, or learning to do something that the computers can do for you, or working to defeat the technology that controls his life. Humanity remains triumphant, if not always victorious, in the battle against an overpowering technology.

Atomic weapons and atomic energy are a unique and overwhelming part of the technology that threatens us. Asimov has frequently used atomic devastation as one aspect of the background for his stories, instead of making it a major component of the plot. Scientists and science fiction writers were well aware of the possibility of nuclear fission long before the Manhattan Project's success became known, so it is not surprising to find references to atomic bombs and radiation in stories written before 1945. "Trends," as we saw, predicted a Second World War of great devastation, but did not specify what types of weapons would be used.

In "Half-Breed" the protagonist "thanked all the powers that were . . . for the fact that war was a thing of two centuries past, for otherwise atomic power would have been the final ruination of civilizaton. As it was, the coalition of World Powers that now controlled the great force of Atomic Power proved it a real blessing and were introducing it into Man's life in the slow, gradual stages necessary to prevent economic upheaval." [16]

"History" (1941) contains a reference to tiny "Drops of Death" falling from spaceships and silently but irresistibly eating out fifteen-foot craters with their powerful radioactivity. "Not Final!"

(1941) has a character mention that atomic power would enable a spaceship to escape even the powerful gravity of Jupiter. In "Black Friar of the Flame" (1942) the great destruction wrought by an "Atomo projectile" plays a minor part in the story, and in "Death Sentence" (1943) Asimov mentions the complete destruction of an ancient civilization by some overwhelming force.[17] In none of these stories does atomic warfare or atomic energy play a decisive role, yet it is clear that the possibility of such developments was often on Asimov's mind as he wrote. He has described his reaction as a science fiction writer to the news of the atomic bomb in *Nightfall and Other Stories:* "The dropping of the atomic bomb in 1945 made science fiction respectable. Once the horror at Hiroshima took place, anyone could see that science fiction writers were not merely dreamers and crackpots after all, and that many of the motifs of that class of literature were now permanently part of the newspaper headlines. . . . Quite apart from the frightening aspects of nuclear explosions . . . I also felt that reality might have a stultifying effect on the field." [18] Science fiction writers would now have to deal with a whole new reality that had intruded into their world of fantasy.

Another Asimov story written fairly early in the Atomic Age is "No Connection" (1948), in which a highly-developed race of bears discovers evidence of a long-vanished species of Primate whose fossils are concentrated in areas of great radioactivity. As they puzzle over what could have caused this strange occurrence, they also learn that a race that inhabits a far distant continent (the "Eekahs," who appear to have descended from chimpanzees) has developed a terrifying new weapon which "involves the bombardment of an element they call plutonium . . . by objects called neutrons." [19] As the story ends, the bear scientists are still trying to understand what connection there could possibly be between all that radioactivity and the concentration of fossils of the Primitive Primates. They are not even wondering about any possible connection between that and the new weapon they have learned about. This story is another example where the urgency of Asimov's message gets in the way of his story-telling.

Pebble in the Sky is set on an Earth made so radioactive by atomic warfare that after fifty thousand years only small areas are habitable, and the population must be maintained at no more than twenty million. This is done by having all citizens report for euthanasia when they reach sixty—or even earlier if illness or accident prevents them from being a productive member of society. This Earth is the outcast world of the Galaxy, feared and hated by the citizens of the other worlds, so that Earth's citizens cannot leave their planet to find a new life somewhere else in the Galaxy. *The Stars, Like Dust* also begins on a devastated Earth but does not stay there. The story moves on to other worlds, and Earth's radio-activity is not as vital an element of the plot as it is in *Pebble in the Sky*.

One Asimov story that is *about* atomic weapons, rather than using them as one aspect of the setting, is the short-short story "Hell-Fire" (1956), found in *Earth Is Room Enough*. A group of scientists has gathered to view the first extremely slow-motion film of the explosion of an atomic bomb. To their shock and horror, the film clearly shows the face of Satan, complete with horns and demonic grin, formed in the mushroom cloud of the explosion. Although Asimov claims no religious affiliation himself, some of his most effective works have strong religious or theological elements because he recognizes the importance of religion in man's history, and because, as he says, he is interested in religion along with many other subjects.

"The Gentle Vultures" (1957), in *Nine Tomorrows*, is another, much longer story with the threat of atomic warfare as its theme. Here Asimov uses the common science fiction idea of Earth's being watched by intelligent beings from more advanced civilizations in other parts of the Galaxy. The Hurrians have been policing the Galaxy for a long time, watching for signs that any planet has developed atomic weapons. Other "large primate" civilizations that have discovered atomic power have always promptly fought an atomic war. Then the Hurrians—peace-loving, noncompetitive, small primates—go in and help the survivors to rebuild their civilization, and also eugenically alter them so that they will be nonaggressive. Then they exact "taxes" from every world that they have "helped." This time, though, the Hurrians have been on the far side of the Moon for fifteen years, waiting for Earth's atomic war, and it still hasn't come. To try to find out why there hasn't been a nuclear war yet, they send a scout ship (a "flying saucer," of course) to Earth to abduct a large primate so that they can study his mind. When the man learns that the Hurrians are waiting for atomic war so that they can pick up the pieces and exact tribute, he calls them "vultures"—and the mental image they receive upsets them so much that they abandon their tentative plan to start the war themselves and return to Hurria, deeply concerned about the fate of the Galaxy. They are positive that large primates whose competitive, aggressive natures have not been gentled by atomic war and the subsequent Hurrian help will be the end of civilization in the Galaxy as soon as they develop space travel.

It is obvious that Asimov's stories cannot be neatly divided into discrete categories—these stories are about atomic energy, and these are about overpopulation, and so on. There is a great deal of overlap, and most stories will contain references to many different sociological concerns. Population control might be effected by technological advances or, failing that, by atomic warfare. Population growth that is *not* controlled will, on the other hand, put great demands on technology to provide enough food and shelter for everyone. Asimov's concern about atomic energy tapered off as the world seemed to adapt to the existence of this threat, and the horror of atomic war became at least a little more remote and perhaps a little less certain. At the same time, the dangers of overpopulation began to come into prominence in his work.

"Mother Earth" (1949), in *The Early Asimov, Book Two*, is an early Galactic Empire story in which the Outer Worlds have to decide what to do about the Earth, the original home of all the inhabitants of the Galaxy (Asimov's now-familiar idea of a Galaxy populated entirely by human beings). Earth's population of sixty billion poses a threat to the comfortably underpopulated Outer Worlds, who fear both immigration from Earth and war. Through a devious plot worked out by one of Earth's leaders, Earth is defeated in a war with the Outer Worlds and put in "quarantine" by those worlds. Earth is thus forced to face and solve her problems instead of relying on the possibility of emigration to the Outer Worlds, or technological help from those worlds, to solve them.

A common method for population control in science fiction is by "rationing" babies, so that each couple has to have permission for a child—and perhaps only the most exceptional parents are allowed to have a second baby. In *Pebble in the Sky* babies are "rationed," but, as we have seen, population control also affects the end of life by decreeing that everyone must die at sixty. It is a serious crime to attempt to evade this mandatory euthanasia.

One of Asimov's most extended and chilling looks at one possible future for Earth is provided in *The Caves of Steel*. This is one of Asimov's two novels which successfully combine the mystery story and science fiction. It is laid in the fifty-first century. The population of Earth has reached eight billion; almost the entire population is crowded into the huge cities, leaving the rest of the land free for agriculture; every aspect of life is controlled in an effort to make the overcrowded conditions as bearable as possible. Each citizen has a "rating" which depends on the importance of his job, and this rating determines the kind of housing, food, and access to community-run amenities that he is entitled to. No one has a private kitchen or bathroom, since they have been abandoned as entirely too wasteful of space and resources. Again, children are rationed; the government decides when a couple will be allowed to have a baby, and whether or not they will be allowed more than one.

Elijah Baley, a New York City detective, is one of the heroes of the book; the other is R. Daneel Olivaw, a robot detective from Spacetown, an Outer Worlds colony set up on Earth. Baley lives in a New York City with a population of twenty million. He sees the "first problem of living" in such an overcrowded world as being to minimize friction with all of the other people who have to live in such close proximity. The best way to do this is for people to be scrupulous in their observance of all the customs and regulations that encompass every part of daily life, so as not to offend or inconvenience their neighbors, from whom there is never any real escape. To accommodate its vast swarms of people, the entire city is thickly built up, with much of it underground, and has been covered over completely, so that people rarely see the sky or the sun, and never without some sort of shielding. This condition has existed for so long that the majority of people on Earth are desperately afraid of the open air.

The fifty Outer Worlds were settled a thousand years before the time of this story, by men from Earth. Now each world has its own civilization and resists any immigration from Earth, in order to keep its society just the way it wants it. Earth, therefore, is hemmed in with its enormous population and cannot find any real solution to its problems. Man has long since lost the urge to colonize any new unoccupied worlds, because of his closed-in existence. Robots are widely used on the Outer Worlds but are feared and distrusted on Earth, and efforts to use them are bitterly resented.

In *The Naked Sun*, the sequel to *The Caves of Steel*, we get a close-up picture of the "ideal" life on one of the Outer Worlds that figured in the earlier work. All of the Outer Worlds are thinly populated and have economies that make use of robots. Solaria, the planet to which Baley is sent to solve a murder, presents a picture of the most extreme dependence on robots. Each citizen of Solaria lives on a large estate of his own, attended by a great number of specialized robots. The human population is twenty thousand while the robot population is two hundred million. Many of the robots are engaged in the industries of Solaria, which include the development and manufacture of robots of all types. In striking contrast to the crowded Earth, where privacy is almost impossible, Solaria has developed a society in which human contact is at an absolute minimum. Even married couples actually "see" each other (that is, are physically present in the same room) only at scheduled intervals, although they share the same estate. All social visits and business conferences are conducted by three-dimensional televiewing, rather than "seeing."

Fetuses are surgically removed from the mother's womb soon after conception and are cared for in a state-run "farm" from then until maturity. Children and parents never know each other. Robots tend to all of the physical needs of the children. The Solarians regretfully admit that they have not been able to train the children to be alone all the time; while they are young they still must be allowed some contact with one another, but they are gradually taught to depend on "viewing" and to do without "seeing." Solarians learn to abhor the very idea of actually "seeing" another person.

The Naked Sun gives a picture of a society that might be regarded as ideal from the point of view of technological advancement, and yet it is clearly not ideal in the human sense. While Earth's overcrowding has led to a timid humanity, with little spirit of adventure or initiative, Solaria's artificial isolation has led to a people with little feeling for each other and no way to work together in an emergency. The advanced technology which permits easy communication with anyone on the planet has actually made real communication—communication of human understanding, empathy, and mutual helpfulness—much more difficult.

Asimov intended to write a third novel to complete the picture he was presenting. It was to have been about another of the Outer Worlds, Aurora, which had achieved a balance between the extremes of Earth and Solaria. It has not been completed because Asimov decided, part way through it, to devote his time to science popularization rather than fiction.

Many of Asimov's stories about overpopulation simply present the problem, not the solution. He appears to feel that no solution will be possible until people are thoroughly awakened to the nature of the threat posed by our growing population. In "Living Space," (1956), in *Earth Is Room Enough*, man has discovered how to transport people to any one of an infinite number of "possible," variant, uninhabited Earths. These alternatives to reality, being infinite in number, enable Earth to take care of a population of one trillion. Each of some three hundred billion of Earth's families lives all alone in the only house on one of three hundred billion alternate, uninhabited Earths; they stay away from the inhabited ones. Unfortunately, competition arises from some of those possible inhabited Earths, and then from surplus population from other planets peopled with alien creatures, making the neat solution to the population explosion less ideal than it had seemed. The story ends right there—with the hoped-for solution disappearing, and no other solution in sight.

Asimov has also dealt with the problem of overpopulation often in his nonfiction works. For example, in "The Power of Progression" he says "I live . . . in the richest nation on Earth, in the period of that nation's maximum power. What a pity, then, that it is all illusion and that I cannot blind myself to the truth. My island of comfort is but a quiet bubble in a torrent that is heaving its way downhill to utter catastrophe. I see nothing to stand in its way and can only watch in helpless horror. The matter can be expressed in a single word: Population." [20]

In "Exile to Hell," discussed previously, one of the characters justifies the extreme penalty for equipment damage by saying, "We live in a crowded world with no margin for error." [21] Of course his "crowded world" turns out to be the Moon, where equipment would indeed be a matter of life and death—and the appalling "Hell" to which criminals are exiled is the primitive, harsh Earth.

While the question of overpopulation does not figure very largely in *The Gods Themselves*, the necessity of continuing to provide all of the energy Earth's two billion people need and have become used to is what stops Earth's politicians and scientists from accepting the idea that the energy-exchange might be dangerous. People regard the Electron Pump as "the key to human paradise" and refuse to believe any crackpot who tries to tell them otherwise.

Throughout his writing career Asimov has shown his concern for the problems that humanity has to face. By examining a few of his stories and novels we have seen the various ways in which he has expressed this concern. Some stories seem to have been written primarily to encourage the reader to recognize and think about some particular problem. Some stories present the problem but suggest no solution; other stories offer possible solutions. Occasionally, Asimov is pessimistic about man's chance of surviving and maintaining his human individuality; more often he has seemed to feel that man's determination to run his own life will somehow win out over any obstacles that science and technology might put in the way.

From 1945 on, Asimov was quite pessimistic about the prospects for avoiding atomic war, but he usually pictured humanity as surviving and rebuilding its civilization. Only an occasional story, such as "No Connection," presents the possibility of man's being completely destroyed and some other species rising to an intelligent, civilized society.

Asimov's major worry in the last twenty years, as far as the fate of humanity is concerned, has been overpopulation, and he has become increasingly pessimistic. He does not believe that humanity will be able to solve this problem soon enough—if ever. But if the problem is not solved intelligently, nature will work out a solution, or series of solutions—warfare, starvation, disease.

Asimov began to write science fiction because he was determined to be a writer, and science fiction was what he knew best and enjoyed the most. As he matured as a writer, science fiction itself was coming to maturity as a serious and responsible type of literature. Asimov and other science fiction authors wrote more and more works that sought to waken humanity to the dangers it faces. As he says in "The Serious Side of Science Fiction":

> All the plagues that threaten us with doom today; from the arsenals of horror bombs and nightmare germs, to the pollution that is poisoning our air and water . . . from the tensions of packing crowds to the lunacies of human prejudice; all, all, all have been treated at length and over and over from every aspect in science fiction. . . .
> But that part of our job is done. We didn't do it well enough. We didn't do it quickly enough. The task was too great; the human population was too numerous . . . too determined on its folly . . . too obstinate in finding sufficient unto the day the evil thereof.
> —Yet, never mind. Too little and too late, but what we could do, we have done.[22]

2. "Elementary, My Dear . . .":

Asimov's Science Fiction Mysteries

HAZEL PIERCE

> I didn't break down in tears. "Just the same you'll do it. You've done mysteries before, haven't you?"
>
> "Of course, I've done mysteries before," he said indignantly. "I've written straight mysteries and science fiction mysteries; novels and short stories; for adults, for teen-agers, and for grade-schoolers."

THE ABOVE exchange appears in *Murder at the ABA*, that Chinese puzzle box masquerading as a mystery novel.[1] The indignant gentleman speaking is one of the characters, a certain Isaac Asimov, who has been groaning over an assignment by Doubleday to write a mystery novel to be entitled *Murder at the ABA*. In addition to the credentials given above, author Asimov in another part of the novel describes character Asimov as a man who "has written on every subject imaginable," who has 163 books to his credit at last count, and for whom "writing is painless."

Whether or not readers take all of these remarks about character Asimov as autobiographical of author Asimov, they can rest assured that the list as given above is true. Isaac Asimov does have to his credit straight mysteries and science fiction mysteries, in long and short forms, for different age groups. Of his first straight mystery,[2] and of *Murder at the ABA*, we shall have little to say, other than to acknowledge their existence. More pertinent here are the science fiction mysteries, and particularly those which Asimov has linked together in series by repeated appearances of an amateur detective or of detective partners.[3]

In his Introduction to *Asimov's Mysteries*, Asimov recalls that in the late 1940s he heard an argument to the effect that science fiction and detective fiction could not be combined successfully because of the different natures of the two genre. The argument proved to be a stimulus, not a deterrent. Since 1949 Asimov has proceeded to combine science fiction and mystery in novels and short stories; to prove his ease in the field, in one short-short, "A Loint of Paw," he spoofs the analytic mind.

In January 1949 *Astounding* published Asimov's first combination, "The Red Queen's Race," now in *The Early Asimov, Book Two.* This story offered a two-pronged problem for the authorities. Dr. Elmer Tywood, professor of nuclear physics, is found dead in the central source chamber of one of the nation's largest atomic power plants. As if the inexplicable death were not enough, the authorities find that the atomic plant has been drained completely of its fissionable matter—not exploded, but drained. The narrator in the story, an unnamed investigator, must answer two questions. Is a crime involved in the man's death? Is international intrigue involved in the draining of the energy source? Presumably all countries are bound by the "Compromise of Sixty-five" following World War III, a compromise which proposed to assure world peace and control of atomic power. However, there is still fear that a person or a combine might exercise an ethical concern about atomic power and plan a series of such drainings of all available power sources.

This first Asimov mystery has a narrator whose method of operation recalls the hard-boiled detective of detective fiction. Working alone, the able investigator from the Bureau uses a tough approach and veiled threats to gain his information. In one of the interviews with a graduate student who had worked with the dead professor, the investigator leans not too subtly on the young man in order to get him to talk. In the words of the investigator, "It worked. I knew it would, because everyone reads mysteries and knows all the clichés."

Not everyone reads mysteries and knows all the clichés, but many of those who do read mysteries certainly know the model first established by Edgar Allan Poe in the 1840s and honed to a fine edge by Arthur Conan Doyle in the 1890s. The pattern is a simple one. A problem, usually a crime or an act with political overtones, presents itself for solution. Between the commission of the crime and the apprehension of the criminal, the march of events in a mystery story strongly suggests that of classical drama. Following the description of the crime and the introduction of the detective (exposition) comes the investigation of clues, witnesses, suspects, and consideration of multiple solutions and complicating factors (rising action). Upon completion of the inquiry the detective dramatically announces his success (climax); his explanation or offering of his proof (falling action) leads quickly to the apprehension or at least the naming of the criminal (denouement).

Obviously there are significant differences between the two. In classical drama emphasis falls on the protagonist's definition of self as he acts in response to the conflict or problem. In mystery fiction the emphasis is on the ratiocinative process itself. A Sherlock Holmes or a Hercule Poirot may merit a reader's interest, but as a personality he is clearly subordinate to the art of detection which he practices. In "The Murders in the Rue Morgue" Poe established this priority by devoting several pages to a discussion of the analytical method before introducing his detective, C. Auguste Dupin. First defining the analytical method as "the moral activity which disentangles," Poe proceeded to emphasize the importance of observation, memory, the careful weighing of observations and inferences, and, most importantly, imagination and judgment. Following the full discussion of the method, Poe then demonstrated that method in Dupin's performance, characterized by a fine balance between reason and mystery, data and action, order and violence.

Although readers accept the subordination of the man to the mind, the detective's personal uniqueness has become a convention. Again Poe set the model with Dupin—brilliant, eccentric, and semisecluded from the world at large. Conan Doyle in Sherlock Holmes gave us a detective of quite similar qualities, but one more sharply drawn in detail, even to the point of a list of twelve "limits" in the second chapter of *A Study in Scarlet*. If such a person is to operate in the general society, he must have a link with more common men. Both Poe and Doyle gave their detectives an assistant-friend, a person of intelligence but less gifted with powers of ratiocination. A foil for the detective, the assistant-friend serves also as a reporter on the detective's more esoteric activities. The ability of the detective to elicit facts and to deduce the right meaning from those facts, with little noticeable effort on his part, casts an aura of magic about him. The assistant, such as Holmes' friend Dr. Watson, stands as the reader's surrogate in this magical world.

Twentieth-century writers have rung many colorful variations on this pattern. The gifted amateur has moved over to admit to his company the police detective, for one, operating within the law but at times outside the system to gain his ends. An offshoot of the single policeman is the police team, whose uniqueness lies not in individual effort but in the team's finesse with police procedure. On the other side of the amateur detective stands the "private eye" or hard-boiled detective. Not one to solve his cases at home in a comfortable armchair or in quiet upper-class drawing rooms, the private eye works in the streets and in high-crime purlieus. Usually a cynical loner, interested in the fee which has been promised to him, he often is forced by events to take an ethical as well as a financial concern in his case, particularly when he must become the only instrument for crude, on-the-spot justice. His methods may well be the ones to which Asimov's anonymous investigator refers in "The Red Queen's Race." At some distance from these detectives is the spy. His operations in an international setting shift detective focus away from domestic issues. Authors of spy novels, while plotting their characters' careers in diplomatic circles or underground organizations, often deemphasize deduction by liberally infusing derring-do and action-adventure.

Along with these several variations of the character of the detective, now common usage, one major shift in the conventional overall pattern has been made to good effect. R. Austin Freeman has discussed the intellectual satisfaction expected by the readers of mystery stories and the pattern which had given yeoman service in fulfilling that expectation. He then offered what he termed "an experiment, an inverted detective story in two parts," [4] an experiment demonstrated effectively in his own Dr. Thorndyke stories. The inverted method first gives the reader a complete description of the crime, its motivation and its commission, plus identification of the perpetrator. In the second part of the story the detective goes through the deductive process, turning already known facts into evidence. The anticipated intellectual satisfaction rests in the reader's ability to pre-guess which facts are hard evidence. No longer an experiment, the inverted detective story is now well-established in the arsenal of conventions available to the writers of mysteries. [5]

Perhaps since many people do read mysteries and do know many of the clichés or conventions, a smart detective can get what he wants from his witness. But a mere knowledge of the conventions is not enough to work out a good mystery story. It certainly will not suffice to work out a good *science fiction* mystery.

How does a writer combine these two genre—one with a firmly set pattern (to the point that it has been termed "formula" literature), the other with a fluid but developing set of imperatives? Readers of science fiction will expect to enjoy variations on a completely different set of conventions from those of mystery fiction: the impact of a scientific invention or discovery on a future era; extrapolation of a contemporary social trend into the near or distant future; galactic settings; alien cultures; focus on the reaction of human beings to machines; time travel both backward and forward into human history; parallel or alternate worlds made credible and scientifically plausible. Readers of science fiction anticipate technical and scientific sophistication balanced with futuristic or prophetic vision. Science fiction promises satisfaction in the imaginative speculation of a new situation, possibly one never to be tested in the reader's real world.

When Isaac Asimov first tested his ability to combine the mystery story with science fiction, he was not alone in that effort; other writers were experimenting, with varying degrees of success. Miriam Allen deFord in *Space, Time & Crime* offers thirteen specimen short stories as testimony of this effort. The authors represented in this volume—Anthony Boucher, Fritz Lieber, Avram Davidson, and others—all published their tales originally between 1949 and 1963. "Crisis, 1999" by Frederic Brown carries the copyright date of 1949, contemporary with Asimov's "The Red Queen's Race." In 1950, Hal C. Clement published *Needle* in book form, following its initial appearance in two parts in *Astounding* (May–June 1949). Alfred Bester's *The Demolished Man* appeared in 1953, the same year Asimov's first robot detective novel, *The Caves of Steel*, appeared in *Galaxy* (October–December).

The authors mentioned above tried out various detective conventions. Frederic Brown's Bela Joad, working in a 1999 world not too different from that of 1949 or today, acts much as the conventional hard-boiled detective. Alfred Bester allows his detective, a professional, the powers of telepathy, thus going outside the conventions of detective fiction to give the detective an unfair advantage over the reader (this kind of authorial magic is what Asimov terms a "pocket frannistan" in the Introduction to *Asimov's Mysteries*). Hal C. Clement in *Needle* uses alien beings as both criminal and detective. His detective, the Hunter, is a symbiotic creature, one who must seek out a compatible human host in whom to exist while he tracks down the renegade symbiote, also housed in a human host. Upon discovering the presence of his "guest," the human Robert Kinnaird helps in tracking down the criminal and bringing him to justice.

What distinguishes Asimov's detective science fiction from that of his contemporaries? What is Asimov's special achievement that merits Sam Moskowitz's accolade: "When it comes to blending the two [science fiction and detective fiction] Isaac Asimov reigns supreme," wrote Moskowitz in reply to A. E. Murch who had lauded both Asimov and Frederic Brown for this accomplishment.[6] One answer lies with the word *blending*. Asimov has balanced the demands of the two genre by building on their common ground.

Both types impose the need for logical, analytical method and for subtle, acute reasoning—applied in the one instance to untangling a puzzle in immediate time and place, the other in speculative time and place. Both exercise the special knowledge of the author. Detective fiction demands a knowledge of police procedures and an understanding of the deductive process; science fiction, of the scientific premises on which the speculative world is based.

A second answer lies with Asimov's own track record. He has been able to draw on his ingenuity without undue strain or awkward repetition. In at least three cases he has expanded an initial appearance of his detective characters into a series without sacrificing either his powers of deduction or his scientific reasonableness. The last four of the Lucky Starr juveniles, the Robot novels, and the Wendell Urth short stories testify to this point. If these three series do not assure his claim to successful mastery of the hybrid form, Asimov has tried several variations on the theme, some illustrated by the non-Urth stories in *Asimov's Mysteries*, to be discussed later.

Several stories, not in *Asimov's Mysteries*, bear mention for the insight they offer on his experimentation, sometimes playful, with different mystery conventions. In "Hostess" (1951, later collected in *Nightfall and Other Stories*), Asimov switched the roles expected by a reader when he has a wife solve the mystery of mental parasites which threaten interstellar peace. Her husband, a policeman with the World Security Board, emerges as a murderer and a cover-up artist for those very minds. "Let's Get Together" (1957), later collected in *The Rest of the Robots*, deals with cold war espionage in a future era. In "Author! Author!" (written as early as 1943, but not published until 1964 in *The Unknown Five*, edited by D. R. Bensen), Asimov spoofed literary detectives who take over and dominate their authors. While these single stories have merit in their own right, the series stories provide the best area for examining Asimov's technique in blending detective or mystery and science fiction conventions.

One might quibble at the inclusion of the Lucky Starr juveniles in a discussion of Asimov's detective science fiction, but this series is worth our notice if only to follow the shift of the title character from the conventional hero of space opera and action-adventure to the hero as cool, rational space detective. The title of the first book of the series is revelatory: *David Starr: Space Ranger* (1952).[7] It tempts us to substitute another well-known epithet, *Lone Ranger*, especially after we read the book and meet John Bigman Jones, friend and cohort of David Starr. Bigman can well serve as a space-Tonto, for he, too, comes from a different culture than the main character, albeit another culture in the galaxy instead of the continent. Together they encounter many exciting adventures and solve all problems. In the second book of the series, *Lucky Starr and the Pirates of the Asteroids* (1953), our hero continues his adventurous exploits, complete with push-tube duel in outer space. The Asimov character in *Murder at the ABA* may well have had similar juveniles in mind when he spoke of writing for "teen-agers and grade-schoolers."

With the third book of the series, *Lucky Starr and the Oceans of Venus* (1954), Lucky begins the shift from space ranger to space detective. (Note that this book was issued in the same year as the robot-detective novel *The Caves of Steel*.) Now more prone to rely on the powers of his mind and on scientific data rather than on cleverness and physical courage alone, Lucky Starr continues to solve the puzzles of his universe: intergalactic conspiracy, conspirators who use telepathic animal extensions of their power, and computers misused to control and to gain power. One brief but telling exchange between Lucky and Bigman illustrates how far Asimov has moved his duo from a Lone Ranger–Tonto relationship to a Sherlock Holmes–Dr. Watson one. At one point Bigman excitedly questions Lucky about something he doesn't understand. Lucky's answer is not the expected explanation but a sentiment worthy of the Great Detective himself: "Actually, it's only a matter of logic."

In the remaining three novels of the Lucky Starr series the two characters retain this relationship, but a new element enters the picture—robots. *Lucky Starr and the Big Sun of Mercury* (1956) and *Lucky Starr and the Moons of Jupiter* (1957) share publication years with Asimov's second robot-detective novel *The Naked Sun* (first in serial form, 1956, and in book form, 1957). The last Lucky Starr book, *Lucky Starr and the Rings of Saturn* followed in 1958.

These three novels present Lucky Starr less as a trouble-shooter and more as a problem-solver for the Council of Science of Earth in their continuing confrontation with the Sirian civilization, a robot-saturated economy. The two "space detectives" solve the stolen robot caper, block the use of Venusian V-frogs to control human emotions, and finally in the last novel they avert a serious galactic struggle when the Sirians move in to establish colonies in Earth's stellar system. While this last novel moves more closely to spy-thriller conventions, the two preceding ones rely more heavily on the personal deductive process. Joseph Patrouch labels *Big Sun of Mercury* and *Moons of Jupiter* as "first-rate science fiction mystery stories that anyone—science fiction fan or mystery fan—can enjoy reading." [8]

Elijah Baley, plain-clothes man, City of New York Police Department, made his first appearance in the pages of *Galaxy* in 1953. His appearance anticipated that of Wendell Urth, Asimov's amateur detective, by just one year. The chronology and close appearance of Asimov's three major detective characters suggest that the author was experimenting with several different ways of wedding science fiction with mystery fiction.

In *The Caves of Steel* Asimov uses the classic pattern of detective fiction: statement of the problem, marshalling of the clues and facts, completion of the inquiry, and explanation of the proof. Setting the pattern into action is the introduction of the detective, Elijah Baley, just before Baley is summoned to Commissioner Enderby's office to receive an assignment to investigate a murder in Spacetown. The murdered man, a Dr. Sarton who worked in robot design, was one of some prominence in Spacetown; the Spacers believe the murderer to be an Earthman, possibly a member of an activist group against Spacer occupation. Outside the City proper, the area called Spacetown has for some time been held in fief by men from the Outer Worlds. The Terrestrial Bureau of Investigation, pleading lack of jurisdiction, refuses the case. Since the murder happened inside the official jurisdiction of the city police department, the Spacers use their political clout to request and get a man from the City as chief investigator. That man is Baley.

This assignment holds a unique challenge for Baley. He is a true product of the conditioning which the City of some 3000 years in the future imposes upon all of its inhabitants. He fears open spaces. He feels uncomfortable in open air. Most of all, he experiences mingled fear and disgust in the presence of robots because they represent an ever-growing threat that they might replace men. To all Earthmen the robots mean loss of jobs, the misery of loss of status, and the lonely sense of displacement. His new assignment requires that Baley face all of these fears. He must go to Spacetown and endure the open spaces and the unconditioned air, especially those disturbing vagrant breezes. An obligatory consideration of the case forces him to take as an assistant a Spacer robot, R. Daneel Olivaw, whose humanoid appearance is so lifelike that he passes undetected even by the chief robotics expert of Earth.

At this point Asimov had to pay considerable attention to an important imperative of science fiction. A story which takes place some 3000 years in the future obviously demands the creation of a world different from the one in which the reader lives today. Setting is always important in science fiction; it must believably fit the future. In *Caves* Asimov begins to build his world from the first page. Particularly during the phase of the investigation which deals with the collection of data and the sifting of clues, Asimov skillfully blends in necessary details of setting.

Asimov does alleviate some possible difficulties in this blending by localizing most of his action in the world of the detective, a world which is not too unfamiliar to the reader. In *Caves* New York City now covers a large area, but more importantly it has burrowed deep underground to become a "tremendous self-contained cave of steel and concrete." While retaining the name New York, it has become "the City" in the minds of its inhabitants. Almost self-sufficient, it is a place where one could live all his life without going outside, a place shared by over twenty million people. It is a microcosm reflecting an overpopulated Earth dependent for certain strategic material on the Outer Worlds, those outlying planets and asteroids originally populated by immigrants from Earth but now closed to such settlement.

The existence of the Outer Worlds and the conflict between them and Earth is not a new invention for this novel. In 1949, Asimov wrote "Mother Earth" (in *The Early Asimov, Book Two*), a short story foreshadowing Baley's Earth at an earlier time when some diplomatic links still existed between Earth and the Outer Worlds. It was also a time in which the feeling of complete inferiority to the men of the Outer Worlds had not yet corrupted Earthmen's view of themselves. In the short story a reader learns many things which become of importance in the novel. We become aware of the genetic practices and the strict population policy of the Outer Worlds. Already the Outer Worlds have perfected positronic robots and have built their economy around them. In contrast, the economy of Earth depends upon the Outer Worlds for scarce materials and an energy supply.

The city of "Mother Earth" also foreshadows the City of *The Caves of Steel* and the effect of it on the people. But there are significant differences. In "Mother Earth" the inhabitants look out of windows on the masses of people. This is a city of windows, not of windowless underground cells. In the novel we experience a City where a "window" is a Medieval affectation, likely to make most people uneasy because it threatens complete privacy, a valued commodity. The earlier city is one of multitudes spread out and up; Baley's City is one of multitudes spread out and down.

In the afterword to "Mother Earth" in *The Early Asimov*, the author responds to his own story saying that "it seems to show clear premonitions of the novels *Caves of Steel* and *The Naked Sun*, which I was to write in the 1950s." One may well call it premonition, but the short story is also evidence of Asimov's economy or utility of invention, an economy we will see over and over again in the science fiction mystery stories of Asimov. While "Mother Earth" does not feature Lije Baley or R. Daneel Olivaw, it could well be considered the initial story of that series, but one lacking the presence of the detective spirit.

The length of the novel afforded Asimov some benefits which he could not gain in the short story. Edgar Allan Poe in his review of Hawthorne's *Twice-Told Tales* warned readers of the nature of the full-length novel, a nature which encouraged it to "deprive itself, of course, of the immense force derivable from totality." By *totality* he is referring to that unity of effect which he himself managed with such excellence in his short stories and poems. Since Asimov, unlike Poe, needed to blend two effects, he took advantage of the length of the novel to fix the setting firmly before turning to the serious work of solving the crime.

Asimov gives us the City in some detail. There is some exposition and direct description of the structure of the City, its cell-like residential areas underground, the yeast vats on the periphery, and the hydroponic "farms." We receive statistics on population (over twenty million) and even a brief history of the growth of the City in which the reader learns that the New York he knows is only 300 years old by comparison with Baley's City of 3000-plus years.

But most exhilarating for the reader is the sense of direct experience which Asimov affords us. With Baley he moves us around the City. We eat in a communal kitchen, use a Personal, smell the pervasive odor of the yeast, shudder at an impolite glance from another person (for a glance, we learn, invades valued privacy). We "run the strips" with Baley and R. Daneel Olivaw as they outfox some Medievalists close on their trail. Moving belts which transport people over the City and which travel from slow to express speeds, these "strips" also offer the youths of the City a challenge to test their courage; this we learn as we join Baley in remembering his youthful adeptness at outrunning his comrades on the strips.

Not only do we learn to know the City physically but we learn to know the people and the things they value. Above all, privacy is jealously guarded, as one may well imagine. Status is one of the keys to happiness, not status based on money or family connections, but on one's rating as a worker. The status ratings bring greater privileges and assure a modicum of comfort for a man and his family. The successful solution of the Spacetown murder will bring Baley a higher rating. Translated into concrete terms, this may mean a seat on the expressway strip during rush hours, a larger living area for the family, or maybe even a choice of chicken or real meat, not yeast food, twice a week at the Section kitchen.

To assure this rating, Baley has only to solve the murder. But solving the murder also means working with a robot. Without R. Daneel success is impossible because the Spacers have dictated his presence. Solution with R. Daneel also seems impossible because Baley is so conditioned by his world to reject robotic existence as being beneficial in any way. To R. Sammy, the office robot who has replaced a young policeman, Baley responds with muted irritation, at times derision. His wife feels revulsion when she discovers R. Daneel to be a robot. Yet the investigation must proceed; gradually Lije Baley's professional training succeeds in controlling his first instinct and he accords R. Daneel a grudging cooperation.

The idea for a robot detective originated in an interview with Horace Gold, so Asimov reports in the foreword to the novel in *The Rest of the Robots.* Asimov had written several robot stories, later collected under the title, *I, Robot.* By this time the Three Laws of Robotics, originally put together in 1940, were well-established and accepted by readers.[9] Asimov had tried and succeeded with some intriguing plots involving robots as characters. One of the stories, in particular, we should notice because it anticipates part of the plot design in *The Caves of Steel.* In "Evidence" the main character, Stephen C. Byerley, is running for political office. His opposition, in an effort to defeat him, accuses him of being a robot and call for evidence to the contrary. They circulate the story that he is the humanoid creation of a brilliant lawyer and biophysicist who had lost his legs, his face, and his voice in an accident. They claim that this man, embittered at the premature loss of a notable career, somehow acquired a positronic brain, grew a body around it, filled it with his own professional knowledge and talent, and then sent it out as Stephen C. Byerley to operate as his surrogate. In spite of the smear campaign, the people accept Byerley; even Susan Calvin, the robopsychologist, testifies to his humanity, but she is never quite sure she is right.

The Caves of Steel owes much to this short story. Like Stephen C. Byerley, the robot detective in the novel "passes" as a human in the City; he even passes the expert inspection of a prominent robotics expert. R. Daneel Olivaw, like Byerley, operates under the Laws of Robotics; also, like Byerley, he has an advanced positronic brain, one capable of making ethical judgments. This latter capability allows him to harm a human being, contrary to First Law, if more sweeping considerations than one man's well-being merit that choice. Most important in this comparison, Daneel like Byerley has been made in his creator's image; in Daneel's case the creator is Dr. Sarton, the murdered Spacer.

From the beginning of their association, R. Daneel seems fated to assume the position of authority over Baley. His efficiency and single-minded concentration on the job at hand give him an edge over the very human Baley, who is struggling also with his personal antipathies. Until Baley's mind is shaken out of its customary assumptions about robots, he is at a disadvantage. The robot, rather than the man, becomes the Sherlock figure; he fits the role of the classic "eccentric" detective, eccentric in the sense of being a deviant from the human norm. Acutely sensitive to possible trouble, R. Daneel responds with the logical action. He makes the "conscious" effort to put the bits and pieces of fact together. Later, although the evidence points against his conclusion, it is R. Daneel who comes up with the first accusation against the real killer.

In the first part of the novel Asimov would seem to be pursuing a pattern we all recognize from detective fiction: the amateur showing up the inefficiency of the professional. In one of Asimov's straight detective fiction short stories, "The Matchbook Collector," one of his characters says it succinctly: "You know ever since Conan Doyle pitted Sherlock Holmes against the Scotland Yard bunglers, there seems to be a notion that the professional can't do anything." [10] Lije Baley finally begins to disprove this notion. After the running of the strips he begins to come into his own; this incident serves to remind him that he is operating in a familiar milieu, his City. When the murder investigation turns up a link with Medievalist groups working underground for a return to the simpler nontechnological life, Baley has leads to follow in the society he knows best. He overcomes the paralysis which had clamped down on his professional imagination during the first two days of his relationship with the robot. He even comes to the point where he can say to himself of R. Daneel, "but he's a machine . . . no more human than a lump of wood is."

Near the end of *The Caves of Steel* Asimov does weaken the blend of mystery and science fiction by introducing a new and unanticipated element. Unexpectedly, the Spacers call off the murder investigation, informing Baley of their decision through R. Daneel. Asimov would have us believe that their main objective was not to find the murderer but to woo Baley's mind toward a tolerance of robots. With this accomplished, they then widened that tolerance to the point where he could entertain, even could express to Enderby, the idea that Earth might consider a new wave of emigration to the still-empty worlds in space. By necessity, this project would involve both leaving the safety of the City and accepting the help of robots in colonizing the new worlds.

Asimov does salvage his detective story, however, when he allows Baley to close the case in his own way. By interpreting literally the hour at which the case is to be closed, Baley uses the remaining time to wrap up the case, thus satisfying his professional pride. He does discover the "murderer" without sacrificing attention to the new project of inducing a change in social attitudes. The revelation of the facts as evidence shares the readers' attention with the author's concern for the "second chance" afforded the criminal. The science fiction side of the story has the last word as Daneel says to the culprit, "Go, and sin no more!"

In the sequel *The Naked Sun*, Asimov himself recognizes his accomplishment in the brief foreword to the novel in *The Rest of the Robots*. He modestly states that he once again "achieved a perfect fusion of the murder mystery and the science-fiction novel." Whether the first novel was a *perfect* fusion is debatable, as mentioned above. The sequel, on the other hand, does achieve a unity which supercedes that of the first robot novel. *The Naked Sun* first appeared in 1956 in *Astounding*, a three-part serial in the October through December issues; it came out as a book in 1957, three years after *Caves*. Like its predecessor, *The Naked Sun* features Elijah Baley and R. Daneel Olivaw collaborating on a murder case, this time on one of the Outer Worlds.

The unity achieved in *The Naked Sun* is explainable in several ways. First, Asimov uses less time to present his two main characters, who are well known, at least to his fans who have read *The Caves of Steel* (one obvious advantage of a series). Second, he does not have to be so detailed in his explanations of the people in the Outer Worlds, their way of life, or their psychology. Above all, he need not spend half his book readjusting Baley's attitude toward acceptance of robot help. Since the adjustment occurred in the first book of the series, it now requires reaffirmation only. True, Baley has other new adjustments to make: he must learn to control the panic engendered by flying; he must come to terms with the unique customs of Solaria; and, most of all, he must conquer his fear of being in the open. These are problems built into the movement of the plot and are easily absorbed into the mystery pattern.

As in *Caves*, the story in *The Naked Sun* falls into the pattern of the classic detective story. A murder occurs on Solaria, one of the Outer Worlds; Elijah Baley is sent to investigate. He finds a society quite different from his own on Earth. Rigid restrictions on immigration and strict genetic control assure Solarians of a steady level of population, one small enough to allow each citizen roughly 150 square miles of land. Theirs is a robot economy, ten thousand robots per human being. Working in the mines and on the land and in the houses, these robots produce all necessary energy, food, and personal services. The physical and social isolation of the human population has gradually bred out the need for direct contact; indeed, the touch or even the immediate presence of another human being is repugnant to Solarians. Even the thought of such contact causes revulsion. Solarians maintain communication with each other by means of trimensional images which give the illusion of being in the same room with the person one is visiting. The custom is called "viewing," in contrast to actual "seeing."

The murder on Solaria is the first in two centuries. Solarian security finds itself incapable of coping with such an extraordinary occurrence. Because his success in the Spacetown murder (*The Caves of Steel*) has earned him a reputation in the Galaxy, Solaria requests Earth to send Elijah Baley to handle the investigation of their murder. An official in the Justice Department gives Baley his charge: find the murderer. He also gives a *sub rosa* assignment: keep eyes and ears open to the general situation on Solaria so that he may report to Earth upon return. In *The Naked Sun*, unlike the late introduction of the second problem in *Caves*, Asimov introduces this thread of the plot early. Also, it fits more naturally into the detective fiction pattern—the international intrigue of the spy thriller grafted onto the localized puzzle of the mystery story.

As before, R. Daneel Olivaw from Aurora, the largest and most powerful of the Outer Worlds, joins Baley as his assistant. Once on Solaria the two detectives slowly gather data, even though they are barred from visiting the scene of the crime or from interviewing suspects except by trimensional image. In Solarian society, as mentioned above, direct access to another's personal presence is practically unknown, even between spouses who meet only on "assigned days." Asimov obviously is working a science-fiction variation of the locked-room situation in detective fiction.

The bare facts of the case come from Hannis Gruer, head of Solarian security: the identity of the murdered man; the facts that no murder weapon was found but that a positronic brain-damaged robot was on the scene; the fact that the murdered man's wife was found bending over the body. The robot, governed by First Law, cannot possibly be suspected of the murder. The chances of any one person's attempting and gaining access to the man are nil because of the elaborate network of robots around each human being on Solaria—not to mention the extreme psychological aversion the murderer would have to overcome merely to approach the victim. The only possible human suspect is the murdered man's wife Gladia. But again, no weapon which could have served the purpose of murder was found, and she had had no time in which to dispose of any such weapon.

After Gruer's report Baley recognizes the seemingly insurmountable difficulties facing him. His only move now is to fall back on the commonplaces of detection, and his response is almost a cliché: "Murder rests on three legs, each equally important. They are motive, means, and opportunity. For a good case against any suspect, each of the three must be satisfied." A faithful reader of detective fiction will easily recollect this truism from speeches of countless fictional detectives, be they amateurs or professionals. At first, the statement seems almost an unwarranted one, until we recall that Asimov must also keep up the logic of the science fiction side of his tale. His character is speaking to someone from a different culture; he is operating in a country where murder is known only in an academic sense. The study of motive, means, and opportunity is unnecessary, hence forgotten. The reminder of basic police procedure illuminates both the detective and the science fiction parts of the novel.

Find motive, means, and opportunity. The path seems simple. But complications soon arise. Baley discovers the existence of subversive elements in this ostensibly tight social organization on Solaria. These people wish to change the "old ways, the good ways," the customs and traditions of which the murdered man was an advocate. The suspicion now arises that Dr. Delmarre, being a Traditionalist, was silenced for political reasons.

Because these political reasons may have intergalactic ramifications, R. Daneel Olivaw from Aurora is excluded from the briefing session. For some inexplicable reason the Solarians do not know that Daneel is a robot. This blindness is incongruous in a society where human beings live so closely and depend so completely on robots. (Either Asimov nods a little here, or else he wishes to emphasize that habit breeds inattention.) They do, nonetheless, regard Daneel as important, accepting him as the representative of Aurora, a government which somehow may be involved in the underground intrigues with which Solaria is threatened. The intergalactic politics smack so obviously of twentieth-century cold war or international politics that the situation threatens to jeopardize Asimov's fusion of science fiction and mystery by suddenly assuming some conventions of a thriller.

To some extent the thriller and the detective story work to contradictory ends. The thriller, unlike the detective story, operates without absolutes. Often at the end no one will be brought to justice, for the idea of justice becomes relative. What is just in one political or social entity is not necessarily just in the opposing entity. The "hero" of a thriller may be a very insignificant person, one quite ordinary who by chance or choice has been caught up in the net of international machinations. The elevating aura of tragedy is denied to him because chance too often determines his actions. Yet he faces and makes many decisions which will tragically affect the lives of many people. In the serious thriller, formula and procedure are of little help.

Surprisingly, Asimov moves us back to the original purpose—a science-fiction detective story—with the very character whose absence at the briefing allowed the digression into galactic politics. R. Daneel Olivaw's absence gives Asimov the opportunity to subordinate the robot detective more completely to the human detective than in *Caves*. No longer the "pocket-frannistan" able to store, sort, and produce instant information for Baley, the robot serves him as the source of background information: Solaria's geography; its social and cultural mores; biographical notes on Solarian officials; and any supplementary data which Baley needs. As the novel unfolds, the need for Daneel's peculiar gifts lessens while the necessity for human imagination grows.

Especially is this state of affairs evident when a second murder attempt occurs, this one on Gruer himself, in full "view" (not in "sight") of Baley and R. Daneel during another interview by trimensional image. This murder attempt accomplishes several things. It partially disables R. Daneel, whose stable existence and operation depends upon his adherence to the Laws of Robotics. Seeing harm come so dramatically to a human being briefly puts Daneel into the robotic equivalent of shock. It thus reduces his effectiveness as an equal partner. By this episode Asimov turns his full attention to the human detective and to the problem calling for human deductive powers. Lije Baley, his own professional training as his sole resource, is jolted into action. Concentrating on the immediate problem—murder and attempted murder—he lets the problem of subversion sort itself out naturally in the course of the investigation.

The internal problems of Solaria and the secondary assignment given to Baley by the Justice Department prove to be mutually supportive. With their advanced robot economy, low population, and excessively long life span, the Solarians have come to a dangerpoint in their social existence. What seem to be Solaria's strengths in the Galaxy are in fact its weaknesses. As Lije Baley solves the original murder and the second murder attempt, he incidentally uncovers the sociological dilemma underlying these crimes, and this discovery allows him to fulfill the second assignment.

Many writers of science fiction give in to a didactic urge. Since science fiction frequently operates as prophetic vision, an author often feels impelled to use the vision to warn his readers of the portents visible in contemporary life. Asimov yields a little to this urge in Baley's report to Albert Minnim of the Justice Department. He parallels the two societies, Solaria and Earth. Earth is a "turned-inside-out" Solaria. Both worlds are at dead ends—Solaria through personal isolation, Earth through cultural isolation. Both worlds must break their molds and introduce new ways of doing things. Each world is a distorted mirror-image of the other.

The metaphor of a mirror-image led to the title of a short story in which the detectives make their third appearance. "Mirror Image" first appeared in *Analog* (May 1972) and later in *The Best of Isaac Asimov*. In the introductory remarks to this book, Asimov implies that the short story was a command performance, written at readers' requests for a sequel to *The Caves of Steel* and *The Naked Sun*. Since some readers expected a third novel in the series, they have been only partially satisfied. Pleading the limitations of time, Asimov delivered the shorter length, but one which does afford a third look at the continuing development of the man-robot relationship.

The problem in "Mirror Image" is impending death, not of a person or of a civilization, but the death of a reputation. Two eminent mathematicians possess identical scholarly papers explaining a startling discovery in their discipline. Both propose to deliver the paper at an important convention. The paper will add considerable luster to the reputation of either man by contributing to the older man's already high place in the profession and by giving impetus to the younger man's rising prominence. Each claims the paper as his own; each accuses the other of stealing it after having been invited to read it as a consultant. Each offers to forgive and forget if the other will forego all claims on the contents.

This unpleasant contention has erupted aboard a space ship enroute to the convention. In the age-old tradition of all ships, the captain as sole authority must act the part of Solomon. To avert the future scandal, he must decide to whom the paper really belongs. He enlists the aid of a passenger on the starship, one R. Daneel Olivaw of Aurora. Olivaw in turn requests and receives permission to make an unscheduled stop at Earth so that he might consult with plainclothesman Elijah Baley.

A key factor in the case, one which Baley uses to keen advantage, is the presence of two robots, property of the two mathematicians. They reinforce the title-metaphor of mirror image by being identical robots, made in the same year at the same factory to the same specifications. Unable to interview the two scientists (they are Spacers and arrogantly reject any contact with an Earthman), Baley interviews the two servant-robots. They corroborate their masters' stories, as expected. To lie and thus cause harm to the master goes against First Law; in this instance the harm to reputation is as important as injury to person. By skillful questioning based on his knowledge of the First Law, Baley pushes one of the robots to the point of stasis, out of commission, thus finding the vital clue to the guilty man.

The clue still has to be turned into evidence. Only after Olivaw has returned to the starship, faced the two men with the fact, and received the confession of one, only then does Baley know that his deduction is accurate. In this story Asimov works a variation of the classic armchair detective. Baley collects facts while sitting in his office; he plans his course while sitting in his office; and he interviews the robots via micro-receiver set up in his office. At no time does he physically work at fact-gathering. Even the final confrontation of the detective and the guilty party is done second-hand through Olivaw. Baley himself operates purely on the intellectual level, resting his case on his powers of deduction alone.

"Mirror Image" demonstrates one reality about detective fiction not illustrated by Asimov heretofore. Stories of detection need not be based on sensational situations to be good stories of detection. While murder or political intrigue may create more excitement for a reader, the less sensational but nonetheless knotty problem allows the author to place a greater emphasis on the deductive process per se. In "Mirror Image" the mode of detection satisfies dyed-in-the-wool devotees of both mystery and science fiction.

Yet another Asimov character, Wendell Urth, made his appearance at the same time that Lucky Starr turned space detective and Lije Baley began his association with R. Daneel. The four Urth stories—"The Singing Bell" (January 1955), "The Talking Stone" (October 1955), "The Dying Night" (July 1956), and "The Key" (October 1966)—all first appeared in *The Magazine of Fantasy and Science Fiction* and later were collected with other mystery stories in *Asimov's Mysteries*.

Wendell Urth, Professor of Extraterrology at Eastern University, is a worthy candidate for admission to that select group of thinking machines and problem-solvers *extraordinare*. Like such gifted amateurs as C. Auguste Dupin, Sherlock Holmes, Augustus S. F. X. Van Dusen, Dr. John Thorndyke, and Hercule Poirot, Wendell Urth possesses the true detective spirit, but without the official label of *detective*. Police authorities and citizens alike call upon the talents of these characters. They untangle puzzling situations which may or may not be criminal but are almost always threatening social stability in some way.

As has been stated before, detective fiction devotes little space to characterization, except for the detective himself. The author usually feels the responsibility to establish his detective as a person of perspicacity with the most impeccable credentials in his own field and with a record of achievement in activities requiring deductive ability. Asimov discharges this duty admirably. He draws Wendell Urth as a man of independent mind to the point of extreme eccentricity. An eminent extraterrologist, he has never been in space, even to the Moon, averring that space travel is foolish. In fact, he shuns all travel by artificial means, preferring to go no farther than his own feet can carry him. He lives in a dim room cluttered with book films, star charts, maps, papers, and a personal collection of artifacts from the far-flung reaches of the solar system. While he works semi-isolated from the world, mentally he roams the known reaches of the solar system. His personal appearance is deceiving. Certain words attach themselves to him: *round, pudgy, snubby, stubby, stumpy*. Asimov works with images of roundness: a round body, a round face, the round nubbin of a nose on which round glasses perch. But behind this unprepossessing appearance is a mind of superior quality.

Three of the Wendell Urth stories include a second character, H. Seton Davenport of the Terrestrial Bureau of Investigation. As with Conan Doyle's Inspector Lestrade, G. K. Chesterton's Valentin, and other descendants of Poe's Prefect of Police, H. Seton Davenport serves to draw the superior mind of Urth into the official investigation. Asimov also uses Davenport as a physical foil for Urth. With his dark hair and prominent nose, his controlled and solemn mien, and the scar marring his right cheek, Davenport suggests a man used to dangerous situations, far removed from the dark and quiet seclusion of Professor Urth.

In Wendell Urth we have an extreme case of the armchair detective. A man who refuses to stir from his own premises except to walk to his classroom is not a man one expects to do the laborious job of clue-collecting. To accommodate his character's special eccentricity, Asimov changed the sequence of his plot from that we have been used to in the previously discussed stories. For the classic pattern he substituted R. Austin Freeman's "inverted story in two parts." In the first part of each story Asimov gives his reader the commission of the crime with the criminals fully identified. In some cases, we even experience the entire situation through dialogue and action rather than through exposition. We are given all the facts which Urth later will turn into hard evidence. In the second part of the story we follow Urth in this task.

The shift to the inverted pattern eases somewhat the work of fusing detective conventions with science fiction. Since in each of the four stories the criminal either lives or works in space, the inverted pattern allows Asimov to tell his science fiction story before any need for deduction arises. He has only to play fair with the reader by placing all necessary facts and pertinent circumstances before him. Jacques Barzun gives his opinion that "in any combination of the detective interest with anything else, the something else must remain the junior partner." [11] This subordination need not occur with the inverted pattern. In the first part of the story science fiction can definitely be the senior partner, with the emphasis on the nonterrestrial settings, the alien life-forms, or the scientific premise on which the action later will turn. In the second part of the story, once we have met Wendell Urth in his cluttered study and have admired his artifacts from Callistan or his Galactic Lens, then detection becomes the senior partner.

In "The Singing Bell," Louis Peyton, archcriminal à la Moriarty or Flambeau, plans to recover a cache of Singing Bells from the Moon and to murder the man who has enlisted his help in the project. The Singing Bells, rare rock formations which produce beautiful harplike tones when stroked, command huge prices from collectors on Earth. Since the importation of the Bells is strictly controlled, Peyton stands to reap great financial benefit from this load of contraband. He carefully plans the trip to the Moon by scheduling it during the month in which he habitually retreats to his mountain hideout. Under the established pattern of his life he can cover up this instance of aberrant behavior which includes murder. For the reader there is nothing kept back about the trip to the Moon, the murder, the victim, or the criminal. H. Seton Davenport in the conversation with Wendell Urth reveals that the police know everything we know, except they can't *prove* it.

This situation is, of course, the Perfect Crime perpetrated by the Master Criminal which can be broken only by the Master Mind. In this story Urth does not "solve" anything. He does the only imaginative thing possible to crack the case: he sets up a simple situation in which he forces the criminal to trap himself by another established pattern of behavior, thus betraying himself to the police who then can test him with the psychoprobe.

"The Talking Stone" departs from the most common crime of mystery fiction, murder, and turns to smuggling. When a disabled spaceship stops at a repair station, the mechanic stumbles by chance on a smuggling operation being perpetrated by asteroid miners. Their chilly response to his casual, friendly overtures piques his curiosity, which becomes all the more sharpened when he inadvertently steps into the wrong area on the ship. There he sees an outsized silicony, a rock-eating organism especially adapted for life on uranium-rich asteroids. Vernadsky, the mechanic, senses a mystery and relays his suspicions to a friend, a space-patrolman. Together they track down the ship which the mechanic had only half-repaired so that it would break down in a predetermined area in space. They do find the ship. They also find a dead crew, for a meteor has hit the ship. The silicony is alive, but it also dies after giving a cryptic message about the location of its "home": "There," it says, "Over there."

The two men report their find to H. Seton Davenport, who in turn calls on Wendell Urth. With the death of the smugglers there is no longer a crime, but a crucial question remains to answer. Where in space is the asteroid so rich in uranium to support a silicony of such size? Without leaving his study, Urth finds the meaning of the creature's last words. Thus he is able to direct Davenport to the location of the hidden record of the coordinates of the asteroid—in a most obvious place, of course. In "The Talking Stone" Asimov has worked a science-fiction twist on Poe's strategy in "The Purloined Letter."

In 1956, Asimov published the third Wendell Urth story in as many years, "The Dying Night." First, he gives the necessary background information for motive, means, and opportunity for murder. Romano Villiers, a brilliant but embittered astronomer of Earth, has discovered a startling method for mass transference. At a World Astronomical Convention he shares his feat with three old classmates: Kaunas from Mercury, Ryger from Ceres, and Talliaferro from the Moon. Later, Villiers is found dying by Professor Mandel, one of the officials at the convention. Villiers' dying words point to one of the three classmates as the murderer, although all three seem well-protected by alibis. When all clues, suspects, and paradoxes have been presented to the reader, Asimov brings in Wendell Urth, this time using Professor Mandel instead of H. Seton Davenport as the "bridge" between the two parts of the story. As in "The Singing Bell," Urth solves the problem by utilizing his knowledge of each man's conditioned behavior. He forces the murderer to reveal himself by an involuntary reaction to Earth's sun.

"The Dying Night" differs significantly in other respects from the two preceding stories. Here the reader does not know who the murderer is, nor has he witnessed the preplanning or the actual commission of the murder. Also, at the end of the tale Asimov breaks, or at least "bends," one of the lesser conventions of the mystery story—no love interest. After carefully building Urth up as the Brain whose sole concerns are his profession and his deductive exercises, Asimov gives him a heart. He humanizes Urth at the end when the professor requests a trip by mass transference to a place close by. To the amazed scientists he shyly explains, "I once—quite a long time ago—knew a girl there. It's been many years—but I sometimes wonder . . ."

"The Key" brings H. Seton Davenport back to work with Wendell Urth. Starting *in medias res,* Asimov uses a lengthy flashback to explain the predicament. Identical first and last paragraphs hold the sequence of events of part one firmly together, serving as verbal bookends: "Karl Jennings knew he was going to die. He had a matter of hours to live and much to do." Jennings and his partner Strauss of a privately subsidized Moon expedition have found a Device in an area where no human landings have ever been made. They conclude that it must have come to the Moon in an ancient landing, perhaps one made by a far superior alien culture.

The Device, an extrasensory object, will take a charge from honest human emotions and in turn will allow the one holding it to change the attitudes of people around him (shades of the V-frogs of Lucky Star exploits). Both men realize the importance of this Device and wish to appropriate it. Strauss wants it for the use of the Ultras, an elitist conservative group of social planners who are urging drastic population controls. Jennings sees it as a tool for reliable, very altruistic men to use for the benefit of all, not for one small, radical group. Jennings' emotions are idealistic; therefore, the Device reacts in his hands as it will not for Strauss. In the ensuing struggle, emotions of both men rise to a high pitch. The amplification of Jennings' emotions by the Device destroys Strauss's mind, even as he mortally wounds Jennings physically. Sensing his impending death, Jennings fights to stay alive until he can hide the Device safely and leave some key to its location. It is important that the key be so designed that only the proper persons can decode it and find the Device.

H. Seton Davenport ultimately receives the cryptogram, which Jennings had succeeded in scratching on a card before he died. He takes the card to Wendell Urth. By coincidence, Urth had known both Jennings and Strauss as students in his classes at Eastern University. Remembering Jennings' weakness for puns, Urth ferrets out the meaning of the symbols on the card. Also, his knowledge of Strauss's cold, unemotional personality allows him the opportunity to explain in philosophical terms the potential good which the Device can bring to humanity, if used by the right people.

As in "The Dying Night," Asimov invites his readers to close their acquaintance with Wendell Urth on a note more personal. In the conclusion of "The Key" we get a glimpse of a Wendell Urth who is not always in control of situations. The nature of his fee for this case is a strange one. He requests that no notice of his help be publicized. If it is, his niece may hear of it and make his life miserable. As he describes her, "She is a terribly headstrong and shrill-voiced woman who will raise public subscriptions and organize demonstrations. She will stop at nothing," including making his life unbearable. To leave our worthy detective on such a note may seem frivolous, but it indicates something about Asimov's developing attitude toward the conventions of detective fiction. He felt freer to play with them, as is witnessed by the cryptogram based on puns; he also felt freer to dilute them with other considerations. Although the early emphasis had been on Professor Urth's formidable mental powers, in the later stories the working-out of the crime shares partnership with the tactics of humanizing Urth.

Asimov's nonseries science fiction mysteries provide additional information about his blending techniques. Of the remaining nine stories in *Asimov's Mysteries*, one is not a mystery at all, its inclusion based on the fact that its sequel is a mystery. "Marooned Off Vesta" (1939) does not lie within our purview here, but reference to it is necessary for understanding "Anniversary" (1959). Three spacemen meet twenty years after they had been marooned off Vesta in a disabled spaceship (note the twenty years which separate the dates of publication of the two stories!). They discover that the insurance company, after all this time, is showing inordinate interest in the bits and pieces of the wrecked ship. This piques their interest, so they turn amateur detectives. By using Multivac, the mile-long computer which is the depository of all information, they piece together the puzzle, identify the item sought, and locate it in a box of souvenirs in the attic of their host's home. Asimov equally balances interest in the science fiction story with the deductive interest.

One of the tales features H. Seton Davenport as the primary detective, operating without Wendell Urth's aid. "The Dust of Death" (1957) deals with the death of a much-unloved scientist about whom all of his associates "talked murder." The solution, ably executed by Davenport and a colleague of the victim, revolves on mistaken identity—not of a person, but of a tank of gas in a chemistry laboratory. Again Asimov reminds his readers through Davenport's explanations to a scientist that a criminal needs motive (everyone had that), "the chemical knowledge required to commit the crime" (everyone had that), and the opportunity (and everyone had that). This would seem to rule out the possibility that the murderer turned on the wrong tank of gas (they are all painted different identifying colors) unless he were color-blind, an unlikely prospect for the work required. Davenport and the assisting scientist finally pinpoint the culprit who had fallen into the trap of habit and had used a mixture of gas which would have been proper for Titan, his last working station, rather than for Earth.

"Obituary" (1959) provides no mystery and no process of detection but does set up a perfect "crime." A man who has mastered the duplication of matter in time sets up his own death so that he may read and live to enjoy his own obituary. His wife takes advantage of this feat to rid herself of her obnoxious mate—the perfect crime. "Starlight" (1962) also has no real mystery. Asimov uses a gimmick similar to that in "Obituary" by presenting a man who consciously plans a perfect crime, this time using hyperspace as the getaway route. He miscalculates, thus outwitting himself in the process. In the foreword to "What's In a Name" (1956), Asimov agrees that this is not a science fiction mystery, but it uses a tenuous connection with science. A library becomes the scene for murder; the victim is an unlikely one, a librarian with no obvious enemies. The solution depends on the investigator's recognizing a vital clue hinging on a major science work.

Asimov gives full rein to his penchant for humor in two of his mysteries. (Humor is a rare commodity in either mystery or science fiction.) "Pâté de Foie Gras" (1956) provides him with an amusing vehicle for some elementary lessons in science as well. The unwary reader thinks he is reading a futuristic version of The Goose That Laid The Golden Egg. Suddenly at the end he finds himself inside the story being asked by the narrator for suggestions as to how the Goose accomplishes its "enzyme-catalyzed nuclear process" that "manages to convert any unstable isotope" into a stable one (thus creating "a perfect method of radioactive ash disposal"). The effect which the narrator hopes for, and begs from the reader, is disbelief. However, both the reader and Asimov are perfectly aware that any solution to this little "joke" would solve the real-life dilemma of radioactive dumping. "A Loint of Paw" (1957), as mentioned earlier, turns on a pun. Whatever mystery is contained in this short-short story warrants only the slightest attention from the reader.

The detective spirit in "I'm in Marsport without Hilda" (1957) definitely takes a junior partnership, as does the serious science fiction element in it. The story involves Max, Class A Agent in the Galactic Service, tapped to catch a smuggler, but the primary interest is in the agent's futile attempts to engage in some extramarital hanky-panky in Marsport. The deductive process teases the reader's ingenuity, based as it is on the principle of free association of language. This allows Asimov to come up with lines such as, "Gay lords hopping pong balls," and "Saved and a haircut above the common herd something about younicorny as Kansas high as my knee." Interest in this palls, however, in competition with the attention generated by the very human situation of a man trying his hardest to yield to temptation and ending up yielding only to frustration. In the foreword Asimov offers this story as proof that he can write a science fiction love story, a claim which devotees of love stories may well challenge. Certainly it is a claim which devotees of mystery stories might wish to disclaim.

One must accord Asimov the credit of having faced the challenge of blending science fiction with mystery fiction in several modes. He has written short stories, short-shorts, novels; he has given us the blend in single tales, in series with a detective-duo, and in series with the amateur-professional combinations. Second, he has treated many of the classic conventions of detective fiction: the locked-room plot, the "perfect crime" plot, the mistaken-identity situation, the cryptogram gimmick, and, perhaps most importantly, he has done successful variations on the personality of the detective. He has adapted his ability to write a well-planned technological story, based on solid scientific facts, to writing a well-planned deductive episode. He has successfully used the two major patterns of the mystery formula—Poe's classic pattern and Freeman's inverted pattern; to a lesser degree, he has succeeded in utilizing some of the best features of the spy thriller.

Most of all, while using the above detective or mystery story conventions, Asimov has not, for the most part, neglected to give his readers scientifically solid science fiction stories. Notable in this effort is his description of setting, both physical and psychological. Often he may interrupt the action to insert needed scientific information in the form of exposition or dialogue between two characters. This habit is not incompatible with the mystery genre, which also relies heavily on the reader's knowing all the facts, some of which must be given in exposition. If the facts happen to be scientific ones, Asimov is most capable of supplying these in understandable prose that does not talk down to his readers.

In the foreword to *The Caves of Steel* in *The Rest of the Robots*, Asimov proposes that he has written "a completely fair murder mystery, a thoroughgoing science fiction story, and an example of the perfect fusion of the two." He leaves it to the reader to decide whether his claim is valid, while suggesting strongly (with tongue-in-cheek, one assumes) that *he* would vote "yes" to all three counts. One may perhaps demur, particularly on *perfect* fusion. But any reader of the whole of Asimov's science fiction mysteries must agree that he has written a body of stories which both delight and instruct, which puzzle and challenge the detective spirit in each one of us, and which are scientifically plausible and satisfying to the science fiction fan.

3. The Use of Technical Metaphors in Asimov's Fiction

MAXINE MOORE

SOMEWHERE IN the wilds of deepest, darkest New York City there lives a man who, according to a dust jacket blurb, has been described as a "natural wonder" and a "national resource"—a man so prolific in his writing that it is not safe to say how many books and stories he has written because before your figure can be published, he will have written several more and will have outmoded your datum; a man who has dared to claim that science fiction is the only relevant form of literature today; and a man whose name is pronounced with a "z" but spelled with an "s." His name is Isaac Asimov, and "he was always a strange one, Isaac was." [1]

Asimov not only writes science fiction—among many other things—he also defines it, defends it, describes it, and discusses it. He places his own work in a broad category he calls Social Science Fiction—"that branch of literature which is concerned with the impact of scientific advance upon human beings." [2] And, when accused of possible intentions toward deeper significance in his works, he denies it in doggerel and pugnaciously claims that "I Just Make Them Up, See!" [3]

But despite his doggerel, and in spite of his insistence in the autobiographical sections of *Opus 100, The Early Asimov,* and elsewhere that his stories simply bubble out of his brain like the froth from the tap, there are some readers who might suspect him of modestly dissembling. Either there is more of art than of raw subconscious in the overall body of his work, or else he is fortunate to be the owner of a highly organized and well-trained subconscious. In any case, from the days of his precocious youth to the completion of *The Gods Themselves,* his work displays an exceptional coherence, unity of concept, and consistency.

Asimov's star reached its zenith during the halcyon days preceding the "New Wave." It was a time of tremendous intellectual excitement for science fiction writers and their fans, who, all together, formed a tight, closed corporation of technologically oriented elite. They spoke among each other in an esoteric lingo that only they could comprehend, sharing special things that reinforced the values of the impending space age. Just such an esoteric comment was one made by Asimov to the effect that science fiction was the only relevant literature for today's world, but it did not remain among the "inner ears"; instead it survived the olden golden days to bemuse or irritate a new breed of science fiction reader. But more of that later.

The 1940s, 1950s, and early 1960s saw the fullest flowering of hard science fiction, and since this was the period to which I relate most fondly, I call it the period of "High Science Fiction" to distinguish it from the "Old" or developing stages and from the New Wave that is now in the ascendency. High Science Fiction combined strong social awareness with a positive attitude toward scientific development and a decidedly experimental approach to writing. Since their readers were not generally of the literary persuasion, these writers followed the "plain speech" requirements of technical writing and strove above all for clarity—at least on the surface level. Beneath that level lurked implications obvious enough to readers of a technological bent. In some cases, in which the author himself contained both scientific and literary background, there were still further depths to be plumbed—but never at the expense of clear, plain, straightforward language that every fan could relate to. For this reason, the language of High Science Fiction is deceptively simplistic, and among literary critics it does not stand up well in comparison to the more poetic renditions by such as Harlan Ellison, Robert Silverberg, and other New Wave writers.

One of the problems faced by Asimov and his colleagues during these decades lay in the varied nature of their readers. New fans sprouted up from among high school boys who spent their mowing money on "sci-fi" pulps and *Popular Mechanics* and looked forward to the possibility of becoming spacemen themselves. In addition to these eager youngsters were the grown-up fans who had cut their teeth on what Asimov calls adventure and gadget science fiction.[4] The youthful readers required a good story in simple language with plenty of accurate technology of the kind that made science both a palatable and a promising discipline. The older fans demanded increasingly sophisticated treatment of psychological, sociological, political, philosophical, even religious themes and concepts. Asimov, Arthur C. Clarke, Robert Heinlein, Robert Sheckley, Frederik Pohl, James Blish, and others satisfied both audiences, combining "simplistic" language with metaphorical, symbolic, and structural systems based on physics rather than metaphysics. Even as science fiction dealt with the same subjects found in major literary works, and sometimes arrived at the same general conclusions, it did so from a different point of view and through a different matrix.

In this chapter I will discuss Asimov's works as "hard" science fiction and explore some of the technological metaphors that he uses so skillfully. Before leaping right into the deep end of the subject, however, I will provide a springboard by noting some comments made by various critics about Asimov's stories and novels and by describing some of Asimov's literary attitudes as they appear in his essays and articles. For purposes of analysis, the novels will be presented not in the order in which they were written, but in accordance with their approximate chronological position in the development of Asimov's Galactic Empire. Selected short stories will be brought in as they relate to concepts under discussion or as they illustrate ideas or techniques.

In any mention of the major science fiction writers, Asimov's name invariably appears. In any discussion of contributions to the idea pool or the language stock of science fiction, the positronic robot, psychohistory, and perhaps Thiotimoline will be accorded due homage for their considerable influence. Somehow, though, Asimov's work does not appear to be taken quite seriously by the academic community that has recently extended tentative—and wary—notice to science fiction. I refer mainly to English departments, since the social sciences, which do not generally function as arbiters of literary excellence, had put science fiction to good use somewhat earlier and with less embarrassment. English professors, however, tended to ignore the genre altogether or to consider it as a phenomenon of American Culture along with Westerns and detective stories. Secret SF fans who had slipped onto the faculty tended to keep their literary perversion to themselves. A few science fiction pieces eventually crept into freshman English classes, often in the hands of daring young teaching assistants who were not, after all, in line for tenure. Bold students, during the student-liberation movement of the Sixties, began to raise cynical eyebrows over the absence of their favorite story form. In some classes *Farenheit 451* began to appear, glorifying literature and Ray Bradbury, then Kurt Vonnegut and Harlan Ellison made their way into a few upper-level English courses, in which the literary imperatives were most often served by such writers as H. G. Wells, Jules Verne, Aldous Huxley, George Orwell, C. S. Lewis, and perhaps Walter M. Miller, Jr. Though a Clarke or a Heinlein novel almost always appeared, Asimov was often omitted in junior-senior science fiction courses (except, of course, for "Nightfall" which with its Emersonian argument is a must). Once the social aspects of his novels were exhausted, what was left to discuss? He lacked the mysticism of Clarke, the hairy-chested sexuality of Heinlein, the theological interest of C. S. Lewis and Walter Miller, the mainstream associations of Huxley and Orwell, or the historical value of Wells and Verne. His importance was undeniable, his brilliance and versatility acknowledged, and his science fiction criticism valuable, but the literary quality of his work was questionable. English professors found it difficult to discuss his novels from a purely literary standpoint.

For the sake of illustration and argument, we might look at some of the comments found in recent science fiction scholarship. In an article Robert H. Canary discusses future history as it relates to literary realism. He distinguishes between linear history and cyclic, and uses Heinlein and Asimov as examples of the latter. Though he notes the usefulness of this mode in some instances, he says of Heinlein's *The Moon Is a Harsh Mistress*, "To some extent, of course, Heinlein is simply exploring the historical parallels as an easy way of lending emotional force to his story—something one might say even more accurately of some other such stories, like Asimov's *Pebble in the Sky*, with its unmotivated parallels to the New Testament." [5] I would emphasize "unmotivated parallels to the New Testament" as evidence that Professor Canary had not given a full reading to *Pebble*, for the parallels are anything but unmotivated, especially in light of the function of its protagonist, Joseph Schwartz, as a "savior figure." In any case, if the cyclic approach to history is valid at all, one assumes that an author can pick his own cycle, and the New Testament period is hardly sacrosanct.

Asimov testifies to a personal leaning toward this type of story, remarking that "in the . . . chess-game type of social science fiction it is frequently found convenient to take advantage of the fact that 'history repeats itself.' Why shouldn't it? Given the same rules and the same starting position, the element of repetition must obtrude." Going on, regarding *Pebble*, he notes that "most thoughtful readers had no difficulty in recognizing the fact that I was retelling the history of Rome and Judea. I even had Earth governed by an Imperial Procurator." As he describes at least one of his motives, he was simply "following the chess-game theory in which all games start from the same point." As to the question of whether history does repeat itself, Asimov in the same article claims and demonstrates that it does so with "surprising specificity." [6]

Professor Lyman Tower Sargeant describes the *Foundation* trilogy as "clearly a Utopia in the general sense of a nonexistent society located in space and time," but, he continues, "I cannot see any way of putting a good-bad label on the place except by my personal reaction which is highly ambivalent. . . . It is a Utopia, but it is not either an eutopia or a dystopia." [7] According to Sargeant's definition of Utopia, it would be necessary to confine Asimov's Utopian concept to the First Foundation society on Terminus and the mysterious Second Foundation, for the Galactic Empire itself is merely a setting, deriving its evolving social conditions from that same cycles-of-history pattern mentioned above. Only the two Foundations involve a planned society—a factor included in Sargeant's definition. The problem here is that neither Foundation knows the course of the plan, so they—at least the First Foundation—also simply follow the cyclic pattern, recapitulating Earth's dark ages, Renaissance, and so forth, repeating the functions of the Arab world as preserver of culture and science. Thus the Foundations are less a "nowhere" than a "rewhere," as is the Empire itself. To classify the Foundation evolution as eutopia or dystopia, one must so classify Earth's own historical development. The Utopian—or eutopian—era aimed at by the Seldon Plan is yet to come, and Asimov has not yet seen fit to describe it as a ficticiously existing reality.

Asimov's fellow science fiction writer, Poul Anderson, discussing the "science" aspects of writings from the hard science fiction era, is also buffaloed by the *Foundation* trilogy. Is it a *"quasiscience,* using a galactic background to treat of history and politics; or is it about the imaginary science of 'psychohistory'; or is it an extrapolation of historiography, which is a real science?" [8] Anderson elects to classify it as a quasiscience, remarking that "you—or the Good

Doctor—may disagree." And, of course, I do, for the following reasons. Clearly, Anderson is concentrating on the aspects of history and politics, yet Asimov, in the *Foundation* trilogy, repeatedly stresses his use of the science of extrapolative statistics—a science already burgeoning in the field of insurance and elsewhere throughout the past forty or fifty years—and the science of symbolic logic, also a well-developed science and an important aspect of computer programming.

The Robot series also comes in for some critical comment. Gary K. Wolfe, somewhat affronted by Asimov's statement that "science fiction is the only real literature of ideas," rebuts by writing that the standard practice of the hard science fiction writers, including Asimov, "has been to trace the possible effects of a given limited concept and scarcely to deal with the actual ideas that may lie behind such a concept at all." [9] He notes that in *I, Robot* the stories will "touch upon an interesting social or psychological problem raised by the presence of robot workers in human society; more often, as in *The Caves of Steel*, the effect is merely that of toying (albeit with mathematical precision) with an idea that is potentially serious. . . . Seldom does Asimov ever touch upon the larger dimensions of the basic idea he is working with—for example, the entire concept of artificial intelligence and the implications of that concept in regard to various aspects of human behavior." This, I believe, is a classic case of a situation well described by Patrick G. Hogan, Jr.:

> The greatest danger in developing a thesis touching the philosophical limitations of science fiction is in one sense that which is on occasion generated by the contrary claims of the literary critic and those of the writer, whatever the nature of the latter's creation. . . . Carefully documented studies as well as casual reviews are prone to discover the presence of ideas or concepts quite likely foreign to authorial intent, or to bemoan the absence of what the critic would have included if he had been creative enough to have been doing the writing. [10]

To this I might add still a third problem: that of a critic criticizing an author for not doing precisely what the author is indeed doing, and that at great length, for the Robot series explores in depth and from various viewpoints the entire concept of artificial intelligence and the implications of that concept in regard to various aspects of human behavior, among other things. It should be added here that Professor Hogan's first caveat regarding the discovery of ideas possibly foreign to authorial intent can also be invoked in rebuttal to what I am about to do.

Any discussion of Asimov's works should be preceded by a recognition of his own statement to the effect that "I Just Make Them Up, See!" His autobiographical tidbits include a disclaimer of any intentional significance beyond face value, though he prudently admits that others might be more qualified than the author to judge whether or not deeper meanings lurk below the surface. At the risk of causing Dr. A. to "go away," I will state categorically that I am quite skeptical in regard to his disclaimer (I feel no obligation to believe anyone born in early January), especially in light of his repeated use of certain themes, metaphors, and techniques that display something more than mere creative eruptions. It is true that given his personal background and education, certain social themes and technological metaphors come naturally, but an integrated tidiness about the entire body of his fiction suggests that Dr. A. indeed knows what he is about. Even in the face of his disclaimer, he discusses several aspects of his own style and thematic concerns in his essays. For these reasons, I have often suspected Dr. A. of a certain coyness in this regard, and have wondered whether critics who have seen his remarks have missed some literary possibilities in his works by having relied on them. At any rate, I shall without compunction probe the obvious and explicate the uncomplicated, cheerfully assuming that anyone who writes so much fiction cannot be all honest.[11] And if one is to make any of the errors described by Professor Hogan, it would seem better to discover things not present than to overlook possible treasures that may be buried in an author's efforts.

In his "Introduction" to *Nebula Award Stories, No. 8*, Asimov wrote that "science fiction is relevant; it is important; it has something to do with the world; it gives meaning to life; and it enlightens the readers. And it has all these characteristics as no other form of literature has!" [12] He stated further that science fiction is the only form "that deals primarily and basically with change," that because it stimulates thoughtful contemplation about the future of earth, man, and self, it "is relevant to the present as nothing else is and performs a service for mankind that nothing else can." He then proffered the question, "does it not follow that ordinary fiction is becoming increasingly irrelevant?" In "When Aristotle

Fails, Try Science Fiction," he wrote that science fiction is the only literature of relevant ideas, since it is "the only literature that, at its best, is firmly based on scientific thought," and that while Homer and Aeschylus are "well worth discussing . . . even fun," their "eternal verities" are "precisely what science fiction doesn't deal with." [13]

It is apparent from his remark that while there are enough matters in Homer and Aeschylus, et al., to "keep an infinite number of minds busy for an infinite amount of time, . . . they weren't settled and aren't settled," he is linking these and other literary forms with such ancient and futile bones of contention as "how many angels can dance on the head of a pin." In short, if literature fails to help humankind through the here and now and into a better future, it is, though perhaps great, nevertheless irrelevant in a world where change prevails. He uses as an analogy the fact that "the faster an automobile is moving, the less the driver can concern himself with the eternal beauties of the scenery and the more he must involve himself with the trivial obstacles in the road ahead." [14] His primary complaint about mainstream literature, however, is that it deals in absolutes that cannot be proven false. The scientific method, while it "doesn't even pretend to define what Truth (with a capital T) is," does offer "a way of determining the false" and punctures pretensions for all to see. [15]

Professor Wolfe feels that Asimov's claims, while "perhaps a necessary feature of any literature that has long been ignored or even suppressed by the literary establishment" may "begin to sound rather shrill and hysterical." He further notes that "these eternal problems ('verities' is a false and misleading term) still appear in varying degrees in even Asimov's best work," and he questions the logic of "such accepted values of science fiction as rationalism and extrapolation" being "exclusive of the values of art" and indeed wonders why the " 'ideas' of science fiction should be rigidly scientific in nature." [16]

It is as though the author and the critic were speaking two different languages. Professor Wolfe refers to "eternal problems," noting that "verities" is a false and misleading word, despite the fact that Asimov definitely says and means "verities"—that is, "Truth with a capital T." What Asimov claims is that most literature deals in verities, absolutes, and Truth instead of with problems.

One of Asimov's most famous short stories addresses itself directly to this matter of absolutes. "Nightfall," written in rebuttal to

Emerson's Transcendental Idealism, pits observed human nature, with its age-old tendency to panic, against Emerson's optimist statement regarding the appearance of the stars. Professor Michael N. Stanton points out that "Emerson's and Asimov's stars are very different things. The passage from 'Nature' shows the stars and the Universe they light as symbolic—could man be jolted from his ruts of habit, he would acknowledge both the might and glory of his Creator and his own vital belonging to the Cosmos." [17] Asimov's stars are equally symbolic, regardless of how precisely he states the laws of gravity, and it is his claim in "Nightfall" that humankind has always resisted change with a determination approaching religious fervor—in fact, often religious in nature. Asimov writes:

> To a man who lived his life as his father had done and all his father's fathers as far back as his knowledge went, it would inevitably seem that there was a "natural order" of things. This natural order was prescribed either by the innate qualities of the human being and his world (if we listen to the Greek thinkers) or it was imposed by the greater wisdom of some supernatural being (if we listen to the Judean thinkers). In either case, it could neither be fought nor changed. [18]

Although he notes the existence of religious change, he has this to say:

> Religious revolutions, important though they are, cannot be creators of nonstatic societies. Each new religion, however scornful of the claims to absolute knowledge and absolute authority on the part of the older faith, is firm in the belief that now, at least, the truth *has* been found, and that there is no ground for any further innovations. [19]

Thus it is only with the greatest difficulty that humans are jolted from their ruts of habit, and then only to scurry desperately into a new rut. In "Nightfall" the scientific community is aware of the millennial madness that accompanies the appearance of the stars; it is prepared; it has even attempted to condition itself. But not even its wildest flights of extrapolation has prepared it for the reality of galactic immensity. Professor Stanton refers to the attitude expressed in "Nightfall" as "the modern and existential," and believes that it implies man's "utter isolation and alienation" from the Universe—his fearful rage against "the dying of the light." [20]

Stanton's article points out the role of John Campbell in the writing of "Nightfall," and in that light I think it is important to bear in mind that this is one of the few stories by Asimov in which such an apparently dim view is taken. In an early series of short stories beginning with "Homo Sol" (1940), collected in *The Early Asimov, Book One,* Asimov dealt with human panic and delineated it as one aspect of man's capacity for group action under emergency conditions. In his famous short story "The Last Question," found in *Nine Tomorrows,* humankind is anything but alienated from the Universe. Indeed, Man becomes the *dieux en machina* which creates the Universe and reverses entropy.

So cheerful is Asimov's usual fictional mien that it would be not at all out of line to treat "Nightfall" as a satire, designed to take a sly poke at Emerson in particular and Idealism or absolutism in general rather than as an expression of the darker elements of modern existentialism. Emerson looked toward the eventual perfectibility of mankind and society. Asimov indicated that the "motions and impulses of humanity: hate, love, fear, suspicion, passion, hunger, lust and so on . . . will not change while mankind remains Homo sapiens." [21] From the day in 1949 when Joseph Schwartz is catapulted into the future, through the day Susan Calvin teaches robot "Lenny" to say "mama," to the day Arkady Darell returns home to Terminus, Asimov's humanity never outgrows these qualities. Not even in "The Last Question" is Emersonian perfectability necessarily implied.

Even so, Asimov is not without his own absolute—though it is an open-ended one that permits an optimism of a kind altogether different from that of Emerson. Despite his rejection of a "natural order of things," Asimov through his works reveals a staunch belief in the Law as an ultimate factor in man's relationship to the Cosmos. He states that "to the ancient Greeks . . . science was not the study of the blind laws that governed the motions of matter and its components. Instead, it was simply an aspect of beauty. Its final aim was purely and statically intellectual. . . . The educated Greek hoped to appreciate the design of the universe . . . rather than see it as a handy device which impious man could seize and use to increase his own comfort." [22] His use of the term "blind laws" might be contrasted to the telic tenor of most of his works. Somehow, the laws of nature, of physics, and of human behavior all interact purposefully, and humankind with all its foibles participates actively (though often ignorantly) in, and perhaps ultimately benefits from, the directed currents of history.

Standing as he does at opposite ideological poles from Emerson, Asimov's attitudes show considerable similarity to those of Benjamin Franklin, who likewise did not anticipate perfected humanity and who likewise expressed faith in the progress and improvement of society in spite of, if not even because of, these very imperfections. By those definitions that give the name of "optimist" to one who believes in the essential goodness of man and the perfectability of mankind, Asimov, like Franklin, would be labeled as "pessimist." Few writers, however, display the kind of tolerance for the flaws of human beings found in Asimov's works. So many of his tales deal with the problem of prejudice—and in one essay he writes that "race prejudice is becoming a dangerous anachronism. We are treating with an outmoded emotional attitude a group of humans who outnumber us badly . . . (and on moral grounds we never did have a leg to stand on)." [23] In his stories of the far future, humans are still plagued by their fears and hatreds of other humans or other entities, and though he never provides a moral leg for them to stand on, he does show at length the reasons for their feelings and implies that so long as the reasons exist, the emotional attitudes will also exist. A few individuals, such as Elijah Baley, will free themselves, but most, like Toran Darell, cannot. A few, like Dr. Leebig, will helplessly turn into destructive moral monsters. Yet always the reasons will be presented so that even when we deplore, we must understand the fears and phobias that clog the ethical judgment.

While in several instances in his novels Asimov decries or satirizes absolutism, "Nightfall" is his definitive fictional statement on the subject. His impatience with the Greek Idealist philosophers expressed in his essays is the natural product of a mind steeped in the values and virtues of the "scientific method" and its corollary rejection of *a priori* Truths. His respect for inductive logic permeates both his fiction and nonfiction, and he gives no house to "intuition" in the Platonic sense nor to deductive logic.

Elijah Baley, of course, claims to have intuitions that contribute to the solution of crimes in *The Caves of Steel* and *The Naked Sun*, but when Robot Olivaw makes "intuitive leaps," Baley shrugs them off as the mere inductive processes of Olivaw's positronic computer brain. [24] Asimov's detectives Baley, Olivaw, and Wendell Urth are all shown to be using inductive reasoning of the highest order, and Baley deludes himself when he contrasts his own "hunches" to Olivaw's mechanistic thought processes.

The basic device of the *Foundation* trilogy—Hari Seldon's accumulation of vast masses of statistical particulars and his consequent generalizations and extrapolations of them—exemplifies the inductive, empirical, relativistic modes of the scientific method. Thus, the Robot and detective series and the *Foundation* trilogy, constituting the major portion of Asimov's works, are patently anti-Platonic, and anti-Emersonian as well. Indeed, one of his early short stories, "The Red Queen's Race" (in *The Early Asimov, Book Two*), bases its plot on the static attitudes of the Greek Idealists, and he uses them also in the satirical characterization of the dilletante, Lord Dorwin, in *Foundation*—a true eighteenth-century devotee of the Ancients.

In the humanities in general, but especially in the field of literature, there is a leaning toward aesthetic tradition that involves majestic Truth, Beauty, and Right. The scientific community, by its own definition of itself, is committed to relativism. The gulf between is wide and deep, as has been pointed out by C. P. Snow and others. When scientific standards are melded with literature, the result is somewhat jarring to the palate of one who believes in the existence of true aesthetic standards. Thomas L. Wymer offers a perceptive view of "Nightfall" when he writes that "like the Enlightenment it argues for the critical examination of traditional assumptions, most of which are rejected as the products of prejudice and superstition, and it champions the quest for a body of truth which can be confirmed by direct observation and demonstration and tested by universal applicability." [25] Wymer's observation of Asimov's link with the Enlightenment also expresses the values of the scientific method as it was conceived of by those eighteenth-century thinkers who rejected intuition and deduction and opted for experimentation, empiricism, direct observation, and induction. As Asimov has pointed out, this was the age in which modern progress began.

It is not surprising that the advent of the essentially Romantic New Wave in science fiction coincided with the easing of the genre into the halls of academe. It stands to reason that Asimov's cheery, tongue-in-cheek Determinism receives little sympathy from readers who find in Harlan Ellison's gumdrops-in-the-works a more appealing concept. True, as Asimov has noted, the New Wave writers "have a stronger literary background and are more interested in stylistic experimentation and in the new freedoms with which sex and inner consciousness may be explored," while at the same time they are "not as science oriented as the writers of a generation ago." [26] Though perhaps more stylistically experimental in terms of science fiction, the New Wave writers are more traditional in terms of mainstream literature and are thus more acceptable. But beyond that, the dramatic conflict between individual free will and the forces of Fate, Necessity, or Circumstance—a conflict that can exist only if free will does in fact exist—is part and parcel of the type of literature which accords with the traditional aesthetic standards professed by the literary discipline.

On the surface of Asimov's fiction there lie rousing good tales of galactic scope, full of interplanetary politics, intrigue, and suspense. Readily visible beneath this active veneer is the layer of social comment dealing primarily with the varied facets of xenophobia, but laced with dashes of acrophobia, claustrophobia, agoraphobia, and all the other phobias that humankind is heir to. These concerns rest on the deeper stratum of Asimov's view of individual and mass psychology. Repeatedly he demonstrates the effects of conditioning on human behavior, yet he does not confine himself to the rigors of Pavlovian or Skinnerian conditioning. Rather he provides his humankind with an organic, i.e., built-in, capacity for rising above conditioning: an ethical factor genetic in nature and thereby common to all living things as a survival trait. And below this, at a basaltic level, lies Asimov's own fairly systematic "philosophy" of reductive materialism and mechanistic determinism.

These levels persist throughout Asimov's fiction and are thoroughly interrelated. His concept of reality, and whatever there is of "message," is expressed through the story line on the one hand and the science metaphor on the other, and the two are so integrated that, as demonstrated above, it is easy to miss those points being made through the hard science imagery. Though as a bona fide mathematical moron I can only skirt the edges of these areas, I am convinced that a technological approach is essential to a full enjoyment of Asimov's style and content. My exposition then will be necessarily limited in this respect, but, I hope, may open some doors for further development.

The order in which I usually range Asimov's novels accords not with the chronology of their composition but rather with their position in the development of the Galactic Empire. The Thiotimoline group, including *The End of Eternity*, serves as a sort of prologue to Earth's entry into space and dismisses the matter of time travel. The Robot group depicts Earth's earliest explorations of near space and establishes the self-isolation and -insulation of the parent planet. *The Stars, Like Dust, The Currents of Space,* and *Pebble in the Sky* show the beginnings of Galactic Empire and the reestablishment of contact between Earth and her estranged descendents. The *Foundation* trilogy begins at the full flower of Empire, traces its fall, and points toward its renascence. *The Gods Themselves* goes beyond galactic concerns and links together three universes, presenting one of the more complex nonhuman life designs in Asimov's repertoire. In dealing with certain concepts developed in the novels, I will discuss a few short stories that bear out the theme or motif.

One of the most amusing and amazing products of Asimov's imagination is the famous mock technical paper, "The Endochronic Properties of Resublimated Thiotimoline" (in *The Early Asimov, Book Two*). Written in 1947 while he was preparing for his Ph.D. orals, "Thiotimoline" exhibits several thematic elements that appear and reappear in his later fiction and therefore provides an excellent introduction to his technical techniques. First, there is the science report format itself; second, the mock footnotes; third, the chemical itself as "hero"; fourth, and most important to this study, the reversal of cause and effect.

Asimov has told the story of the origins of "Thiotimoline" both in *The Early Asimov* and *Opus 100*. Having spent years developing an entertaining prose style, he was now faced with the prospect of writing a dull, dry, stuffy dissertation. "Thiotimoline," he reports, was to give him practice in writing badly. And so it did to perfection, for few things are as dull, dry, stuffy—and hilarious—as this soporific satire. In organization, thoroughness of detail, and coherency, it is a fine specimen of "tech" writing. In style it is, unfortunately, typical—not only of science papers but of those appearing in literary journals as well. It does bring up two characteristics of Asimov's fiction, one by contrast and one by comparison.

The contrast, of course, lies in the difference between the turgid prose of "Thiotimoline" and the clarity, simplicity, and precision of his fiction and nonfiction, even when he is dealing with complex subjects. His is the plain speech style that was intended by the seventeenth- and eighteenth-century science writers in their rebellion against the rhetorical excesses of previous centuries. Today that lucid style is associated only with popularizers, while scholarly writing in all fields, science and humanities alike, has reverted to turgid rhetoric, without even the benefit of metaphor or sentence balance. Asimov is not alone in his use of plain speech, for it characterizes many of the technically oriented writers of hard science fiction.

The comparison involves the organization of Asimov's serial fiction, which tends to follow the pattern of lab experiments. Take, for example, the Robot and *Foundation* groups. In the first book of each, *I, Robot* and *Foundation*, the lab conditions are provided and the ground rules set up. Terms are defined. The Three Laws of Robotics are explained and the results of weakening or strengthening each Law are tested; the statistical technology of psychohistory is defined and established on Terminus and three instances of its successful operation are put forth. In the second book of each group, *The Caves of Steel* and *Foundation and Empire*, the technological "hero" is field-tested. A major variable throws a monkey wrench into the works—a properly programmed robot is involved in a murder, and a mutant empath disrupts the progress of the Seldon Plan; in each case, the situation is partially salvaged by the end of the novel. The third book of each group, *The Naked Sun* and *Second Foundation*, resolves the problem by correcting errors, by refining techniques, and/or by redefining terms.

Overall, of course, the parallel to the traditional fiction formula is apparent: the situation is established; conflict arises, destroying order; and finally the climax and resolution conclude the work. The difference lies primarily in the fact that mainstream fiction purports to imitate life, while Asimov's fiction imitates the laws of physics. To restate, in mainstream fiction the ground rules and parameters are inherent in whatever "slice of life" the author chooses for his backdrop, while Asimov must fabricate a backdrop that incorporates physical law, a variant which appears to violate that law, and a resolution which demonstrates that law to be fundamentally inviolable.

On this basis it can be said that in each of these series a technological device is the primary "hero" that moves through each as human "herolets" come and go, the device-hero is threatened by the forces of disorder, and it survives in the end. Thus the tragic mode is virtually impossible in Asimov's fiction since the hero element, device, or idea is part and parcel of the law of the universe itself and therefore as indestructible as the universe. The suspense lies in the discovery of whether or not the hero is in fact in accordance with cosmic law, and in how that technological hero affects humanity as a whole. The comic mode, on the other hand, is quite feasible and it prevails in Asimov's work. Hence, we may enjoy

Thiotimoline, the thirstiest hero on record, as it rampages through a series of comic incidents, creating catastrophe for humans in its determination to resolve its own categorical imperative.

The reversal of cause and effect set up by "Thiotimoline" is of considerable importance because it establishes the ground situation for two novels, *The End of Eternity* and *Pebble in the Sky*, and for Asimov's own most beloved short story "The Last Question." All these works feature an effect which brings about its own cause. The possibility of effect preceding cause is ridiculous on the face of it in a context of linear time. On the other hand, if time, like space, is itself a multidimensional phenomenon which human perception can detect only longitudinally—that is, if past, present, and future, like length, breadth, and depth, all coexist simultaneously—then the idea of cause and effect becomes meaningless. Under these conditions it would be perfectly logical for a given condition in one time frame to draw forth a response from another, just as American political freedom once drew forth European suppressed persons, or just as a positively charged element will attract a negatively charged one. Thus, in "resublimated properties" the later inevitable addition of water can cause the previous occurrence of dissolved Thiotimoline; in *The End of Eternity* time travelers can hitch their wagon to a star that will later provide nova power; in *Pebble* the needs of decayed and impoverished Earth in the days of Galactic Empire can draw forth a Joseph Schwartz from the twentieth century's dawn of atomic science; and in "The Last Question" it becomes clearly feasible for humankind to develop the means for its own creation.

Cause and effect, then, as we know it, is a function of linear time, which is by no means a proven concept. Asimov's play of cause and effect is the function of a concept of time, the dimensions of which interact with the dimensions of space, rather than one of time as mere duration, or a fourth dimension of space. Needless to say, in such a context, "free will" must undergo redefinition or else be relegated to the realm of human wishful thinking. Asimov offers such a redefinition. Also affected by this concept is that type of human morality that relies on action and consequence, sin and responsibility. Science fiction in general contains a view of morality that differs somewhat from the traditional, but Asimov, more than any of the other writers, puts human morality in its very specific place: *second* (the First Law of Robotics dealing with the person-to-humanity ethic as opposed to the Second Law of Robotics, which deals with person-to-person morality and with social variables).

"The Resublimated Properties of Endochronic Thiotimoline" sets up a new kind of space-time continuum—a "Thio-time-line"— the "End-o-chronic" nature of which proceeds into *The End of Eternity*. In this novel, the ground situation of the simultaneity of past, present, and future has enabled humankind to harness the power of Nova Sol to create and maintain a "corridor" through time, extending from the twentieth century to the end of the solar system's million-or-so-year future. Within this closed corridor an elite corps of men, a temporal priesthood of sorts called the Eternals, travels from one time to another making adjustments that result in "reality changes," the purposes of which are to thwart space travel and to maintain the status quo of Earth as a "closed corporation." Now Asimov provides the laws that govern the situation he has set up.

First we have the Corridor itself, which, as Asimov describes it, is analogous to the current sent through a copper wire from a generator (Nova Sol) to the terminal (Earth in the late 1930s). The "kettles" in which the Eternals travel through time operate like electrons, that is, the kettles themselves do not move, but rather each sets up a vibration that activates a kettle in the adjacent time frame, thereby creating a moving line of force, or a current. The Corridor is depicted as a straight circuit throughout the novel. Only toward the end is it revealed that there is a loop in the circuit, created by the fact that the inventor had learned the secret of time travel during his youth as one of the Eternals and had gone *back* in time to invent the device.

The Corridor, then, is governed by the physical laws of electromotive force. The second law to be observed is the Law of Minimals, the Principle of Parsimony, or Occam's Razor. To effect a reality change in a given period of time, the Eternal goes back in time, steps out of his time-proof Corridor into the temporal world, and commits an act that will result in changing the future. First, however, he must compute the probabilities that would derive from possible acts so that he can put forth the minimum possible effort to achieve the minimum satisfactory reality change in the future.

Third, we have the laws of inertia. Each reality change creates a warp or stress on the fabric of time, which is one of the reasons for applying Occam's Razor. Whatever act the Eternal commits in the temporal world exerts a certain force which extends itself into the future with a momentum appropriate to the force until it is counteracted by the "mass" of time itself and gradually subsides. Thus a given reality change will be so planned as to exert its greatest force at the crucial moment and to wear itself out as soon as possible.

Therefore, and fourth, time is postulated to have a certain tensile strength. It can be "warped," as can the metal span of steel, but the warp generates energy in the material which must be dissipated within the context of the law of conservation of energy. Repeated reality changes eventually begin to build up excessive energy within the fabric of time. When the young inventor-to-have-been, having learned the technology of time travel, must travel back to the twentieth century to invent time travel, all these forces combine to create a short circuit, and the Corridor ceases to have ever existed.

So once and for all, Asimov dispenses with the matter of time travel, with its closed corporation, its esoteric elite, and its forces of conservatism, in favor of space travel and its connotations of liberty and expansion. But the "laws" Asimov has established in his world of time travel appear to remain in effect throughout his subsequent worlds of space development: the simultaneity of past, present, and future; and the concept of time as subject to the same laws of stress and inertia that three-dimensional space is heir to. These Asimovian time laws, then, form the ground situation for succeeding novels.

The End of Eternity is a statement of liberalism and a protest against such powers of conservatism as elitist or esoteric groups, economic, political, or religious, or any force that exerts a coercive influence on the mass of humanity. In theme it relates to Asimov's 1948 short story "The Red Queen's Race," which was written immediately after "Grow Old with Me," the short story that later became the novel *Pebble in the Sky*.[27]

Time travel having been dismissed, human technology now gives rise to the robot, establishing a partnership that opens up first the solar system and then the universe for human exploration. The Robot series chronicles this beginning stage of the Galactic Empire.

Before going on it might be helpful to review one of the important technological developments of the early twentieth century. Human experiments with electricity go far back into history, beginning perhaps with the discovery of static electricity in amber by the early Greeks. Industrial harnessing of electrical power began with eighteenth-century experimentation and came to fulfillment during the nineteenth century with the development of the telegraph and telephone and the prolific work of Edison—all, however, limited to "wire-bound" technology until Marconi's discoveries in radio. Even this development was limited in usefulness until Lee de Forest developed the triode in 1905 and thereby ushered in the Age of Electronics with all its banes and blessings. Before De Forest the diode structure characterized all electrical equipment—two terminals, anode and cathode, connected by metal wire or some other medium of conduction. De Forest added a third element to this system when he perfected the audion tube which featured, in addition to anode and cathode, a grid with a fluctuating charge. Since then, the invention in 1948 of the transistor has proffered vast improvement but no departure from the triode structure introduced by De Forest. Though Marconi took the first step toward freeing communication from wire-bound technology, it was De Forest who made it feasible, and for this he is called the Father of the Age of Electronics.

The triode provides a possible metaphorical parallel to physical nature in regard to the play on determinism and free will, and there is enough evidence from Asimov's fiction that he might consciously or unconsciously be using imagery based on this principle to warrant our using the "electrical approach" for our analysis. Let us say, for example, that the "life force" generates violent agitation in the "filament" of humanity, and "free electrons," or individuals, are shaken loose, driven sometimes entirely out of the filament, or "line" of humankind. These free electrons are headed toward some "positive" goal, the "plate." The grid—of space-time, circumstance, Necessity, or the "yes-no" attitudes involved in human interaction—*controls* the flow of free electrons by its ability to change polarity. When negative it repels most of the negative electrons, or individual elements, forcing them to remain in or near the mainstream filament. When positive it enables a limited flow of free electrons through to the positive plate, and the plate current increases.

In *The End of Eternity* Asimov presents a diode culture, its power source, or EMF, located in its own eventual destruction—Nova Sol—its current passing through the heavily insulated Corridor of Eternity, and its "electrons," the individual Eternals, utterly confined. The Galactic Empire might be likened to the original development of radio, and its "radiation" of humankind to the stars seen as a liberation from the closed circuit of time travel. In subsequent novels Asimov controls the free will functions of individuality by way of variations on his universal triode, its full development culminating in the transistor-like structure of Hari Seldon's Foundation terminals. Though the *Foundation* stories predate the transistor by some five years, the transistor and the audion share the same principles. Hence, the dictionary definition of the transistor, which is far more concise than those found in physics texts, might be useful in the following analyses, especially those of the *Foundation* trilogy. A transistor is

> A three-terminal semiconductor device used for amplification, switching, and detection, typically containing two rectifying junctions and characteristically operating so that the current between one pair of terminals controls the current between the other pair, one terminal being common to input and output.[28]

The Robot series explores at length the endless parallels between the human brain and the computer function of the machine. Beneath the surface of lighthearted robot stories and detective novels, Asimov studies the ethical problems inherent in programmed and conditioned humankind—the strength of cultural demands (Second Law) when tested against the needs of humanity as a whole (First Law).

I, Robot (and various robot stories excluded from that book) introduces the reader to the positronic robot, the Three Laws of Robotics, and that ultimate human robot, the "predestining" Susan Calvin who instills into every robot a "Puritan work ethic" and determines the required strength of each of the Three Laws.[29] We learn that a properly programmed robot cannot harm a human being, we are shown why not, and we see how variations in the strength of the Three Laws affect that premise. In addition, the evolution of the robot from the mute but sensate Robbie to the ultrahumanistic Stephen Byerley, World Coordinator, is revealed through a series of tales that recapitulate in their structure the evolution of literature from simple folk tale through Medieval theological exemplum and Renaissance Greek tragedy to complex contemporary short story style. The ultima Thule of robotic development, "The Last Question," is not included in *I, Robot* but should be borne in mind as the finale of Asimov's fictional universe.

In each Robot tale the manipulation of the Three Laws sets up stresses in the mechanism of the positronic brain, resulting in reactions and behavior decidedly emotional in nature. The relationship between the programmed brain and the emotional reactions is, I believe, fully demonstrated by Asimov, and it leads into the robot-human parallels developed in *The Caves of Steel* and *The Naked Sun*. The two detectives who appear as uncommon sidekicks in *Caves* and *Sun* are the properly programmed android robot and the culturally conditioned man. Each displays the "hang-ups" resulting from his conditioning and from the interplay between the imperatives of protection of humankind, obedience to human law, and self-interest. Their phobias, manias, preconceptions, prejudices, and panics are paralleled throughout.

Both novels juxtapose R. Daneel's "positronic" ethic to "copper" Baley's "electronic" (negative) ethic, and both are contrasted to the heavily insulated and nonconductive mentalities of those characters who are fixed and bigoted in their cultural milieus, unable to communicate, radiate, receive, rectify, or transform. These insulated elements, such as Leebig, the murderer in *Sun*, are simple diodes with a binary, yes-no, closed circuit, culture-bound morality, while the anode-Olivaw and the cathode-Baley, played against the yes-no grid of humankind, are able to expand beyond such insularity into a life-promoting ethic.

In *Caves* the murder occurs on Earth, when a Spacer roboticist, part of a Spacer colony attempting to persuade claustrophiliac Earthmen to colonize new planets, is killed. The obvious suspect would be an Earthman who detests the arrogant superiority of the Spacers and fears robots. Earth detective Elijah Baley is teamed with Spacer robot detective R. Daneel Olivaw, to solve the murder. Baley lives underground among a teeming population whose conditioned phobias are so deep that they have become cultural properties. The true matter of suspense, aside from who-done-it, lies in whether or not Baley can break cultural conditioning for the greater good of humankind in general. That he does so results, in *The Naked Sun*, in his being sent offworld (like the Biblical Elijah), again with R. Daneel (after the prophet Daniel, whose health and wholesomeness and devotion to the Law aroused hatred among the heathen) to solve a murder on Solaria—a "hot-house" planet whose Spacer inhabitants are as heavily laden with culture-phobias as "hot-house" Earth, perhaps more so.

Caves contains a chemical metaphor of some interest in that the Spacers hope to encourage dissatisfied Earthmen to colonize new planets with the help of robots, thereby forming a "C/Fe" (pronounced "see fee") culture. Daneel explains: "Carbon is the basis of human life and iron of robot life. It becomes easy to speak of C/Fe when you wish to express a culture that combines the best of the two on an equal but parallel basis." The diagonal that separates the two elements symbolizes "neither one nor the other, but a mixture of the two, without priority" (48). Such a mixture (depending on the formula and upon the word "priority" having nothing to do with "amount") can, of course, result in steel, an alloy in many ways superior to either of its constituents.

With extreme subtlety Asimov draws the parallels between man and robot—such subtlety, indeed, that it is quite possible not only to overlook them but to deny them altogether. Nevertheless, for every difference Baley claims between himself and Daneel, Asimov provides a situation that reveals them to be essentially alike. Even in the simple matter of curiosity, the same action is presented with different semantics. For example, when Baley visits the Spacer domes, he finds himself "goggling at the size of the rooms and the way in which space was so carelessly distributed" (68). Subsequently, it is reported that Daneel, visiting an Earth community dining room, "had been gazing at the interior of the kitchen with cool absorption" (100). We have here Baley's viewpoint to deal with, and Baley is convinced that humans and robots are indeed at opposite poles. When he asks whether Daneel can smile, it is "in sudden curiosity" (100). When Daneel inquires about contact lenses, it is "in order to learn more of Earth's peculiar customs" (175).

The Spacer roboticist Fastolfe tells Baley that "the essence of the robot mind lies in a completely literal interpretation of the universe. It recognizes no spirit in the First Law, only the letter" (74), when told that Daneel had drawn a blaster on rioting humans. He tells Baley that Daneel has been programmed with a drive for justice, to which Baley replies that justice "is an abstraction. Only a human being can use the term" (75). Daneel himself defines justice as "that which exists when all the laws are enforced," and claims that "an unjust law is a contradiction in terms." When Baley reads to Daneel from the Bible the passage in which Jesus forgives Mary Magdalene, Daneel professes ignorance of the terms "forgiveness" and "mercy" (148–49), yet he never shows rancor over a slight, and when he is slapped by suspect Clousarr, he tries to dodge the blow and then remarks, "That was a dangerous action, Francis. Had I not moved backward, you might easily have damaged your hand. As it is, I regret that I must have caused you pain" (159). In the end Daneel shows that he does understand such abstractions as mercy and the spirit of the law when he realizes that "the destruction of what should not be, that is, the destruction of what you people call evil, is less just and desirable than the conversion of this evil into what you call good" (191). To his own seeming surprise, he echoes the words of Jesus and tells the murderer, "Go, and sin no more!" Regarding Daneel's literal interpretation of the First Law, he later tells Baley that "we were never under any delusions as to which was more important, an individual or humanity," and that "there are degrees of justice, Elijah. When the lesser is incompatible with the greater, the lesser must give way" (174). Compare to this the definition of justice indicated by an Earthman, the police commissioner Enderby. Discussing a young man suspected of destroying a robot he says, "R. Sammy took his job away. I can understand how he feels. There would be a tremendous sense of justice. He would want a certain revenge. Wouldn't you?" (165). Here the human's idea of justice as revenge contrasts to that of both Elijah and Daneel.

Early in the book we find that Baley, having taken a battery of aptitude tests, was "capable enough, efficient enough" and possessed of a high loyalty index (56), while much later he notes Daneel's "queer mixture of ability and submissiveness" (160)—traits that precisely match his own. If Baley thinks Daneel is literal minded, he has only to look back on a certain very literal interpretation of the Biblical story of Jezabel, which had driven his romantic wife into the Medievalist Society. When he notes that Daneel never smiled (63), he later challenges the robot to do so. "R. Daneel smiled. . . . His lips curled back and the skin about either end folded." Baley reacts: "Don't bother, R. Daneel. It doesn't do a thing for you" (100). Much earlier, however, we learn that Baley himself is a sardonic man with a "long, grave face" (33) who rarely smiles, and much later, when confronted with the prospect that he himself might be under suspicion, "the corners of Baley's lips pulled back a savage trifle" (183).

Such parallels go on and on in *Caves* and to an even greater extent in *Sun*, for Asimov seems intent on demonstrating that the human being is a programmed being—including his virtues, his ethic, and his "spirit" as well. Baley, with all his Earth conditioning, is less bound than other humans because his father had been a victim of the system. Moreover, Baley is both practical and materialistic. Thus, just as Daneel is "converted" to the ethic of mercy, Baley is also converted to the space-oriented ethic of human progress. In each case, the conversion consists only in the character being provided with additional data to which his brain is receptive.

As the transitional *The Caves of Steel* presents Earthman versus Spacer on the Earthman's own home ground, *The Naked Sun* places Baley and Daneel on an isolated world in which the worst aspects of Spacer individualism have been grafted onto the worst aspects of Earth insularity. Just as Earthmen in *Caves* huddled together in vast apartment complexes where "natural Solariums" excluded air but admitted sunlight in only the wealthiest homes (53), Asimov now moves Baley to "Solaria," where Spacers live as far apart as possible in personal insularity, unable to tolerate the near presence of another human. Here a horticultural metaphor prevails in which only one blossom proves to be viable—a "Gladia" which is transplanted to a healthier environment. The horticultural metaphor demonstrates that the hothouse culture of the solarium is not a survival medium.

The Naked Sun also provides some "triode" possibilities. For one corpse there are three murderers. The wielder of the weapon, the immediate murderer, is culturally deficient—her Second Law is inadequately programmed. The weapon itself, a properly programmed robot, suffers from the revealed limitation in the Laws of Robotics: ignorance. Unable to fit his role in the murder into his strong First Law, he becomes insane despite his "innocence" of intent. It is subsequently demonstrated that R. Daneel's programing is more finely balanced. He, too, is instrumental in a human death, but his Third Law provides him with a self-protecting common sense that prevents unwarranted pangs of conscience.

The "true" murderer is, of course, the villain of the piece, even though he was nowhere near the scene of the crime.[30] He is the engineer of this and still other and greater crimes. His cultural imperatives outweigh all other factors; his Second Law comes first, his self-protective Third Law comes in second, and his First Law—the protection of humankind—comes in a far third, or goes off the track altogether. His binary, yes-no moral vision cannot cope with a multidimensional human ethic.

But Elijah Baley can. By an effort of will generated by his First Law directive, he is able to free himself from his cultured phobias and to overcome his earth-bound imperatives. He is a human being first, an Earthman second, and an individual last. As a result he is a free element moving toward a positive plate—the only true individualist. Having established humankind as robotic in nature, Asimov abandons the positronic robot as a major element in the continued growth of the Galactic Empire. The groundwork has been laid for the further discussion of free will in the Greater Galactic novels.

Between the Robot group and the *Foundation* trilogy falls another trio of novels that trace the spread of humanity through space by leaps and eons. *The Stars, Like Dust* portrays the pioneering period during which Earth is still known as the source of humankind. Probably no more than a quadrant of the Galaxy has been colonized, and the autonomous worlds, resembling feudal duchies, Scottish fiefs, or Latin-American ranchos, are gradually being gathered in by a Kahn-type conquerer. This is one of Asimov's weaker novels, featuring a love story that provides a delightful couple of hours' reading and is otherwise hardly worth mentioning.

The second book, *The Currents of Space*, leaps forward to the beginning of the Galactic Empire when Trantor is gradually gathering the inhabited systems into its fold. At this stage, Earth has been forgotten as the source of mankind—except among anxiety-ridden Earthmen living among Earth's radioactive ruins. For some the anxiety is too much. They develop terraphobia, taking to space as Spacioanalysts and avoiding planets. One such Earthman discovers that the sun of slave planet Florina, where the slaves are all of a pale, fair-haired complexion, is in the prenova stage as a result of having passed through one of the carbon currents of space. As part of the political and economic tug-of-war among Florinian liberationists, Sarkian slave-holding economic interests, and Trantorian imperialists, the Earthman is captured and brainwiped. This tale of espionage, murder, and suspense—and some romance—makes for excellent reading, but its science and sociology are too overt to require analysis here. A nice irony is presented when fair-haired slave planet Florina's rescue results in part from the meddling of a dark-skinned Spacioanalyst from "Libair" who feels sympathy because he and the Florinians represent the extremes of color among Galactic humanity. The book, first published in 1952, uses as its device the steady-state theory of solar continuity.

The third member of the Development trio is Asimov's earliest novel, *Pebble in the Sky*, published in 1950.[31] The setting is the height of Empire after "hundreds of thousands of years of expansion through space" (18). The influence of "Thiotimoline" can be seen in this tale when, as an aftermath of World War II, a half-baked lab experiment in the new field of atomic energy sends forth a deadly ray that shunts one Joseph Schwartz into the far future. Schwartz, an elderly Jewish tailor with a predilection for Browning, has already experienced one traumatic migration on account of racial persecution; now he is again uprooted and involuntarily emigrated into another.

In the latter-day Earth when he arrives, the forces of xenophobia are overwhelming, and Asimov brings forth repeatedly and graphically the conditioning factors that have brought them about: the myths, mistakes, private interests, religious bonds, and so forth. In this context Schwartz is destined to become a "savior," and toward this end he has certain powers—a forced-in historical perspective and a telepathy that provides him with an insight into his fellow man similar to that attributed to Jesus. Because history is "cyclical," the conditions are similar to those in Judea under the heel of the Romans. Because those cycles are "spiral," however, conditions are not the same, but instead partake of all subsequent political and religious developments. Schwartz is by no means a misdrawn "Christ figure"; he is a "savior figure," of which many and varied have appeared throughout human history. Thus Schwartz the Jew has a name meaning "black," and the downtrodden Earthies are a mixture of helots, "Polacks," "niggers," "chinks," "redskins," and other subjected groups. The "Earthie squaw" is named "Pola," and her father is engaged through his science in the same sort of "consciousness raising" that Chopin accomplished through his music. Far from limiting its attention to the New Testament period, *Pebble* features parallels to Moses, Lincoln, and other liberators—not all of whom necessarily died to make men free. The allusions range from the *Quo Vadis* persecutions to the "Old Schwartz Joe" of the American South.

As in "Thiotimoline" we are faced with the premise of the coexistence of past, present, and future. Asimov demonstrates in many of his works—and thoroughly explains in *The End of Eternity*—that the so-called errors of humankind or of nature, or the apparent deviations from that which is considered to be the norm, create the means for their own correction. Thus the experimentation leading to the Atomic Age which results in the ravaging of Earth also results in the Space Age by which humankind escapes to the stars; the experiment that eventually leads to Earth's position as a radioactive, backward, superstitious, and despised world also sends forth a Schwartz to "rectify" the error in the far upwhen. Here the myth of Pandora receives technological affirmation: for every ill effect released in the human quest for knowledge, a "savior-element" is also emitted.

In some ways *Pebble* is Asimov's richest novel, not only for the vast amount of food for thought presented by the varied sociological problems touched upon—racism, prejudice, euthanasia, brain tampering, and so forth—but because of the care expended on the characterization of Joseph Schwartz. He is one of the "free" elements liberated in a controlled universe—free, that is, in the sense that he has been "knocked out" of his atomic orbit like a beta particle. Like Elijah Baley, Schwartz is subject to such a situation because, as a particle previously subjected to social bombardment, he is on the outer fringes of the social atom and is not utterly bound to the twentieth-century American nucleus. Thus the laser-like ray emitted by the careless experimenter can readily knock him into a new orbit, and he will again be able to make the necessary adjustment to a strange environment and to patch up the split between Earthman and Spacer, like the good tailor that he is.

In line with the principles of Conservation of Energy, Asimov notes in a throwaway line toward the end of *Pebble* that the same mischief-making ray that knocked Schwartz into the day-after-tomorrow still races through the Galaxy, causing ships, and even one planet, to disappear mysteriously (150).

It is in the *Foundation* trilogy that the electronic imagery becomes apparent, and in *The Gods Themselves* that the triode metaphor is made explicit. Throughout the tales of Galactic Development, Asimov has contrasted the confinement and self-destructive potential of conservative absolutism and insularity to the *controlled* freedom of individual action, when that action is directed toward the goal of benefit to humanity rather than to the group or to the self. In each instance, the concept of the fixed future serves as backdrop to those individual actions and to the occurrence of seemingly random events as well.

The *Foundation* series provides a broad-sweep view of this interplay between fixed future and free will. The First and Second Foundations are the terminals of a massive triode, as demonstrated by the name given to the planet base of the First Foundation, "Terminus," and the mysterious locale of the Second Foundation, "Star's End." The "yes-no" grid of the forces of history, circumstance, and human mass psychology permits but *controls* the exercise of free will and of individual action.

As usual in Asimov's trilogies the first book, *Foundation*, sets up the parameters and ground rules for Asimov's metaphor. The spiral of history has expanded from the tiny Fall-of-Rome cycle to the massive Galactic crash, but is still repeating itself with variations. Sociomathematician Hari Seldon can now reckon with a population comparable to electrons, and therefore statistically predictable. During his trial Seldon points out the inertia involved in historical trends (1:1:6), and the mass involved in the fall of empire, so that even social trends are presented as analogous to the Laws of Gravity.[32] Though Seldon, like saviors before him, reveals a great deal to his listeners, and even more to his disciples, he conceals the major aspects of his plan, and to effect that plan he sets up two "terminal" foundations at opposite ends of the galaxy.

The First Foundation, the Arabia of the galactic Dark Ages, preserves the physical sciences, especially the atomic sciences, and remains a source of intellectual power that gives it physical ascendancy over the weakened body of the Empire. A series of saviors, such as "Salvor" Hardin, keep Seldon's plan functioning smoothly.

Foundation and Empire depicts the advent of an emotional factor, the Mule, whose role in the Galactic experiment as a so-called random factor is, I believe, clarified by comparison to the role of Dua in *The Gods Themselves*, to be discussed below. Just as Dua is called "Little Em" or "Left Em" (intellectualized emotions), the Mule might be seen as a majuscule Left Em: the *mem*, symbol for water, the humor of the emotions, the thirteenth, or unlucky, letter, and the symbol for mutual inductance. The Mule's "EmF" (emotional force) interferes with, deflects, and nearly dampens out the current of psychohistory, until the currents are rectified by the Second Foundation.

The Mule himself is an emotional cripple. "My meagerness is glandular; my nose I was born with. . . . I grew up haphazard; wounded and tortured in mind, full of self-pity and hatred of others" (2:11:26). As a mutant he possesses the power of emotional control, not only over others, but over himself. He describes his power: "To me, men's minds are dials, with pointers that indicate the prevailing emotion. . . . I learned that I could reach into those minds and turn the pointer to the spot I wished" (2:11:26). Thus he reaches the emotions by way of the mind.

Just as "perception" is a quality attributed primarily to Dua in *The Gods Themselves*, the Mule describes "a special facet of emotional control." He explains that "intuition or insight or hunch-tendency

. . . can be treated as an emotion" (2:II:26). Thus in the *Foundation* as well as in the Robot tales and *The Gods Themselves*, mind and emotion are closely linked.

In the guise of a clown—traditionally a disruptive element—the Mule proceeds to conquer the First Foundation and is on the point of discovering the secret location of the Second when he is brought to a halt by a woman, Bayta Darell. There is no problem, of course, in associating this name with the "beta particle"—a high-speed electron or positron, especially one emitted in radioactive decay, similar to the situation of Joseph Schwartz.

Decay is the prevailing condition of the atomic society of Terminus, the First Foundation. Bayta, reviewing the Seldon Plan, describes the old Galactic Empire as "falling apart of the triple disease of inertia, despotism, and maldistribution of the goods of the universe." And, she continues, "Now . . . every vice of the Empire has been repeated in the Foundation. Inertia! Our ruling class knows one law; no change. Despotism! They know one rule; force. Maldistribution! They know one desire; to hold what is theirs." Bayta's father-in-law confirms the diagnosis: "There's no hope in the flab-sides of the Foundation. . . . Not enough spunk left in the whole rotten world to outface one good Trader" (2:II:11).

So the atomic power culture of the Foundation, in a state of decay, has emitted one "Bayta particle." She will, in the end, "strike" Ebling Mis, who has discovered the location of the Second Foundation and is about to impart his finding to the Mule. By knocking out the Ebling particle, Bayta, in effect, defeats the Mule and saves the Seldon Plan. Again, as in *Pebble*, a catastrophic condition provides the means by which its own ravagings can eventually be rectified. It might be noted too that this action takes place in a vacuum (as in a vacuum tube), since Bayta triumphantly informs the Mule, "All your victories outside the Foundation count for nothing, since the Galaxy is a barbarian vacuum now" (2:II:26).

The problem of free will is one of the open issues in the *Foundation* trilogy, as it was a covert theme in the Robot group. In the trilogy, several characters are actively concerned about the implications of the Seldon Plan in regard to free will. In *Foundation and Empire*, Imperial General Bel Riose desires to attack the Foundation but is told regarding the Seldon Plan, "without pretending to predict the actions of individual humans, it formulated definite laws capable of mathematical analysis and extrapolation to govern and predict the mass action of human groups," and that "the place, time, and conditions all conspire mathematically and so, inevitably, to the development of Universal Empire," with the Foundation as its nucleus. Bel Riose indignantly reacts: "You are trying to say that I am a silly robot following a predetermined course into destruction. . . . We stand clasped tightly in the forcing hand of the Goddess of Historical Necessity. . . . And if I exercise my prerogative of freewill? If I choose to attack next year, or not to attack at all? How pliable is the Goddess?" He is told, "Attack now or never. . . . Do whatever you wish in your fullest exercise of freewill. You will still lose." And, of course, he does (2:ɪ:3).

But the larger concern with free will is that of Toran Darell, son of Bayta and father of the redoubtable *enfant terrible*, Arkady, in *Second Foundation*. Toran Darell hates the mysterious Second Foundation. After the death of his wife, "he knew that he could live only by fighting that vague and fearful enemy that deprived him of the dignity of manhood by controlling his destiny; that made life a miserable struggle against a foreordained end; that made all the universe a hateful and deadly chess game" (3:ɪɪ:14). In secret he devotes his widowed life to finding the way to identify and destroy a Second Foundationer. Only when he has solved this problem can he cope with the question, "When can a man know he is not a puppet? *How* can a man know he is not a puppet?" (3:ɪɪ:21). It is the arch irony of the tale that Darell's obsession is an essential part of the Second Foundation's efforts to restore the Seldon Plan.

And speaking of "arch," there is an interesting similarity in the names of the three generations of Darells. The name of Bayta's husband and of her son is "Toran," while her granddaughter's name is Arcadia, or Arkady. If "Toran" may be related to torus, we have a "toroid generated by a circle; a surface having the shape of a doughnut." When Toran Darell relates to his fellow conspirators his (and Arkady's) reasons for believing the Second Foundation to be located on Terminus, he describes the Galaxy as a flat, lens-shaped object: "A cross section along the flatness of it is a circle, and a circle had no end" (3:ɪɪ:21). Also, a torus is a "mound-like" structure—a convex form, like the galaxy in side-view. His brilliant daughter "Arcadia," in her journey from Terminus through Kalgan to "Star's End," might be seen as an "arc," a "luminous discharge of electric current crossing a gap between two electrodes." Moreover, she might be seen as a concave form; to the Second Foundationers, Arcadia and Toran are "the two poles of a hyperatomic motor; each being inactive without the other. And the switch had to be thrown—contact had to be made—at just the right moment" (3:ii:22). And the Second Foundation saw to that.

If the Foundations are two terminals, a ready-made grid is provided at the Kalgan space port, at the apex of Arkady's arc through space, but Arkady, a free but controlled particle, escapes through it to reach her destination on the metallic home-plate of Trantor, in the midst of the Second Foundation. Here she remains until time to make contact with her opposite pole on Terminus.

What then is the ultimate aim of the Seldon Plan? The First Speaker, Preem Palver, describes it: heretofore, "control of self and society has been left to chance or to the vague gropings of intuitive ethical systems based on inspiration and emotion. As a result, no culture of greater stability than about fifty-five percent has ever existed, and these only as the result of great human misery." In the future, an Empire "will have been established in which Mankind will be ready for the leadership of Mental Science," which is said to be "a benevolent dictatorship of the mentally best" (3:ii:8). Toran Darell depicts the brain as "the source of a myriad, tiny electromagnetic fields" in which "every fleeting emotion varies those fields in more or less intricate fashion" (3:ii:20). Thus we are dealing with the brain as an electrical device that produces ethical systems based on two elements—inspiration and emotion. As such, the brain is a diode structure with limited control, while it exists in a triode universe that is a controlled entity. When the human mind ceases to be "binary" and acquires the "control grid" of ethical awareness, it will be harmonious with the universe and the leadership of Mental Science will exist as a Second Galactic Empire in the inner universe of the individual mind.

Second Foundationer Preem Palver remarks that the flaws in the secrecy of the Second Foundation "remained unnoticed because Seldon had spoken of 'the other end' [of the Galaxy] in his way [sociologically], and they had interpreted it in their way [physically]" (3:ii:22)—an excellent statement perhaps of the problems of interpretation inherent in a totally literary or even humanistic approach to hard science fiction.

Speaking of Preem Palver, it might be well at this point to bring up a nontechnical aspect of Asimov's work, one that reinforces the technological imagery and the emphasis on Law that permeates the stories and novels. Without mentioning the name of Asimov, Leslie Fiedler has remarked in an essay that "the universe of science fiction is Jewish; the wise old tailor, the absurd but sympathetic *yiddishe momme*, plus a dozen other Jewish stereotypes, whiz unchanged across its space and time." [33] It is obvious, of course, that the above references are to Joseph Schwartz and Mrs. Preem Palver. Asimov is the first to agree with Fiedler's observation, though he writes, "I didn't think of Jews, particularly, in connection with robots, wrecked spaceships, strange worlds with six suns, and Galactic Empires. The subject didn't come up in my mind." Of Schwartz he says, "I didn't come right out and say he was Jewish, but I've never found anyone who thought he wasn't." He relates further that when it was necessary to have a character who, "for nefarious purposes of my own, I wanted the reader to underestimate," the trick was to "give him a substandard version of English, for then he would be dismissed as a comic character with at most a certain limited folk wisdom. Since the only substandard version of English I can handle faultlessly is the Yiddish dialect, some of the characters in *The Foundation Trilogy* speak it." [34]

Notably, the characters who are "free electrons" in Asimov's tales (Schwartz, Baley, Palver, and others) are subtly Jewish in flavor. Though they carry what he calls a "cultural stigmata (you should excuse the expression)," they are able to rise above it when necessary and to become citizens of humanity. [35] Though they break with the deadwood of tradition, they nevertheless carry the living branches of tradition with them wherever they go, and Asimov's use of extensive historical allusion in his cycle-of-history mode shows humankind as a species that retains its heritage even to the end of time. But heritage is one thing, and cultural conditioning is another, for the latter apparently has its roots so deep in the human psyche that Asimov has created a special short story to deal with the subject.

"Unto the Fourth Generation" depicts a secular, business-oriented young adman on his way to make an important sale, who finds himself distracted by the variant spellings of the name Lewkowitz, Levkovich, Lafkowitz, etc. [36] Striking out in pursuit of the source of the Name, he finds himself in a timeless mist in the heart of Brooklyn, where his racial heritage appears in the ghostly person of his great-great grandfather who has come to bless him. Light but poignant, "Unto the Fourth Generation" provides a parable of ethnic psychology quite in keeping with Asimov's many studies of human conditioning.

Still another short story might be mentioned before moving on to *The Gods Themselves*. A delightful exposition of the backstage workings of Fate, combined with the possible exorcising of a personal pain-in-the-neck, may be found in the whimsical short story "Spell My Name with an S," a plea no doubt made all too often by the author himself (and collected in *Nine Tomorrows*). Though it carries overtones of fantasy and the occult, the story features a very sincere numerologist who insists that his art stands on a solid scientific base—the same base, in fact, used by Hari Seldon to plot the future of the Galaxy, that of statistical extrapolation trimmed down to personal utility through the judicious application of Occam's Razor. Here Asimov tells of a dead-ended government employee named Zebatinsky who, in embarrassed desperation, consults a numerologist. After much computation the numerologist prescribes that the client's name be changed to Sebatinsky. The change sets off a perfectly logical chain reaction among the client's professional associates and superiors that quickly results in a promotion and prospects for continued advancement. None of the steps involved is ever revealed to the client, but the reader is treated to a revelation of cause and effect that is as enlightening as it is amusing. Despite the numerologist's efforts to convince his client of the scientific facts behind his art, the client, ignorant of the logical chain of events, will forever retain a superstitious belief in the occult. His attitude, and his refusal to take the numerologist's scientific explanation seriously, is a comic version of the near-tragic one of the pharisaic Earth Secretary and his cohorts in *Pebble*, as it is described by Schwartz: "They won't listen. Do you know why? Because they have certain fixed notions about the past. Any change would be blasphemy in their eyes, even if it were the truth. They don't want the truth; they want their traditions" (152).

In the context of Asimov's pro-intellectual bent, it is notable that he sometimes emphasizes the necessity of ignorance. In the *Foundation* trilogy, it is essential to the workings of the Seldon Plan that the Foundationers be kept completely in the dark regarding the projection of events, lest they disturb the statistical matrix by the very act of willfully trying to bring the event to pass. The opposite condition exists in *The End of Eternity*, wherein the select group of Eternals do have a way to foresee the future and, as a result, to meddle with it in a way that brings about their own end. Another dimension is presented in *The Gods Themselves*, where the Rational entity, Odeen, must remain ignorant of the true function of his marital triad until he figures the matter out for himself—at which point the triad fulfills its function. The same conditions exist in the short story "Profession" (in *Nine Tomorrows*), in which young George Platen, who is "abnormal" because he is unable to be "programmed" for his career by the use of education tapes, is placed in a "Home for the Feeble Minded," there to remain until he figures out for himself that the so-called "feeble-minded" constitute Earth's only source of original ideas.

In all three of these instances, Asimov points out that the fruit of knowledge must ripen before it is plucked—if it is to be plucked at all. While vast quantities of information can be ingested by the human brain, either by way of explanation or by a sort of "electroplating" process, one does not effectively understand the material until he assimilates it for himself. So frequently does Asimov inject this resistance factor of ignorance that one is tempted to suspect him of having noticed in himself a tendency toward sudden and illuminating syntheses of long-accumulated "bits" of information. This type of mental process is, of course, the basis for most detective stories, and applies to Elijah Baley's self-proclaimed "intuitive" solutions as well as to Wendell Urth's rational step-by-step analyses of accumulating evidence.

The title of Asimov's most recent novel is taken from a quotation, "Against stupidity, the gods themselves contend in vain"; but to that quotation Asimov has added a question mark. The stupidity of both humankind and the alien beings of the para-Universe in *The Gods Themselves*, even as it brings both races near to catastrophe, ultimately leads to the creation of a tri-universal power hook-up that provides benefit for all concerned.[37]

The denizens of the para-Universe are among Asimov's most unique life designs. The marital triad—consisting of the Rational, Odeen (odd-even); the Emotional, Dua (two); and the Parental, Tritt (three)—would seem to be his entry into the age-old game of dividing the human being into mind, spirit, and body. But Asimov's triad forms a triode of sorts, in which "the Emotional supplied the energy . . . the Rational the seed, the Parental the incubator" (95). Eventually, these three entities fuse to form a single individual whose name is Estwald. I would not dare to claim that this name intentionally points to Lee De Forest, but the syllable *wald* does mean "forest," while *est* can translate as either "east" or "it is."

The metaphysical division of the human being has long been a subject of scholastic debate in religion, philosophy, and literature. It is one of those "eternal verities" that Asimov himself decries. However, the triad of Estwald rests on an empirical rather than a philosophical base, and the relationships it suggests are analogous to those found in the physical world. Through the three-part structure of the novel, the Estwald triad is paralleled to the energy exchange among three universes in which the Earth universe is described as "a highway but not the terminus in either direction" (271), a function served by the Emotional, Dua, in the Estwald triode. The initial two-way energy exchange between the Earth universe and Estwald's para-Universe threatens dire catastrophe to Earth but cannot be disconnected because of a political and scientific power play among jealous factions on Earth. When the third element, the cosmeg-Universe, is brought into the union and set up on the Moon so as to operate in a vacuum, the power requirements of all three universes are filled—the assumption in the novel being that the flow of energy into the supposedly lifeless cosmeg-Universe might induce a big bang, "setting up a new kind of Universe that will eventually grow hospitable to life" (271).

The relationship within the Estwald triad might again come right from the dictionary's definition of the transistor. The three individual members form a three-terminal semiconductor which contains two rectifying junctions, and it operates so that the relationship between one pair of beings controls the relationship between the other pair, with one individual being common to both input and output of energy. It would not stretch the imagination too much to speculate as to whether a similar force governs the relationship among the human mind, emotions, and biological urges.

The Estwald triad has problems, however, that result in a shocking imbalance. The Emotional member, overintellectualized, gets out of control and nearly destroys the unit. On the other hand, this same Dua, the Emotional, provides most of the triad's capacitance for amplified consciousness, flexibility, and perceptiveness, just as a transistor provides amplification, switching, and detection.

The explicit "alien" sexuality that permeates this central section of the novel is delightfully satirical, even as it provides a serious comment on the relationship of body, mind, and emotion. Asimov describes it from the point of view of Dua: "She never expected to feel for either Odeen or Tritt the sheer intensity of longing they felt for each other. She could melt alone; they could melt only through her mediation" (92). The attraction between the square, stolid, conservative "right-ling" Tritt, and the oval, knowledge-seeking, adventurous but uptight "left-ling" Odeen identify them as possessing opposite charges. The direction of the "seed" from Odeen to Tritt identifies Odeen as a negative pole and Tritt as the positive. Dua, the mediator, carries both positive and negative capacity, a quality, indeed, that adds to her charm in the triad, if not to her comprehensibility.

In *The Gods Themselves*, as in the *Foundation* trilogy, there is an intriguing emphasis on secrecy. The responsibility for guiding the triad into the eventual merger that means death for the three and life for the individual Estwald rests with the Rational left-ling, Odeen, but he is never told the facts of the transformation and does not know that the triad will form a "Hard One" with its final sexual "melt."

> To put it together properly and permanently, just so, the Rational must reach a certain *pitch* [italics mine] in development. That pitch is reached when he finds out out, *for himself* [Asimov's italics], what it's all about: when his mind is finally keen enough to remember what has happened in all those temporary unions during melting. If the Rational were told, that development would be aborted and the time of the perfect melt could not be determined. The Hard One would form imperfectly. (166)

This necessary ignorance appears to be Asimov's rationale for the human tendency to "see through a glass, darkly."

The numerology of the triad offers yet another view of their relationship. Tritt, the biological right-ling, includes in his number three all three primary numbers; thus, as the triad's "Parental," he is capable of reproducing all three. Dua, the Emotional mid-ling, is included in Tritt, but excludes him—and Asimov shows that the sympathy or attraction between them is limited. Nevertheless, as sexual mediator, Dua links Tritt's three-ness to Odeen. Odeen, the Rational left-ling, is not given a numerical value, though he is, so to speak, the prime, or first, member of the triad as far as leadership is concerned. Instead he is designated as the "odd-even" member, which enables him to relate equally, though differently, to Tritt's three-ness and Dua's two-ness. By this numerological trick, each of the three is provided with a linkage factor: Tritt is inclusive, Dua mediative, and Odeen relative. Only as Estwald does the triad assume unity. Pursuing the metaphor of number, we might say that the biological aspect of an individual includes both emotion and intelligence; the emotional aspect is largely mental or imaginative, but provides both mind and body with their only path to ecstasy; while the intellectual aspect, ideally, controls both emotions and biological urges.

The actions of the triad reveal that both mind and body are ruthless in regard to the fulfillment of their needs, while the emotional element contains the ethic of concern for others. Thus it is Dua who tries to save the Earth universe from catastrophe, even at the risk of sacrificing herself, her triad, and her para-Universe. The outcome of the trilogy suggests that though this effort on the part of uncontrolled emotionalism fortunately fails, Dua still provides the warning that enables the Earth-universe to save itself by creating a universal triad.

The "electronic" approach to Asimov's works is a limited one, of course, since the "chemical" or "nuclear" approach might also reveal metaphorical possibilities. Though he draws from various fields of science, he often uses them as mere plot devices rather than as metaphorical or structural bases. In "Thiotimoline," chemistry serves as both plot device and metaphor; in the Robot group, computer technology provides the base for extrapolation, though the metaphor of this series lies in the predestining role of Dr. Calvin. Nuclear physics is extrapolated in *Pebble in the Sky*, astronomy in *The Currents of Space* and *The Gods Themselves*, statistics and symbolic logic in the *Foundation* trilogy.

As always, the question arises as to the author's intent—as to whether he is consciously constructing a galactic triode, for example, in order to demonstrate his concept of free will in a determinist context. As previously noted, two things work against this probability. First, Asimov claims no such intention; second, both the Robot group and the *Foundation* trilogy were first composed as separate short stories over a long period of time. In addition, we have Asimov's own word on the influences exerted by John Campbell on, among other things, the famous Three Laws of Robotics. On the other side of the question, however, stands the internal evidence of the works themselves. Regardless of the order in which they were written, the novels fall into place in the chronology of the Galactic Empire as though Asimov had conceptualized them from the very beginning. The electrical potential is clearly present in *The End of Eternity*, the *Foundation* trilogy, and *The Gods Themselves*, since Asimov makes use of electronic imagery in a way that is clearly intentional. Whether it is justifiable to focus upon these images and devices and to elevate them to metaphors in the face of Asimov's demurrers might be seen on the one hand as a critical fallacy such as that described by Professor Hogan, and on the other as a valid mode of extrapolating extrapolative literature.

Whatever Asimov's conscious intent, his consistency of theme is impressive and bespeaks a directed subconscious so orderly in the arrangement of its own conditioned preoccupations that it might well function on its own while Dr. A. fingers his compulsive typewriter. Moreover, the technology involved is most likely so ingrained in his mental processes that it can emerge in the structure of a novel with minimum conscious effort. So much for "apological" remarks. I am in any case concerned less with the author's intent than with the reader's prospects for enrichment, and I am convinced that Asimov's work contains a wealth of literary possibilities when approached on its own terms, namely, that in science fiction, "science" comes first.

4. Asimov's *Foundation* Novels: Historical Materialism Distorted into Cyclical Psychohistory *

CHARLES ELKINS

AMONG SCIENCE FICTION series, surely none has enjoyed such spectacular popularity as Isaac Asimov's *Foundation* stories. Asimov has been awarded a Hugo "for the best all-time science fiction series," and many science fiction aficionados describe their first encounter with Asimov's novels in religious terms. Alva Rogers' response is typical: the *Foundation* stories, he says, "are some of the greatest science fiction ever written, with a Sense of Wonder in the underlying concept that is truly out of this world." [1] Despite genuine questions which serious science fiction critics, such as Damon Knight, have raised with regard to the *Foundation* trilogy's "underlying concept," it continues to go through printing after printing.

Nevertheless, it is difficult to put one's finger on precisely what element or elements so fascinate readers. From just about any formal perspective, the *Foundation* trilogy is seriously flawed. The characters are undifferentiated and one-dimensional. Stylistically, the novels are disasters, and Asimov's ear for dialogue is simply atrocious. The characters speak with a monotonous rhythm and impoverished vocabulary characteristic of American teenagers' popular reading in the Forties and Fifties; the few exceptions are no better—e.g., the Mule, who, in the disguise of the Clown, speaks a pseudo-archaic courtly dialect, or Lord Dorwin, who speaks like Elmer Fudd, or the archetypal Jewish Mother who can say, "So shut your mouth, Pappa. Into you anybody could bump" (3:II:15). [2] The distinctive vocabulary traits are as a rule ludicrous: *God!* is replaced by *Galaxy!*, and when a character really wants to express his

---

* This chapter first appeared in a shorter version in *Science Fiction Studies* #8 (March 1976).

disgust or anger, he cries, "Son-of-a-Spacer!" or "I don't care an electron!" (1:v:1). To describe the characters' annoyance, arrogance, or bitterness, Asimov uses again and again one favorite adjective and adverb, *sardonic(ally)*:

> Sutt's eyes gleamed sardonically (1:v:1)
>
> Mallow stared him down sardonically (1:v:4)
>
> Riose looked sardonic (2:i:5)
>
> [Devers] stared at the two with sardonic belligerence (2:i:5)
>
> "What's wrong, trader?" he asked sardonically (2:i:7)
>
> The smooth lines of Pritcher's dark face twitched sardonically (3:i:2)
>
> But Anthor's eyes opened, quite suddenly, and fixed themselves sardonically on Munn's countenance (3:ii:20)

Evidently, all people in all time periods will be sardonic. In the twelve-thousandth year after the founding of the First Galactic Empire, characters still use terms drawn from the western—e.g., "lynching party" (2:ii:7)—and slogans imported from the political slang of the times, e.g., "lick-spittle clique of appeasers out of City Hall" (1:iii:2).

Nor is this merely a question of literary niceties. If language is both a symbolic screen through which we filter reality and an instrument by which we explore and change reality, then Asimov's style is totally inappropriate. He has imported a watered-down idiom of his time—the banal pseudo-factual style of the mass circulation magazines—into a world twelve thousand years into the future, with no change at all! The consciousness of his characters, as it is objectified in speech shows absolutely no historical development and hence fails to evoke in the reader any feeling for the future universe they inhabit.

The *Foundation* novels also fail by Asimov's own definition of what he calls "social science fiction." In an essay written shortly after their publication, Asimov defined it as "that branch of literature which is concerned with the impact of scientific advance upon human beings." [3] In another essay Asimov argued that science fiction "deals with the possible advance in science and with the potential changes—even those damned eternal verities—these may bring about in society." [4] These precepts do not square with his novels. There is no indication in the *Foundation* stories that scientific advances—e.g., traveling faster than light, developing atomic technology, predicting and controlling human events, and controlling minds—have *any* effect on people. Man remains essentially the same; the springs of human action are unchanged.

This conflict between Asimov's precepts and practice is a consequence of contradictory notions he holds about the nature of historical change. Despite his contention that science fiction deals with change and, moreover, that "scientific-economic change is master and political change is the servant" so that "technological changes lie at the root of political change," [5] Asimov does not believe in significant change. More precisely, he does not believe that scientific advances will entail any changes in men's mutual relationships: "hate, love, fear, suspicion, passion, hunger, lust . . . these will not change while mankind remains"; history repeats itself (in large outline at least) "with surprising specificity." [6] Citing Toynbee's cyclical theory of history as a basis for social theorizing and extrapolating from it into the future—a procedure which Toynbee explicitly rejected [7]—Asimov creates a future political structure modeled on the Roman and British empires. "In telling future-history," he relates, "I always felt it wisest to be guided by past-history. This was true in the 'Foundation' series too." [8]

That past history should serve as a guide for future history is a dubious assumption at best. It certainly undercuts any notion of significant change. Moreover, it is a fetter on the imaginative possibilities of the speculative novel. Instead of events growing out of the inner logic and premises of the narrative situation, the plot and characters are forced to conform to a predetermined template. Thus, not only is the concept itself questionable, but its use as a structuring and thematic device leads one to suspect a deficiency in imaginative vision. As a guiding framework for science fiction, it has, as a rule, disastrous consequences. Damon Knight rightly argues that it is not science fiction "any more than the well-known western with rayguns instead of sixshooters. . . . It's of the essence of speculative fiction that an original problem be set up which the author is obliged to work out for himself; if the problem is an old one, and he has only to look the answers up in a book, there's very little fun in it for anybody; moreover, the answers are certain to be wrong." [9]

Considering these problems, then, to what can one attribute the extraordinary success of the *Foundation* trilogy? I would suggest that the "Sense of Wonder in the underlying concept" which so captivates readers is a *concept of history* which is, in its grand sweep, similar to one of the main ingredients of Marxism—historical materialism—which had captured and is capturing the imagination of millions (although Asimov's use of it, as I shall argue, is a crude caricature of this concept, a simplistic distortion similar to other varieties of "vulgar" Marxism of the period when the *Foundation* stories were being written). The perspective of historical materialism entails the assertion of overriding historical laws. In its cruder versions it involves the old puzzle of historical inevitability (predestination) versus free will, which itself flows out of the often unsuccessful yet desperately necessary—and therefore always repeated—struggles of men to control their personal futures and the future of their societies. Consider this discussion of freedom versus necessity between the old, powerless patrician, Ducem Barr, who understands the implications of Seldon's Plan, and the eager, ambitious, and headstrong General of the Galactic Empire, Bel Riose:

Barr: Without pretending to predict the actions of individual humans, it [Seldon's Plan] formulated definite laws capable of mathematical analysis and extrapolation to govern and predict the mass action of human groups.

Riose: You are trying to say that I am a silly robot following a predetermined course into destruction.

Barr: No, . . . I have already said that the science had nothing to do with individual actions. It is the vaster background that has been foreseen.

Riose: Then we stand clasped tightly in the forcing hand of the Goddess of Historical Necessity.

Barr: Of *Psycho*-Historical Necessity. . . .

Riose: And if I exercise my prerogative of freewill? If I choose to attack next year, or not to attack at all? How pliable is the Goddess? How resourceful?

Barr: . . . Do whatever you wish in your fullest exercise of freewill. You will still lose.

Riose: Because of Hari Seldon's dead hand?

Barr: Because of the dead hand of the mathematics of human behavior that can neither be stopped, swerved, nor delayed. (2:1:3)

The logic of history is equated with the logic of the natural sciences. Bayta, the woman who eventually thwarts the Mule's efforts to locate the Second Foundation, says, "The laws of history are as absolute as the laws of physics, and if the probabilities of error are greater, it is only because history does not deal with as many humans as physics does atoms, so that individual variations count for more" (2:11:11). From the *Encyclopedia Galactica* one learns that Seldon's Plan can be reduced to "The synthesis of the calculus of n-variables and of n-dimensional geometry" (3:ii:8). Using incredibly complex mathematics, Seldon's Plan predicts the fall of the decadent First Galactic Empire (read Roman Empire), the rise of the Traders and Merchant Princes (read bourgeoisie and nationalism), the growth of the First Foundation (read postindustrial, bureaucratic-technological society), its interaction with the long-hidden Second Foundation, and the eventual creation of the Second Galactic Empire, a civilization based on "Mental Science" (read Asimov's utopian vision?).

It's a fascinating concept. At least on a superficial level, the conceptual parallels with classical Marxism are clear. Donald Wollheim, despite his crude caricature of Marxism, is correct in his "conjecture that Asimov took the basic premise of Marx and Engels, said to himself that there was a point there [i.e., in Marxism]—that the movements of human mass must be subject to the laws of motion and interaction, and that a science could be developed based upon mathematics and utilizing all the known data." [10] Is not Seldon's discovery precisely that which Marxists claim to have made? In his speech at Marx's funeral, Frederick Engels asserted that "just as Darwin discovered the law of evolution in organic nature, so Marx discovered the law of evolution in human history. . . . Marx also discovered the special law of motion governing the present-day capitalist method of production and the bourgeois society that this method of production has created." [11] Similarly, just as Seldon concentrates not on the individual but the masses, so—as Lenin says—"historical materialism made it possible for the first time to study with scientific accuracy the social conditions of the life of the masses and the changes in these conditions. . . . Marxism indicated the way to one all-embracing and comprehensive study of the processes of the rise, development, and decline of socio-economic systems. . . . Marx drew attention and indicated the way to a scientific study of history as a simple process which, with all its immense variety and contradictions, is governed by definite laws." [12]

It is this concept, that history has "definite laws" which cannot only be made intelligible but can give insight into the course of future historical events, which so intrigues both the readers of the *Foundation* novels and those who study Marxism. Whether embodied in Seldon's Plan or the concept of historical materialism, this idea is the very stuff of drama, for it inevitably raises the question of human free will versus historical determinism, a problem fraught with dramatic tension from Sophocles' *Oedipus Rex* through the present.

In the 1930s the mechanistic conception of Marxism was founded on such works as Plekhanov's *The Role of the Individual in History* (1898), Bukharin's *Historical Materialism* (1921), or Kautsky's *The Class Struggle* (1910), and canonized in Stalin's *Anarchism and Socialism* (1906). Stalin, for example, argued that "since modern collective work must lead inevitably to collective ownership, it is self-evident that the socialist order must follow capitalism with the same inevitability *as day follows night*." [13] It was precisely this crude conception of historical materialism that dominated the thinking of a large majority of American radicals and concerned social activists throughout the Thirties and into the Fifties, in and out of the Communist Party. (Much of Marx's and Engels' writings were still untranslated; the German Marxists' and Antonio Gramsci's works were unknown; most of Georg Lukács' essays were unavailable. What Marxist theory Americans received was basically what was filtered through the USSR under Stalin.) Obviously, this was an interpretation of history containing built-in contradictions and producing psychological as well as political tensions. On one hand, it created an impression that there was an inevitability to history which would run its course without any need for action. On the other, it encouraged a feeling that intense activity was necessary to bring about the fulfillment of the inevitable end.

This dilemma—given a predetermined outcome, to act or not to act—is exactly what Asimov's characters experience. It generates the dramatic tension in his novels. If Seldon's Plan is correct, the correct interpretation of history, what actions should the characters take when faced with the necessity of making crucial decisions? The hero of the First Foundation, Salvor Hardin, decides to wait until the "crisis" itself (an attack by another planet) limits his choice to one and only one course of action. He argues:

> . . . the future isn't nebulous. It's been calculated out by Seldon and charted. Each successive crisis in our history is mapped and each depends in a measure on the successful conclusion of the ones previous. . . . At each crisis our freedom of action would become circumscribed to the point where only one course of action was possible. . . . As long as *more* than one course of action is possible, the crisis has not been reached. We *must* let things drift so long as we possibly can. (1:III:2)

Hardin is content to follow the logic of Seldon's Plan; he will do "one hundred percent of nothing." By contrast, other characters, such as Bel Riose and Dr. Darell, resist the implication of the Plan and of historical inevitability: "he [Darell] knew that he could live only by fighting that vague and fearful enemy that deprived him of the dignity of manhood by controlling his destiny; that made life a miserable struggle against a foreordained end; that made all the universe a hateful and deadly chess game" (3:II:14). Ultimately, resistance is futile; all actions merely confirm the inevitability of Seldon's Plan.

The engrossment, the "Sense of Wonder" evoked by the *Foundation* trilogy, lies in the reader's discovery of this fact. Again and again the question is raised (by the characters and the reader): Is Seldon's Plan still operational? Has the Mule's interference negated the Plan? And time and again, just as Oedipus and Sophocles' audience come to understand the power of Apollo over man's destiny, Asimov's characters and readers come to comprehend the full implications of "Psycho-Historical Necessity." This understanding evokes a mixture of futility and awe.

Wollheim is on the right track in pointing out the probable Marxian "influence" on Asimov. Asimov must have been aware of Soviet Marxism: his parents immigrated from Russia in 1923, six years after the October Revolution. Moreover, 1939, the year Asimov began writing his future history, was the year of the Soviet-Nazi Pact, and he has recalled how he was caught up in the events unfolding in Europe.[14] If Asimov was at all aware of the pervading political and intellectual milieu of the New Deal decade, he would have been exposed to the clamorous controversies between the Left and Right as well as within the Left of the time (e.g., the passionate debates generated by the disillusionment of many prominent intellectuals with the Stalinist brand of Marxism and the American Communist Party's submission to the Soviet dogma[15]). While Asimov does not mention any involvement in radical politics, Sam Moskowitz credits him with helping to found the Futurian Science Literary Society in 1938, a society which James Blish says "was formed exclusively for those who were either actual members of the Communist Party or espoused the Party's policies." The members "did endorse the Marxist view of change, or whatever version of it the American CP was wedded to at the time."[16] To what *degree* Asimov was acquainted with Marxism at first hand is not of great import. He was certainly aware both of some of its slogans and of its power to arouse allegiance among intellectuals and crucially alter the tempo of world history.

However, awareness is one thing, understanding another. What Asimov accepted as the "underlying concept" of the *Foundation* trilogy is the vulgar, mechanical, debased version of Marxism promulgated in the Thirties—and still accepted by many today. Indeed he takes *this* brand of Marxism to its logical end; human actions and the history they create become as predictable as physical events in nature. Just as those scientific elites in our world who comprehend nature's laws manipulate nature to their advantage, so, too, the guardians and the First Speaker, who alone understand Seldon's Plan, manipulate individuals and control the course of history. "Psycho-history is," as Wollheim quaintly puts it, "the science that Marxism never became" [17] (a point to which I will return). With the proviso that neither Wollheim nor Asimov has understood Marxism (and that one should substitute "mechanical pseudo-Marxism" for their mentions of it), it is precisely this treatment of history as a "science" above men which accounts for the *Foundation* trilogy's ideological fascination and evocativeness as well as for its ultimate intellectual and artistic bankruptcy.

Reading the *Foundation* novels, one experiences an overriding sense of the inevitable, of a pervading fatalism. Everything in the universe is predetermined. Unable to change the preordained course of events, man becomes, instead of the agent of history, an object, a "pawn" (using Asimov's chess metaphor)[18] in the grip of historical necessity—i.e., of the actualization of Hari Seldon's calculations.

Except for the Mule, a nonhuman, only those who understand Seldon's Plan—the First Speaker and the twelve guardians—are free. They, the elite, are the only ones free to determine history, to make certain that Seldon's Plan is realized; so that in six hundred years the Second Foundation produces an elite group of psychologists "ready to assume leadership" and to create the Second Galactic Empire. The ignorant masses (those with whom Seldon's mathematics is supposed to deal) would resent "a ruling class of psychologists" because "only an insignificant minority . . . are inherently able to lead Man through the greater involvements of Mental Science" (3:II:8). Hence, it is imperative that the Plan be kept secret. No psychologist is permitted in the First Foundation. Seldon "worked with mobs, populations of whole planets, and only *blind* mobs who do not possess any foreknowledge of the results of their own actions. . . . Interference due to foresight would have knocked the Plan out of kilter" (1:III:2). Throughout the *Foundation* trilogy the masses are held in supreme contempt. They are described as "the fanatic hordes," "the featureless . . . mob"; their primary quality seems to be "incoherence" (1:v:14). The masses must be governed by a higher authority; they are not fit to rule themselves. This is the First Speaker's job: "For twenty-five years, he, and his administration, had been trying to force a Galaxy of stubborn and stupid human beings back to the path— It was a terrible task" (3:II:8).

The sense of fatality and futility evoked in the *Foundation* novels is a consequence of the reader's recognition that not only will Seldon's Plan remain hidden but even those who preserve it are almost overwhelmed by its complexity. A few will be free; the rest will be under the thumb of those who can understand the Plan. The First Speaker (and clearly Asimov himself, along with many other science fiction writers such as Robert Heinlein) envisions a society organized not according to the principles of equality but according to a hierarchy of merit. It is a society similar to the one urged by Saint-Simon, the French utopian thinker; he also argued for a society governed by *savants* (mathematicians, chemists, engineers, painters, writers, etc.), who would form a Council of Newton and, because they were men of genius, would have the right to determine human destiny.[19] In the *Foundation* trilogy the masses merely follow. Unable either to discover or to comprehend the Plan's "synthesis of the calculus of n-variables and n-dimensional geometry," the great majority of mankind is at the mercy of complex forces which they can neither understand nor control, and surrender their freedom to a techno-bureaucratic elite. Asimov thus expresses a modern version of Saint-Simon's ideology, namely, the necessity of society's being governed by a technocratic elite.

The realization that Seldon's Plan and the Second Foundation will remain a mystery, and that the Second Galactic Empire will come to pass despite the actions of the great mass of humanity, gives Asimov's *Foundation* trilogy its aura of fatalism. *Que sera, sera.* It seems to me that this attitude is one of the major reasons for the endurance of the *Foundation* novels, just as it is one of the fascinations inherent in a crude reading of Marxism. In many ways, fatalism is an attractive way of coming to terms with one's world. It implies and evokes a certain passivity. It is, in essence, a frame of adjustment which cautions man to submit to the inevitable. At its worst, this attitude encourages a slavish submission to circumstances. At its best, fatalism and its assumptions have been the basis for the tragic hero's confrontation with Fate and his sublime but ultimately futile struggle to control and overcome it. But Asimov's characters are not tragic heroes. They are nondescript pawns, unable to take their destiny into their own hands. There is no fear or pity to evoke a tragic catharsis. Instead there is complacency. The *Foundation* trilogy ends on a note of one-upmanship. After all that has happened, history is still on its course and Hari Seldon wins again.

Thus, the similarities of the underlying concept of the *Foundation* novels with even a vulgar Marxist version of historical materialism shed some new light on their fascination and staying power. However, one must also conclude that Asimov's failure to grasp the complexities of historical materialism and of the humanistic emphasis of Marxism constitutes their major intellectual and artistic deficiency. This needs to be emphasized because critics who have juxtaposed the *Foundation* novels with certain tenets of Marxism argue that the validity of the "underlying concept" and the strengths of the novels lie in their deviation from Marxism. In so doing, these critics continue to propagate a thoroughly distorted view of Marxism and thus produce a misleading evaluation of Asimov's achievements.

For example, Wollheim's argument that Asimov's psychohistory is the exact science that "Marxism thought it was and never could be " [20] entails a doubly preposterous comparison. To take Marxism first, Marx and Engels never claimed for their theories the status of "exact science." They were always careful to describe the "laws" of historical development as "tendencies." Marx warns that his theory of the capitalist mode of production assumes "that the laws of the capitalist mode of production develop in pure form. In reality there is always an approximation." [21] Similarly, Engels writes that no economic law "has any reality except as approximation, tendency, average, and not immediate reality. This is partly due to the fact that their action clashes with the simultaneous action of other laws, but partly due to their own nature as concepts." [22] So much for Wollheim's assertion that Marxism claimed to be an exact science.

Second, to focus now on psychohistory, Wollheim fails to point out that those who articulate Seldon's Plan consistently confuse *determinable* and *determined*. Note that Ducem Barr says that Seldon's mathematics can simultaneously "predict" and "govern" the action of large groups (he doesn't say how this happens). Seldon's Plan is designed not only to predict future galactic history but to *prevent* the long anarchy which would follow the collapse of the First Galactic Empire. Its power to control rests on the ability of the elite who guard the Plan to calculate all the possible variations, to keep the Plan secret from the rest of humanity, and to intervene, if necessary, to keep the Plan operational. To those who do not understand Seldon's "little algebra of humanity" (3:II:8), man's destiny appears fixed and inevitable. Man is seen merely as an *object* of history rather than, dialectically, as a *subject and object* in the making of history.

For Marxists, however, history is neither *determinable* nor *determined* by a set of abstract equations. History is people acting. People come to understand historical "laws" because in their action they simultaneously change history—each other and their social institutions—and are changed by it. Marx came to the conclusion that "the logic of history was thoroughly objective and communicable. It could be grasped by the intellect, and at the same time— since it was the history of man—it was capable of modification as soon as men understood the nature and process in which they were involved: a process whereby their own creations had assumed an aspect of seemingly internal and inevitable laws [Seldon's Plan!]. History therefore culminated not in the intellectual contemplation of the past, but in a deliberate shaping of the future." [23]

For Marx and Engels, the choices people make about their lives, their morals, their *praxis* (creative action), and their knowledge of their particular situation—all of these are included in the "laws" of social development. Marx believed that capitalism would be replaced by socialism because it not only had fatal economic limitations but also because those limitations would lead the great mass of humanity—not merely an elite—to adopt his theory as a guide to action. Marx did not relieve men of moral responsibility: "Underlying the whole of his work providing the ethical impulse that guided his hopes and his studies was a vision and theory of human freedom, of man as master of himself, of nature and of history." [24]

Behind Seldon's psychohistory lies the assumption—shared by Asimov—that mankind will not fundamentally change, that basic human drives are universal and eternal. Marx disagrees. His optimism is based on a rejection of this cyclical view of history. History sometimes may, but as a rule does not—and certainly does not have to—repeat itself. This rejection may help explain why some critics acquainted with Marxism are so exasperated by what they see as the essentially conservative nature of much contemporary science fiction. For example, Franz Rottensteiner charges that "present day science fiction, far from being *the* literature of change, is as a rule very conservative in its method as well as content. While paying lip service to change and offering some background slightly changed in relation to the author's environment, it actually comforts the reader with the palliative that nothing will ever really change, that we'll always be again what we have been before, in this world or the next; as below, so above; as on earth, so in the after life, Amen." [25]

For Marxists, however, technological change inevitably leads to changes in consciousness. If technological change, then change in the means of production; if change in the means of production, then change in the relations of production; if change in the human relations accompanying production, then changes in the super-structure (art, religion, philosophy, politics, etc.); if change in the superstructure, then change in human consciousness. Moreover, *this dialectic is reversible;* at given epochs—such as our own—human consciousness itself intervenes powerfully in changing the basic substructure of society (its materials and relations of production).[26] Marxism not only posits significant social change as men make their history, but Marx insists that *man himself,* literally his physical senses, is subject to alteration. In his intercourse with nature, man changes nature and himself. Marx writes, "The development of the five senses is the labor of the whole previous history of the world." [27] The revolution which brings communism will constitute "a universal act of human self-change." [28] Men will literally be dif-ferent from what they have been in the past.

By contrast, these relationships are not explored in the *Foun-dation* trilogy. Areas of social reality, such as interdependence of specific economic structures, appear as separate autonomous sectors. While Seldon recognizes that economic cycles are variables which his Plan must take into account (1:1:4), and while Asimov depicts the economic power of the First Foundation supplanting the politi-cal rule of the Empire (as if they were two entirely separate condi-tions), the relationships between economic and political power are not clear (2:1:10). The Machiavellian power struggles that constitute the essential plot of the *Foundation* trilogy are expressed almost ex-clusively in psychological terms. Politics and political savvy are equated with psychology (1:II:3); the Mule gains supremacy by controlling his enemies' emotions; the ultimate goal of the guardians of Seldon's Plan is establishing the Second Galactic Empire, which is described as a society ruled by psychologists skilled in "Mental Science" (3:ɪɪ:8). (It could be a "science" because Seldon assumes, as does Asimov, that "human reaction to stimuli would remain constant" [2:ɪɪ:25].) Human misery is not the result of external political, social, or economic oppression; rather it is the consequence of man's failure to communicate (3:ɪɪ:8). Furthermore, *this* failure is not a result of social, political, or economic differences but of the failure of language itself! Things would be fine if man could get along without human speech. Even here, however, Asimov never attempts to make the connections between these elements (the social, psychological, political, linguistic, economic, etc.) clear.

Thus, on one side, there is in Marxism a sense of almost unlimited possibility, of hope, of freedom; on the other, there is in the *Foundation* novels a sense of predestination, of remorseless logic, a pervading fatalism. Except for the elite who understand Seldon's Plan, the rest of mankind are ignorant counters in the grip of an idea which stands over and against them as universal, immutable, external law. From a Marxian perspective this is the very essence of slavery. Unable to comprehend the laws of nature or historical development, man is a slave to these laws, just as any animal is a slave to external circumstances. Uncognizable laws are manifested as "blind" Necessity. Man's freedom is determined by his ability to understand himself and to make his world comprehensible. Once understood, previously mysterious events lose their transcendent nature, their "fetishistic" quality as Marx would say; they become demystified and lose their power to move men through mystery. In striking contrast to Asimov's depiction of Seldon's Plan, it is the possibility that all men can ultimately comprehend those hidden and complex forces at work on them that gives Marxism its vision of hope. It is this comprehension that creates the conditions for freedom. By the same token, it is the reader's recognition that Seldon's Plan and the Second Foundation will remain a mystery, and that the Second Galactic Empire will come to pass regardless of any actions by the mass of humanity, which gives the *Foundation* trilogy its aura of fatalism and complacency.

Yet why not? From a Marxian perspective, Asimov's depiction of the particular future embodied in the *Foundation* stories is an accurate reflection of the material and historical situation out of which these works arose: the alienation of men and women in modern bourgeois society. For Marxists, alienation describes a situation in which the creations of people's minds and hands—whether they be goods or complex social systems—stand over and dominate their creators. Alienation is a consequence of man's impotence before the forces of nature and society, and of his ignorance of their operations. Alienation abates to the extent that man's knowledge and power over nature and his social relations are increased. Thus, in one sense, Asimov's *Foundation* trilogy endures *because* of its fatalistic perspective. It accurately sizes up the modern situation. Reading these novels, the reader experiences this fatalism which, in a Marxist analysis, flows from his own alienation in society and his sense of impotence in facing problems he can no longer understand, the solutions of which he puts in the hand of a techno-bureaucratic elite.

5. Asimov's Golden Age: The Ordering of an Art

DONALD M. HASSLER

> But now he saw and understood it as he never had before, a world in
> which degeneration had gone to the utmost limit. . . . [Humans] were
> the last terrible descendants, the last degenerated product, of the an-
> cient Arctarian colonists who once had been kings of intellect.
>
> Edmond Hamilton, "Devolution" (1936)

Isaac Asimov, in writing the strange mixture of literary history
and autobiography that serves as his commentary for including this
story in his anthology *Before the Golden Age*, describes Hamilton's
cosmic pessimism as a significant influence on his own thinking.
He writes, ". . . for years I had noticed that stories with sad end-
ings, or ironical ones, or paradoxical ones struck me harder than
those with conventionally happy ones, and stayed with me
longer." [1] The comment is brief and immediately followed by Asimov's customary reference to several of his own stories in the same
vein, but the unelaborated reference read in conjunction with
Hamilton's poignant little tale may itself be seen as a provocative
cluster of images that for Asimov constitute loss, a profound sense
of movement in history, and the comic sense that allows humankind to endure these conditions.

Even though the protagonist in the Hamilton story ends up a
suicide, the images that Asimov responded to contain patterns and
comic elements that allow the reader to maintain intellectual and
ironic distance. Actually, Asimov is more explicit about his fascination with these images of ironic juxtaposition and with the tone of
sadness mixed with a certain comic absurdity. In his introduction
to the Hamilton story he writes, "It's the third story by him I
couldn't forget from my teen-age years, and all three had to do, one
way or another, with the origin or development of life, and all took
a sardonic view of mankind." [2] The themes of origin or development invite comparison, and in addition to the three stories by

111

Hamilton there are several other stories remembered vividly by Asimov and chosen by him for this anthology in which science fiction's early historical periods are compared with a certain irony. A Clifford Simak story of 1931, "The World of the Red Sun," was part of the repertoire of that writer that influenced young Asimov. Asimov says of the story, "I could not help but recognize the force of a dramatic and ironic ending. ("The Man Who Evolved" had possessed one, too.)" [3] The story mentioned parenthetically by Asimov is another Edmond Hamilton story and the first in the anthology.

Two other writers, Neil Jones and Nat Schachner, are also represented in Asimov's personalized anthology by stories with strong images of ironic contrast and mutability. The Jones story, "The Jameson Satellite," is early and primitive, but Asimov recalls, "None of the flaws in language and construction were obvious to my eleven-and-a-half-year self, however. What I responded to was the tantalizing glimpse of possible immortality and the vision of the world's sad death." [4] This is pure, nonironic mutability; some irony might be seen, however, when we realize that "the world's sad death" is followed by more progressive development. A phrase that expresses this mutability and irony appears in the third Hamilton story, "The Accursed Galaxy," when the pure-force creature identifies the basic problem in all discussions of mutability—"this strange disease of matter." [5]

Ironic contrast is the key theme in the Schachner story, "Past, Present, and Future" (1937). What is usually considered to be progress—that is, the development to diversification, specialization, and complexity—is ironically shown to be, as in Hamilton's "devolution," a degeneration from an earlier ideal unity. In Schachner's story, a noble Greek observes of men ten thousand years advanced from himself, "Were these the beings of the future? Could a Greek of Alexander's day, steeped in Aristotle and Aeschylos, find sweet companionship with these spindly, feeble creatures who stood before him?" [6]

In an article in the *New York Times Book Review* for America's Bicentennial, Irving Howe described the adamant refusal of our greatest American writers to accept any awareness of history. [7] Howe associated this refusal with our innocent confidence as New Worlders that we are literally the incarnation of a new Golden Age. Unlike the Greek hero in the Schachner story who compares a degenerate future to an ideal Golden past, American writers (as they are ahistorical, Howe argued) fail to make such comparisons of the past to the present. Asimov was quoted in 1967 as saying, "From 1939 to 1949, I thought of myself as a science-fiction writer. From 1949 to 1958, I thought of myself as a biochemist. From 1958 to 1965, I thought of myself as a science writer. Now I don't know what to think of myself; my current interest is history." [8] This is obviously understated. As a young discoverer of the science fiction stories of the Thirties, Asimov responded continually to images of change, development, and history, as we have seen. He was reading Gibbon on the fall of the Roman Empire when he conceived his own most history-oriented fiction, the "Foundation" stories.[9] And finally as a literary autobiographer of the maturing genre of science fiction, Asimov is realizing the full complexities in a historical view of reality and of art.

It is no accident that the title of his most interesting and provocative autobiographical anthology (and he seems to have decided to do many of these) contains the image of the Golden Age.[10] This terminology of a Golden Age has become common in talking about the John W. Campbell era in science fiction, and so perhaps the significance of the image is more culturally widespread. But Asimov's explanation of his use of the image in his title seems to me more searching, suggestive, and profound than merely a culturally determined reflex. Rather I am convinced that the myth of a lost Golden Age and its implications for a view of history are deeply embedded in a complex of literary effects that Asimov makes which are much broader and deeper than merely a response to popular culture of the Forties. In the introduction to the anthology, he discusses the way in which each individual life recapitulates the mythic pattern of sensing and yearning for a lost Golden Age:

> To anyone who has lived a life that has not been utterly disastrous, there is an iridescent aura permeating its second decade. Memories of the first decade, extending back to before the age of ten, are dim, uncertain, and incomplete. Beginning with the third decade, after twenty, life becomes filled with adult responsibility and turns to lead.[11]

Usually the image *is* one of an Iron Age contrasted to a Golden Age, as we shall see later, and Asimov's sensitivity to the pattern seems quite explicit. A few paragraphs later he describes his own personal "golden age":

My own golden age (small letters) lay in the 1930s. It came in the decade just before the Golden Age (capital letters), and it had a glory for me—and a glory for everyone, for it was in *my* golden age that the personalities that molded the Golden Age, including Campbell himself, were themselves molded. . . . There was a rough-hewn vigor about them that sophistication has, to some extent, lost us.[12]

He is talking, of course, about Hamilton, Jones, Schachner, Weinbaum, Simak, and all the others he anthologizes.

The usual pattern is from unified simplicity to complexity, diversification, specialization, even sophistication, as Asimov refers to it. This is exactly the pattern he chooses to isolate and describe in comparing both his own adolescence to his maturity and the adolescence of science fiction in the Thirties to its more mature development since then. Usually, there is irony and ambivalence in such comparisons because certainly the "lead" or "iron" of sophistication has its advantages and the "gold" of unity has its absurdities.

The classic manifestation of the comparison of the Golden Age to the Iron Age emphasizes just this ambivalence. Eighteenth-century *philosophes*, deeply enmeshed in the debate concerning the Ancients and the Moderns, loved and, to a great extent, believed the following quotation from the Roman poet Ovid: "Golden was the first age, which, with no one to compel, without a law, of its own will, kept faith and did the right." [13] But each time the image of a perfect Golden Age (usually lost in the past) presented itself, it was mingled with its opposite, the image of the Iron Age of modern times, less perfect but vigorous and steely in its inventive drive toward progress. This beautifully balanced and mixed attitude of the eighteenth-century toward its own history, the Ancients and the Moderns, the Golden Age versus the Iron Age, is succinctly expressed in the following comment about one of the favorite types of poem, the Georgic: "Nostalgia for an idyllic past (or future) is entirely blended with pride in a vigorous present. The benefits that work can bring are in some ways greater than those accessible in a prelapsarian state, but, of course, the cost too is high. Consequently a man is forced to entertain contradictory feelings: there is no simple solution." [14]

The self-conscious running debate about the relative merits of the Ancients and the Moderns, which was so much a part of the eighteenth-century literature and which is a built-in comparison in any strongly historical view of things, also produced a literary phenomenon that recent critics have labeled the "Burden of the

Past." [15] This burden is related, of course, to the sense of a lost Golden Age; and, I think, Asimov and many twentieth-century writers continue to feel it—or they ignore history altogether, as Howe says, which is simply another way of "feeling" it. The point can be emphasized about this sense of loss that writers with a strong historical sense have always felt:

> Every modern man who has tried "to publish" knows this fear. Since Pope reminded us that epic heroes like Sarpedon were not self-conscious and could act directly and "heroically," we have been self-conscious. And this despairing reticence and uncertainty about what we do, which is really an uncertainty about who we are, may be the great unstated subject matter of modern literature. [16]

Obviously, neither Pope nor Asimov nor the majority of "modern" writers is really very reticent. They forge Iron Age products with great regularity and often with great irony.

In fact, the strong irony is a key symptom for diagnosing an ambivalent attitude toward this comparison of the Ancients and the Moderns. The comparison must be made clearly and incisively, but "modern" limitations must be accepted and worked with— hence, the irony. Pope was witty and ironic about his own fame and his own abilities *because* he was totally serious about maintaining them. Similarly, Asimov's innumerable writings are shot through with wit and irony. Sam Moskowitz refers to ". . . the spontaneous explosions of humor which he employed to reduce his self-consciousness. . . . At heart Isaac Asimov is and always has been a very serious man." [17] Joseph Patrouch touches on the same ambivalent effects in Asimov when he writes: ". . . all Asimovian stories [teach] the value of reason, yes, but that reason is applied to trifles which are completely beside the point of Asimov's main concerns. His stories actually serve to distract us from the real problems which he sees all around us. He cannot take his fiction seriously if he insists on using it in such inconsequential ways at a time when he sincerely believes civilization as we know it is breaking down." [18]

Asimov's career itself in broad outline has moved from art to science writing and popularizing to nostalgia, reminiscence, and categorizing about the career itself and about art. It is almost as though his own writing development has gone from a more single-minded and heroic simplicity to greater diversification, specialization and complexity. He apparently is fascinated by and encourages these cyclical and patterned views of development—progress or degeneration depending on how the development is interpreted. His own central creation of the Galactic Empire and then the Foundation (or Foundations) within that Empire follow this same pattern of movement from a heroic, more unified past to greater complexity and diversification which *can be* interpreted ambivalently as progress. The First Foundation itself experiences these patterns as the *Encyclopedia Galactica* says: "With forty years of expansion behind them, the Foundation faced the menace of Riose. The epic days of Hardin and Mallow had gone and with them a certain hard daring and resolution. . . ." (2:1:2)

The totally determined large overall movement of a patterned history such as the psychohistory of the Seldon Plan, or even the eighteenth-century notion of Necessity as seen in Thomas Godwin's writing, is in itself a kind of unity that individuals must react to with ambivalence. Many critics of Asimov have noted that the individual human being is not important or effective in the large patterns of psychohistory.[19] Asimov's own ambivalence toward this wonderful unity of psychohistory can be seen in his role as writer and writer of this history. To write is somehow to claim individuality and specific complexity from the large world of patterns and cycles. This is doomed to failure, to being an Iron Age activity of diversified progress that will never seem golden when compared to what has been lost. Nevertheless, the individual and the writer must grow and diversify. At least, Asimov certainly toys with the notion that the real hero in history must be the writer, the novelist, the chronicler—evidence is the heroine Arkady Darell, in the final book on Second Foundation, as well as in the narrator's voice in *Before the Golden Age*.

This dynamic of the writer as hero making a tentative order out of decay and degeneration can be seen in the great eighteenth-century historian Edward Gibbon, whose *Decline and Fall of the Roman Empire* provided a model for the *Foundation* trilogy—in as much as any epic work from a lost Golden Age can be a model for an Iron Age commercial venture. In a sense, that kind of Asimovian irony in which I just indulged is very much the topic of this whole discussion. As science fiction matures as a literary genre and becomes conscious of its own history and of literary history in general, it becomes more and more sophisticated and aware of antecedents and models. With this sophistication comes hesitancy and a sense of burden from tradition and the past. Asimov understands his history and uses his history, but as a writer he is changed by it.

In fact, as with Gibbon, the point of view and the understanding of the narrator may be more important to us than what is narrated. This sophistication, on the part both of the writer and the reader, and this Iron Age literary suppleness is certainly a long way from the simple heroic tales from an early Golden Age. A new collection of essays on Gibbon emphasizes again and again the central position of the historian in his history: *"The Decline and Fall of the Roman Empire* continues to be read, not for the precise dates of various emperors, but for Gibbon's own unique historical perspective; the enduring success of the work seems to rest on the singular and powerful imprint of Gibbon's mind on his materials." [20]

I identified Gibbon a moment ago as being a representative for us of a lost Golden Age. Gibbon, of course, believed strongly in continual progress—the kind of progress that will lead to the Second Galactic Empire after the Second Foundation. Perhaps his most famous sentence in the *Decline* leaves no doubt about his belief in progress: "We may therefore acquiesce in the pleasing conclusion that every age of the world has increased, and still increases, the real wealth, the happiness, the knowledge, and perhaps the virtue, of the human race." [21] At the same time, however, Gibbon's great work does trace a decline and fall with tortuous explicitness; he and his contemporaries looked back continually in their works to lost Golden Ages of their own. This is precisely the ambivalence of the Georgic poem, mentioned earlier, and a similar awareness of existence in the flow of time by Asimov has contributed to the maturing of science fiction as a genre.

Even more than his continual ambivalence of tone, however, Asimov's sheer variety of productivity and his continual attempt to make historical and literary placings reminds me of literary characteristics of the late eighteenth century in England when self-conscious, ambivalent geniuses were trying to order the fledgling arts—in particular, poetry in the vernacular. If Edward Gibbon is the prototype for the Iron Age historian in Asimov, then the prototype for the literary hack who elevates his profession by means of sophistication and moral intensity is Samuel Johnson. As it happens, Gibbon and Johnson met frequently in the Club,[22] and now both prototypes may be said to meet easily in Asimov. Key traits in Johnson's *The Lives of the Poets*, which did brilliantly for English poetry what writers like Moskowitz, Brian Aldiss, and Asimov seem to be trying to do in a less "modern" way for science fiction, are the sense of order coming from great variety and the ordering role of the commentator's individuality itself. Lawrence Lipking writes about Johnson's work: "No study of the *Lives* can be convincing unless it confronts their *lack* of any obvious unity, their formal variety, their passages of hack-work, their ability to please readers whose definitions of greatness have nothing to do with each other." [23]

Throughout Asimov's innumerable literary productions, each of them seeming to become more and more self-conscious, the unity resides in the individuality of the historian, as it does for Gibbon and for Johnson. Leo Braudy, in his fine study of the importance of "voice" in late eighteenth-century literature, writes: "They demonstrate that forms and interpretations can be insubstantial and ephemeral guides to a world necessarily ordered anew by each individual consciousness. Perhaps their final lesson is the need to take on personal responsibility for such a construction." [24] The individual voice is so important in Asimov, especially lately in his nonfiction, and it is a voice trying for balanced judgments and meaningful placings.

The deepest unity in any individual voice, however, can only be sensed in tone and shades of imagery. How sad, how feeling, how deep is the vision behind the voice? Here the best illustration and comparison can be found in Johnson and his profound sense of mutability and loss. Again, I am invoking the eighteenth century as a Golden Age (for us), just as they had their Golden Age, and surely as Asimov would like *his* prime looked backed on as a Golden Age. The sensitivity of Asimov to such a vision goes all the way back to his first reading of science fiction, as he tells us; it is like the Johnsonian vision that is permeated with the irony and sadness of the chronicler who is more sensitive than others to what has been lost. With Asimov, as with Johnson, the primary mitigating compensation for the sense of sadness and loss is the temporary power of the writer. Lipking writes:

> Convinced that no man's life would appear happy if we could scrutinize it closely enough, Johnson often assumes misery where he cannot prove it. . . . Literary biography asks not only whether men can be happy, but whether a literary vocation can be successful. . . . *The Lives of the Poets* records the professional histories of men who have tried to do something worthy of a man's attention, and thus implies that a literary vocation may do much to fill the vacuity of human life. [25]

The writing of history reveals—even produces—mutability, sadness, a sense of loss and fragmentation. Only when history is over and destroyed will we experience unity. In the meantime, we settle ironically, even gleefully as Asimov does often, for fragments, loss, and iron rather than gold.

6. Human Reactions to Technological Change in Asimov's Fiction

FERN MILMAN

IN "THE RED QUEEN'S RACE," [1] Professor Elmer Tywood hires someone to translate a chemistry textbook into Greek. He then sends the textbook back through time to ancient Greece by a process he discovered called micro-temporal-translation. Tywood believes that Rome, which had adopted the culture of Hellenic Greece, created an almost perfect civilization—the Pax Romana. What it lacked was a means to eliminate slavery so that all could enjoy its cultural benefits. Tywood feels this shortcoming can be eliminated through technology, using machines to replace slaves. Professor Tywood is attempting to make a culture change—an attempt at diffusion through time.

A change in the culture of a particular society may originate within the society, as in invention; or it may be the result of culture traits borrowed from another society, as in diffusion or acculturation. Invention may be either accidental or deliberate. Technological advances as the result of deliberate planning are a common part of our society today. An example of this is the United States' space program. Of course, no invention can be said to have caused a change in a culture if knowledge of it remains only with the inventor. An invention must be shared with and used by the society as a whole before it makes a culture change. Thus, the invention of the chronoscope in, for example, "The Dead Past" [2] can't be considered responsible for any culture change because the government has suppressed all research into or use of the chronoscope. The possible culture change—loss of privacy—is prevented.

Diffusion is the process by which a trait from the culture of one society becomes part of the culture of another. A cultural trait may spread from one society to neighboring societies—carried by traders, soldiers, missionaries, and so on. A cultural trait will be accepted if it fits the recipient culture, or it may be changed to fit the culture. Concrete cultural traits, such as technological devices and items of clothing, are more likely to be borrowed than cultural ideas as they are more easily communicated. Although diffusion involves occasional contacts between cultures, acculturation is a change in culture resulting from continuous first-hand contact between two different cultures. The relationship between the two cultures is often a superordinate-subordinate one, such as the relationship between Indians and whites in the United States. The superordinate group may use force, either physical or psychological, to get the other group to change. Even without force being applied to them, the members of the subordinate group may find they must change in order to survive because the stronger group has changed the environment.

Many factors affect the acceptance or rejection of a particular cultural trait. Ralph Linton discusses the initial acceptance of a cultural trait by a small group of individuals he calls "innovators" (Ralph Linton, ed., *Acculturation in Seven American Indian Tribes*, Appleton-Century Crofts, 1963). The innovators may be motivated by curiosity, by the novelty of the cultural trait, or by desire for prestige. If a cultural trait is too different from the rest of the society's culture, however, no one will accept it. The people most responsive to a culture change are either those most dissatisfied with present conditions or those who are more flexible and less committed to tradition, such as the young. Often in our culture, a new idea such as an item of fashion is first accepted by the young and then gradually spreads to the rest of the society.

The same processes operate in the spread of a cultural trait from the innovators to the rest of the society. In addition, the spread of a cultural trait to the rest of the group depends on the prestige of the innovators. The most important consideration in the acceptance of a cultural trait is its utility. If people feel a trait is not worth changing established behavior patterns, they will reject it.

Cultures everywhere are constantly being changed by the processes of invention, diffusion, and acculturation. Rates of change differ; some cultures change more rapidly than others. Technology has made rapid changes in our culture. In 1903, for example, the Wright brothers made history with a flight of 120 feet lasting twelve seconds; today, trips to the moon evoke no surprise. Technology has also made rapid progress in conquering disease and in communication.

But the changes technology brings aren't always advantageous. The same technological advances that have brought many benefits to our lives have also polluted our air and our oceans. And no one who has lost his job to a machine can have a completely positive attitude toward technological change. As Alan E. Nourse has pointed out, until this century change has been relatively slow, giving people time to adapt. Now change is much more rapid. Some people are able to accept and make use of change. According to Nourse:

> The vast majority of people, however, have always found change to be frightening, bewildering, or demoralizing. These people, typifying the forces of reaction or conservatism within the society, have sought to ignore, prevent, or control the forces of change in order to maintain a status quo.[3]

Man's feelings about his world are reflected in his fiction, and science fiction in particular deals with attitudes toward science and technology. According to Reginald Bretnor, science fiction is "fiction based on rational speculation regarding the human experience of science and its resultant technologies."[4] As one of the leading writers of technological science fiction, how does Isaac Asimov present man's reactions to technological change?

In his robot stories Asimov shows how people resist accepting the invention of the positronic robot into their daily lives, in spite of their many advantages. There's Robbie the perfect nursemaid, for example. What better nursemaid could a mother have for her child than one designed specifically for that purpose? And Robbie can never harm a child or allow any harm to occur because of the First Law of Robotics.[5]

Another advantage is that robots can function in outer space and on other planets under conditions unsuitable for humans. In "Victory Unintentional," robots are able to make the trip from Ganymede to Jupiter, a trip impossible for humans to make because the ship must have an interior vacuum to prevent explosion in the Jovian atmosphere. The same features that enable the robots to make the trip prevent the Jovians from declaring war against the humans on Ganymede.[6] In "Reason," Asimov gives us a robot able to run a space station which directs solar energy to the planets. This is what Powell explains to the robot Cutie:

> "When these stations were first established to feed solar energy to the planets, they were run by humans. However, the heat, the hard solar

radiations and the electron storms made the post a difficult one. Robots were developed to replace human labor and now only two human executives are required for each station. We are trying to replace even those, and that's where you come in. You're the highest type of robot ever developed and if you show the ability to run this station independently, no human need ever come here again except to bring parts for repairs." [7]

Sometimes the advantage is purely intellectual as with the Machines. The Machines' ability to collect data, analyze, and make calculations enables them to manage the world economy in a way that avoids conflicts, thereby keeping peace. Since, as with other positronic robots, they operate according to the Three Laws of Robotics, everything they do is for the good of mankind. [8]

But do these advantages persuade people to accept the positronic robot and make them want to have these marvelous mechanical servants work for them? No, just the opposite occurs. Having the perfect nursemaid to take care of her daughter doesn't make Gloria's mother happy. She thinks of Robbie only as a machine; she fears it and feels strange having it as a part of her life. These feelings cause her to argue with her husband:

> "You listen to *me*, George. I won't have my daughter entrusted to a machine—and I don't care how clever it is. It has no soul, and no one knows what it may be thinking. A child just isn't *made* to be guarded by a thing of metal."

Her attitude is reflected by the rest of the society. Initially, a law is passed in New York City keeping robots off the streets at night. Eventually, all use of robots, except for scientific research, is banned on Earth.

Asimov gives other examples of people's fear of robots. When robot AL-76 escapes from the United States Robot and Mechanical Men Corporation—the first robot to do so—he creates panic. People think a monster has gotten loose and they gather to shoot it down. [9] United States Robots and Mechanical Men, Inc. tries to eliminate this fear of robots. They allow people into U.S. Robots on guided tours. The idea is to allow "people to see robots at close quarters and counter their almost instinctive fear of the mechanical objects through increased familiarity." [10] The idea is a failure.

Part of this fear of the positronic robot is that the robot is superior in many ways to people and may replace them in certain areas. In *The Caves of Steel*, for example, some people lose their jobs to robots. This leads to antirobot riots. Feelings of inferiority to robots creates prejudice against them. The fear of being replaced by robots leads Dr. Ninheimer to attempt to destroy U.S. Robots.[11] He believes that eventually robots will rob people of their creativity. He tries to justify to Susan Calvin his reason for attempting to destroy U.S. Robots:

> "Your robot takes over the galleys. Soon it, or other robots, would take over the original writing, the searching of the sources, the checking and crosschecking of passages, perhaps even the deduction of conclusions. What would that leave the scholar? One thing only—the barren decisions concerning what orders to give the robot next! I want to save the future generations of the world of scholarship from such a final hell. That meant more to me than even my own reputation and so I set out to destroy U.S. Robots by whatever means."

People's feelings against the robots lead them to form antirobot organizations, such as the Fundamentalists. The Fundamentalists "were those who had not adapted themselves to what had once been called the Atomic Age, in the days when atoms were a novelty." [12] Even the Machines, controlling the world's economy for everyone's benefit, have their enemy in "The Evitable Conflict." This enemy is the Society for Humanity, composed of people unable to adapt to a changing culture. They believe the Machines are destroying human initiative and therefore try to sabotage them.

Even in the areas where the positronic robots are accepted, man tries to maintain control of them. That is the purpose of the Three Laws. This control is not foolproof, however. For example, Donovan and Powell have a problem in sending the robot Speedy to get selenium. The order to get the selenium and the danger to Speedy create a conflict between the Second and Third Laws. This makes Speedy the robot equivalent of drunk.[13] Another problem arises with Herbie—a robot who can read minds. The First Law makes it impossible for a robot to harm a human, even emotionally. This turns Herbie into a liar. He tells people what they want to hear so he won't hurt their feelings.[14] Thus, a robot may operate within the Three Laws and still not be completely under man's control.

Eventually, people begin to accept robots, as is seen in the *The Caves of Steel*. True, there is still antirobot feeling, but robots are now being used on Earth. Robots are in charge of everything outside of the Cities. They run the mines, the ranches, the farms. They pipe water to the Cities from the reservoirs. Finally, they are even allowed into the Cities.

On other worlds, robots are even more a part of society. In *The Naked Sun*, Solaria is a leader in the manufacture and export of specialty robots. The population on Solaria is twenty thousand. The human population, that is. The robot population is two hundred million—a human-robot ratio of ten thousand to one. Each person (or husband and wife) lives on his or her own estate, with robot servants to cater to every need. But this life of luxury, made possible by the small human population and large robot population, has its weaknesses. It has resulted in a prejudice against "seeing"—the physical presence of another human being. The size of an estate and its robot-run self-sufficiency make it possible for a Solarian to live completely alone, with no human contact necessary except for purposes of reproduction. And methods are being investigated that will make even *that* contact unnecessary. From being merely unnecessary, human contact becomes undesirable. This leads to the development of better viewing equipment and finally to the prejudice against "seeing." This in turn leads to a lack of human interaction and cooperation, and to intellectual stagnation. Thus, a technological change has led to changes in other areas of culture as well.

In several of his short stories, Asimov gives other examples of the consequences of the acceptance of invention. The acceptance of the teaching machine, for example, leads to individual learning. Each student has his or her own teaching machine, and eventually, school, as an institution where groups of students gather to be taught by a human teacher, may no longer exist.[15] Some of these consequences occur because people become too dependent on technology. This is the problem in "The Feeling of Power" where, because of his reliance on the computer, man no longer knows how to do simple arithmetic.[16] People believe a man can never do as capable a job as a machine.

Asimov also gives examples where people are doing more than just accepting machines, they are becoming machines. In "Segregationist" robots—Metallos—are so well-accepted that they have been granted citizenship, and people want to become more like them. A patient with a defective heart asks for a metallic replacement rather than one made of plastic that more closely operates like a human heart.[17] In "Profession" people's professions are chosen for them by brain analysis. The knowledge enabling them to perform the profession they have been chosen for is placed within the brain. Learning, as we know it, never occurs. Unfortunately, this method

makes it impossible for a technician to keep up with new developments in his field. If a new machine is invented, the technician
does not know how to use it. A technician who does know the new
machine is referred to as a new model—a term we use for a machine.[18]

The cultural changes resulting from the acceptance of technological inventions aren't always negative, however. In "All the
Troubles in the World," people adjust to the fact that Multivac can
predict crime and that Corrections agents can stop crime before it
is committed. This leads to a decrease in intentions to commit a
crime.[19] In the robot stories, Asimov has shown how resistance to
the positronic robot is followed gradually by acceptance. He gives
another example of resistance followed by acceptance in "Sally,"
which concerns automobiles with positronic brains. These automobiles require only the driver to punch in the destination, everything else is automatic. Since the positronic brain reacts faster
than the human brain, deaths due to automobile accidents are eliminated. At first, people protest when the old automobiles are
banned from the roads, but eventually they recognize the advantages of the automatic automobile—an example of the importance
of utility in the acceptance of a technological innovation.[20]

In *The Gods Themselves* Asimov discusses the acceptance and the
rejection of technological innovations on Earth and on the Moon.
There is the rapid and widespread acceptance of the Electron
Pump on Earth, for example. The Electron Pump is considered an
invention because that is the way Dr. Hallam and others want it
considered. Actually it is an example of diffusion from another
Universe. People readily accept the Electron Pump because it provides free and unlimited energy.

This rapid acceptance of the Electron Pump is unrepresentative
of the general attitude toward technological change, however.
Earth is anti-innovation. This is because the Great Crisis has "left
behind a permanent distrust of technology; a vast inertia; a lack of
desire to risk change because of the possible side-effects" (183). The
acceptance of the Electron Pump is easy; it is extremely useful and
trouble-free. Earthmen aren't ready to accept change; they are
afraid of it. On the Moon the attitude is just the opposite. Technology on the Moon is constantly growing. Lunar scientists find new
sources of food, water, and energy. They must, in order to survive.

This opposition of attitudes toward technological change also occurs in "Mother Earth." On the planet Aurora each home has its own power and utility supply, and as many positronic robots as are necessary to do the work. Earth, on the other hand, opposes robot labor, hydroponic farming, and birth control. The combination of the robot and low population gives the people of Aurora a different life-style than the people of Earth—a life-style of privacy, individuality, and luxury.[21] *The Gods Themselves* and "Mother Earth" can be considered examples of how the members of society who are young and less committed to tradition are those who are more responsive to change. Both the Moon and Aurora can be considered young societies as compared to Earth.

Thus, Asimov has shown how the acceptance of invention depends on the cultural attitude toward technological innovation, and how the acceptance of a technological innovation leads to changes in other areas of the culture. Asimov also gives examples of people's reactions to technological change from outside the society—by diffusion and acculturation. In "Homo Sol" Earthmen from a technologically advanced Earth meet with humanoids from other worlds. The Earthmen are very receptive toward change, but only toward technological change. They accept more than twenty gadgets they see in a museum on another world and adapt the ideas for use as military devices. They refuse, however, to accept the ideas of belonging to the Galactic Federation and peaceful cooperation with beings from other worlds.[22] This is an example of how people more readily accept material items than ideologies from another culture, and how they change these material items to fit their culture.

In "Youth" the Astronomer and the Industrialist discuss the consequences of accepting a thought projector from alien beings. The Industrialist is opposed to this diffusion of an item of alien culture. He fears the changes the thought projector might bring. He associates change with the atomic wars of the past. The Astronomer, on the other hand, wants the thought projector. He hopes it will stimulate cultural change. While the Industrialist believes that preventing any change will maintain the status quo, the Astronomer believes rather that this will result in the culture's decline.[23]

In *The Caves of Steel* the contact between two different cultures is more prolonged, a necessary condition for acculturation. People from the Outer Worlds settle on Earth in Spacetown. For twenty-five years they try to influence Earth to modernize, to adopt the integrated human/ robot society that the Outer Worlds have, believing this will benefit the Galaxy. The Spacers have been introducing robots into the Earth economy, thereby replacing men in their jobs. They hope to create a displaced and dissatisfied group of people who will be receptive to the idea of colonizing other worlds. The Spacers themselves lead lives that are too long and comfortable to risk in the colonization of new planets; Earthmen are too inflexible. Their culture—their living enclosed in Cities—has made it impossible for them to consider leaving their Cities, let alone leaving their planet. It is actually the Medievalists who will be the innovators and begin the change in culture leading to the colonizing of new planets by Earthmen. The Medievalists are the group of Earthmen most opposed to the Spacers. It is they who are responsible for Earth's antirobot riots. The Medievalists want Earth to return to its pre-City ways—to return to the soil. It is the Medievalists who desire change, who want to upset the status quo. They need only have their direction changed from going back to the soil of Earth to going forward—to the soil of other worlds.

In *The End of Eternity* there is a situation resembling acculturation: a superordinate society, the Eternals, force change upon a subordinate society, the Timers. This situation differs, however, from the usual acculturation because the Timers are unaware that the Eternals are introducing changes into their culture. When the Eternals introduce a change, they are creating a new reality. But it is new only from the point of view of the Eternals; for the Timers this "new" reality is the one that has always existed.

Thus, the Eternals have complete control over technological change. Only those technological innovations the Eternals approve of are allowed to remain. Otherwise, the Eternals make a Reality Change, creating a new reality in which that particular technological device has never existed. The Eternals believe they must do this, that they are working for the good of humanity. So they eliminate a mass duplicator that had been invented around the year 30,000 because the society that invented it was never able to solve the problems resulting from it. The objects eliminated in Time are preserved in Eternity. The Eternals are able to use these objects, as they have used the mass duplicator. Allowing these objects to remain in Time, the Eternals feel, would have dangerous consequences. "Man had to be protected from his own too flourishing technical mind" (p. 95). Sometimes changes in another area of a culture affect technological development. A Reality Change made in the 2481st Century to eliminate drug addiction, for example, results in the elimination of electrogravitic space travel. The Eternals' attitude toward technological change and their role in controlling it are expressed by Senior Computer Twissell:

> "The intention of the circle in Time is to establish the knowledge of Time-travel and of the nature of Reality, to build Eternity, ahead of its natural Time. Left to itself, mankind would not have learned the truth about Time before their technological advances in other directions had made racial suicide inevitable." (125)

But the Eternals have been operating under a delusion. Their Reality Changes have not been for the good of man, but rather for "Safety and security. Moderation. Nothing in excess. No risks without overwhelming certainty of an adequate return" (186). The Eternals, by establishing this state of security, have prevented Man from reaching beyond the Solar System until after the 125,000th Century. This has given time for other intelligences, younger than mankind, to colonize the Galaxy. By the time Earthmen reach the rest of the Galaxy, there is no place for them. Man returns to Earth demoralized. By the year 150,000, mankind has become extinct.

In the *Foundation* trilogy, Asimov gives numerous examples of attempts by one society to change the culture of another through the processes of diffusion and acculturation, as well as examples of resistance and acceptance of technological change. The first move toward acceptance of technological change takes place within the First Foundation. Originally, the First Foundation's primary purpose is the writing of the Encyclopedia Galactica—the preservation of the knowledge of the Galaxy through the period of the decline and fall of the Empire. Though they call themselves scientists, the Encyclopedists are only preserving knowledge, not adding to it. It isn't until fifty years after the founding of the Encyclopedia that the Encyclopedists discover they have been working on a fraud. Salvor Hardin takes over leadership of Terminus and technological growth begins.

Hardin begins the task of getting the Four Kingdoms of the periphery to accept the technology of the Foundation. The Foundation is the superordinate society trying to acculturate the Four Kingdoms, the subordinate society. The Four Kingdoms have declined scientifically, as part of the general decline of the Empire. They no longer have atomic power. As is often the case with acculturation, Hardin has to use force. But not physical force. As Hardin often says, "Violence is the last refuge of the incompetent" (1:ɪɪ:5). So he uses psychological force. He gets the Four Kingdoms to accept the Foundation's science by making a religion of it. As Hardin states, ". . . the barbarians looked upon our science as a sort of magical sorcery, and it was easiest to get them to accept it on that basis" (1:ɪɪɪ:1). Otherwise, the Kingdoms would have resisted the acceptance of the Foundation's technology. According to Poly Verisof, high priest of Anacreon and the Foundation's representative:

"... when the old Empire began to rot at the fringes, it could be considered that science, as science, had failed the outer worlds. To be reaccepted it would have to present itself in another guise—and it has done just that." (1:ɪɪɪ:2)

In this way Hardin gets the Four Kingdoms to accept atomic power technology—energy for heat and light and communication systems—run by priests who are trained by the Foundation. The Four Kingdoms have become acculturated, but the Foundation remains in control.

An important way elements of culture spread from one society to another is through trade. The Foundation Traders bring the atomic devices of the Foundation to many other worlds. But a society will reject cultural elements from another society when these elements conflict with the rest of its culture. This is the problem the Foundation Traders encounter when they try to sell atomic devices to Askone. Askone resists accepting technological changes from the Foundation for religious reasons. The Grand Master of Askone tells one of the Traders his atomic devices "are worthless in that they lack the ancestral blessing. Your goods are wicked and accursed in that they lie under the ancestral interdict" (1:ɪv:2). The Askonians identify atomic power and advanced science with the imperial regime they drove out long ago when they set up an independent government.

What the Foundation Traders need on Askone is one of Ralph Linton's "innovators," someone who is particularly motivated by desire for novelty or prestige to accept new technological devices. The innovator is usually someone less committed to tradition or more dissatisfied with the status quo than other members of the society. Trader Limmar Ponyets finds his innovator in Pherl, member of the council of the Elders of Askone, and favorite of the Grand Master. Being the favorite of the Grand Master has made Pherl many enemies; in addition, he is young and his family does not belong to one of the Five Tribes. This combination of circumstances is bound to create problems for Pherl upon the death of the Grand Master. So Ponyets is able to convince Pherl to buy an atomic device—a transmuter—with which Pherl may make all the gold he will need to smooth his path to being next Grand Master. At the same time, Ponyets blackmails Pherl into buying the rest of his atomic devices as well.

So the First Foundation encounters resistance when attempting to bring technological change to the rest of the Galaxy. But the First Foundation itself resists acculturation by the Second Foundation. The Second Foundation represents a different type of technology from the First Foundation. The First Foundation is a world of physical scientists; the Second Foundation is a world of mental scientists. Since technology is the application of science, both Foundations can be considered to be involved in spreading technological change.

The First Foundation resists this control by the psychological technologists of the Second Foundation. Some of the people of the First Foundation search for the Second Foundation. Some of them have become psychologists, presenting a serious threat to Seldon's Plan. For Seldon's Plan is one of acculturation—of the Galaxy by the First Foundation and of the Second Galactic Empire by the Second Foundation. Seldon believes that past emphasis on physical science, and not enough emphasis on society, has never led to the creation of a stable culture. He proposes "a benevolent dictatorship of the mentally best" (3:II:8). Naturally, this would be resented by the rest of mankind. Seldon's Plan is to avoid this resentment without the use of a force that would crush mankind. As a student of the Second Foundation expresses it:

> "The solution is the Seldon Plan. Conditions have been so arranged and so maintained that in a millennium from its beginnings—six hundred years from now, a Second Galactic Empire will have been established in which Mankind will be ready for the leadership of Mental Science. In that same interval, the Second Foundation in *its* development, will have brought forth a group of Psychologists ready to assume leadership. Or, as I have myself often thought, the First Foundation supplies the physical framework of a single political unit, and the Second Foundation supplies the mental framework of a ready-made ruling class." (3:II:8)

Thus, in his fiction Asimov has given examples of all the ways in which technological change may occur. There is technological change from within the society—or invention—as with the positronic robot. And there are examples of technological change by diffusion and acculturation, between societies as in the *Foundation* trilogy, and through time as in "The Red Queen's Race" and *The End of Eternity*. Asimov also cites man's different reactions to technological change. There is the positive attitude and acceptance of technological change by the people of the First Foundation in *Foundation* and the people who inhabit the Moon in *The Gods Themselves*. There are efforts to control technological change as the Three Laws of Robotics control the positronic robot. And there are attempts to prevent technological change, such as the antirobot organizations.

Do all these problems arising from technological change in Asimov's fiction mean that he believes technological innovation is bad for mankind? Entire cultures indeed believe this. It is a view held, for example, by the Trobriand Islanders, and it stems from their idea of reality. The Trobriand Islanders' view of reality differs from the linear one we have. This lack of lineality can be seen in their language, which contains no temporal or cause-and-effect relationships. Thus, they do not say that the *taytu* (a kind of yam) becomes overripe. Overripeness is a quality of something entirely different—a *yowana*. To the Trobrianders, the value of a magical spell lies in itself, not in its results. In our culture, at least up to the present, the line is an integral part of reality—a study must show what it leads to, a history must progress chronologically. The Trobriander's history is a collection of anecdotes, not connected by cause-and-effect relationships or arranged chronologically:

> To the Trobriander, climax in history is abominable, a denial of all good, since it would imply not only the presence of change, but also that change increases the good; but to him value lies in sameness, in repeated pattern, in the incorporation of all time within the same point.[24]

This view is quite different from that presented in Asimov's fiction. For Asimov, when technological change is resisted or prevented, the resulting stagnation is a much worse alternative than facing the problems brought on by such change. In *The Stars, Like Dust* it is the enemy—the Tyranni—who deliberately causes stagnation. The Tyranni have stopped the technological growth of the planet Rhodia and other worlds of the Nebular Regions to keep them from becoming militarily powerful. Gillbret, brother of the Director of Rhodia, explains the results of this stagnation, even if, centuries later, the Tyranni have been defeated:

". . . And when those centuries have passed, we will still all be agricultural worlds with no industrial or scientific heritage to speak of, while our neighbors on all sides, those not under Tyrannian control, will be strong and urbanized. The Kingdoms will be semicolonial areas forever. They will *never* catch up, and we will be merely observers in the great drama of human advance." (p. 58)

That stagnation is the work of the enemy. But stagnation may result from misguided benevolence, such as the stagnation created by the Eternals in *The End of Eternity*. By steering the course of mankind's technological innovations too much along the road of safety and security, the Eternals keep space travel from developing for many centuries. As a woman from the Hidden Centuries explains:

"When we moved out into space, the signs were up. *Occupied! No Trespassing! Clear Out!* Mankind drew back its exploratory feelers, remained at home. But now he knew Earth for what it was: a prison surrounded by an infinity of freedom. . . . And mankind died out!" (185)

Protecting man from the problems of dealing with technological change has led to stagnation, and stagnation has led to the death of the human race.

Asimov also discusses this problem of stagnation in the *Foundation* trilogy. While the Encyclopedists work to preserve the knowledge of man's past, they do nothing to move it forward. This situation brings Salvor Hardin, mayor of Terminus, to express his opinion to the Encyclopedists:

"And you men and half of Terminus as well are just as bad. We sit here, considering the Encyclopedia the all-in-all. We consider the greatest end of science is the classification of past data. It is important, but is there no further work to be done? We're receding and forgetting, don't you see? Here in the Periphery they've lost atomic power. In Gamma Andromeda, a power plant has blown up because of poor repairs, and the Chancellor of the Empire complains that atomic technicians are scarce. And the solution? To train new ones? Never! Instead they're to restrict atomic power.

"Don't you see? It's Galaxywide. It's a worship of the past. It's a deterioration—a *stagnation*." (1:ii:5)

In *Foundation*, stagnation represents a regression to an earlier preatomic technology. This regression is the goal of the Medievalists in *The Caves of Steel*. They want the people of Earth to leave the Cities to return to the soil. Lije Baley believes this would be going

"Backward, in other words, to an impossible past. . . . Back to the seed, to the egg, to the womb. Why not move forward? Don't cut Earth's population. Use it for export. Go back to the soil, but go back to the soil of other planets. Colonize!" (156)

Baley agrees with the Medievalists that Earthmen must leave the Cities and learn to live in the open, but in doing so they must create a new society, not go back to an old one. Not only that, they must learn to accept robots to help them colonize other worlds. Stagnation is also a problem on Solaria in *The Naked Sun*. The Solarians are isolated from one another, specialized, dependent on robots. The intellectual and physical stimulation needed to produce change is absent. Lije Baley gives another reason for the Solarians' stagnation:

"And if isolation isn't enough to induce stagnation, there is the matter of their long lives. On Earth, we have a continuous influx of young people who are willing to change because they haven't had time to grow hard-set in their ways. I suppose there's some optimum. A life long enough for real accomplishment and short enough to make way for youth at a rate that's not too slow. On Solaria, the rate *is* too slow." (216)

Thus, the Solarians lack a group of innovators willing to accept culture change. But Earth, too, even with its "continuous influx of young people" actually is set in its ways. While Earth may seem very different from Solaria, it is really quite similar. While the Solarians retreat from each other, Earthmen retreat from the rest of the Galaxy. They hide within their Cities, afraid even to face the outdoors of their own planet. To end their stagnation, Earthmen must leave their Cities. They have to learn to face the outdoors and the Galaxy.

Asimov has shown that whether technological change comes from within, as with invention, or from outside, as with diffusion and acculturation, we cannot ignore it nor must we try to resist or prevent it. Instead we must learn to live with technological changes because it is inevitable that we will have them. We must reach forward, as Lije Baley comes to believe: "He lifted his head and he could see through all the steel and concrete and humanity above him. He could see the beacon set in space to lure men outward. He could see it shining down. The naked sun!" (223).

7. A Galaxy Full of People:

Characterization in Asimov's Major Fiction

DONALD WATT

FOR A MAN who insists he does not know How to Write, Asimov is a prolific and successful author. He has published over 170 books. He is known to have had as many as a dozen books in press at the same time. A compulsive worker, he prefers the familiar book-lined walls of his attic to sunny vacation resorts, and he argues that his health begins to deteriorate whenever he stops working. But, he says: "As far as writing is concerned, I am a complete and utter primitive. I have no formal training at all and to this day I don't know How to Write." [1]

Asimov's views are perhaps best expressed by one of his own characters, Arcadia Darell, in *Second Foundation:* "What's the use of writing books unless you sell them and become well-known? I don't want just some old professors to know me. It's got to be everybody" (3:II:11). Asimov is a science fiction novelist with no pretensions toward innovative techniques, hidden allusions, or occult symbolism. He is, as he professes to be, a popular writer whose work is immediately accessible to a wide audience.

It is worth asking, then, what it is about Asimov's writing that accounts for his popularity. His readers agree with his belief that, in all likelihood, he will in future be remembered for his science fiction, not for his science nonfiction: "Science is moving so rapidly, my science books will be quickly dated," he has said. "If anything lives, it may be some of my science fiction." [2] My argument is that Asimov's characters are at the center of appeal in his major fiction because they enrich and enliven the science fiction worlds he creates.

Asimov himself attests to the importance of sound characters in his and other science fiction when he discusses sociological problem stories and recommends that the "actual plot of the story, the suspense, the conflict, ought to arise—if this were a first-class story—out of the particular needs and frustrations of people." [3] In his well-known essay on "Social Science Fiction," Asimov recalls his 1952 definition of science fiction as "that branch of literature which is concerned with the impact of scientific advance upon human beings." He defends his definition, saying he finds "intellectual satisfaction" in it, because "it places the emphasis not upon science but upon human beings." [4] In Asimov's view, the stuff of science fiction is the human response to what science and the future have wrought, and this is indeed what his own novels are about.

The *Foundation* trilogy poses two special problems for a study of Asimov's characterizations—fatalism and fragmentation. First of all, the omnipresent specter of Seldon's Plan gives rise to the objection that Asimov's is a determined universe, and that genuine characters cannot come to life within such a fixed environment. Since the inhabitants of the trilogy cannot act outside the statistical probabilities of psychohistory, so the argument goes, the individuals Asimov dramatizes in the Plan must of necessity be flat, acted upon, unidimensional. Even if this argument were accurate, the success of Asimov's characterizations need not everywhere depend upon whether or not his galactic population is fated. Sophocles' Oedipus and Chaucer's Troilus are, to varying degrees, fated characters who are nonetheless aesthetically sound and very much alive.

Not everyone believes the people of the entire trilogy are so fated. Granted, most of the critical reaction thus far to the *Foundation* epic has dealt with Asimov's concept of history as cyclical, implying that it is predictable and hence determined. Sam Moskowitz, for one, says the action in the trilogy is "primarily cerebral. Everything that happens is the result of the machinations of a prime mover, shifting power elements like pieces on a chess board." [5] But Susan Glicksohn explicitly disagrees with Moskowitz and submits that individuals do influence events in the trilogy, that "individuals have meaning within this cycle." [6]

Many of the important characters in the trilogy exhibit various traits and idiosyncrasies which distinguish them as stimulating personalities whether their probable world history has been foreplotted or not, and sometimes even whether their individual responses to certain situations have been rigged or not. Manipulated though many of the trilogy's characters are, their individual initiative and resourcefulness are often necessary to guide or to repair the great Plan. In this, the *Foundation* books introduce us to a number of memorable characters in the Asimov canon.

The second problem the trilogy poses for a reading of Asimov's characters is their fragmentation. The three novels span some four hundred years in future history. As a result, it is impossible for Asimov to remain very long with any of the characters because he must maintain the extended chronological perspective (he wrote the *Foundation* books as a series of stories over a period of seven years). As in Arthur C. Clarke's *Childhood's End*, the long temporal scope of the trilogy limits the amount of development Asimov can allow for individual characters. Despite this, Charles Elkins is perhaps too severe when he says the trilogy's "characters are undifferentiated and one-dimensional." * One may concede that Asimov does often fall back upon stereotypes, but some of the lead characters achieve memorable life in spite of their creator's self-imposed restrictions.

In the first book of the trilogy, *Foundation*, too many of the characterizations are, admittedly, incomplete or simplistic. Gaal Dornick, a country boy in the big Asimovian city, immediately falls victim to Asimov's historical sweep: just as we begin to see his development to a position of importance in the impending post-Seldon era, the chronology leaves him indifferently behind. On the other hand, Asimov overdoes his portrait of effete Lord Dorwin, a foppish representative of an overripe Empire. And Wienis, plotting his maniacal revenge against Hardin, is a rather too transparent villain.

But these mediocre stereotypes are incidental to the succession of thundering Asimov heroes in *Foundation*. Hari Seldon, Salvor Hardin, Limmar Ponyets, and Hober Mallow dominate their respective sections, and though Seldon and Ponyets are sketches, Hardin and Mallow are well-executed portraits, with Mallow coming close to life-size dimensions despite some of his comic-strip gestures. These men exhibit considerable ingenuity as they master the psychology of their opponents. Hardin's words to Jord Fara in this connection are of key importance: "At best, he [Seldon] might indicate the problem, but if ever there is to be a solution, we must work it out ourselves" (1:II:5). The thrust of individual spontaneity and action is what is required to overcome the inertia of the slowly dying Empire. Hardin, convinced the Foundation will suffocate

---

* See his chapter in this book.

under blind faith in Empire *or* in Seldon, triggers a revolt against the Encyclopedists. In "The Mayors" section, he penetrates vanity and vengeance as he resists actionist pressures at home by Sermak and Verisof and invokes his native shrewdness at the right moment to destroy Wienis on Anacreon. Those scenes dramatizing Hardin's crafty psychological in-fighting against Haut Rodric and Wienis are surely one source of Asimov's broad appeal in the trilogy.

Mallow, though, in his rough pride and robust cunning, is the climax and the triumph of *Foundation*'s heroes. He combines the attributes of a Viking chieftain and a Mississippi riverboat gambler. As a Smyrnian, he is sensitive about his non-Foundation heritage and he never makes "the mistake of being overpolite to a Foundation man" (1:v:1). Asimov shows us Mallow's explosive temper as he unequivocally rejects Jaim Twer's plea to release the planted priest, Jord Parma, on Korell: "I've got more to do here than guard missionaries. I'll do, sir, what I please, and, by Seldon and all the Galaxy, if you try to stop me, I'll tear out your stinking windpipe. Don't get in my way, Twer, or it will be the last of you" (1:v:4). Mallow's physical force, though, is ultimately less fun than his Odyssean cunning. He is fully aware of Hardin's crucial advice: "To succeed," Hardin once said, "planning alone is insufficient. One must improvise as well." Concludes Mallow: "I'll improvise" (1:v:3). Improvise he does as he insinuates himself into Commdor Asper's favor in a cool stroke of diplomatic patronage. Calculatingly he assures Asper he has no use for the Foundation's sham religion. "All this mysticism and hocus-pocus of the missionaries annoy me, and I'm glad you refuse to countenance it. It makes you more my type of man" (1:v:5). Later, Mallow adds to and improves his improvisation by exploiting Korell's economic dependence on the Foundation, which he has caused, to resolve the third Seldon crisis.

A character such as Mallow must be seen in the perspective of Asimov's early career. As Asimov embarked on his career as a science fiction writer, he came to know John W. Campbell, editor of *Astounding Stories*, well enough to recognize the new realism Campbell encouraged among his contributors. Under Campbell's influence, Asimov says, science fiction became "more than a personal battle between an all-good hero and an all-bad villain." Campbell sought to displace the common science fiction stereotypes, such as the mad scientist and his beautiful daughter, "the cardboard menace from alien worlds, the robot who is a Frankenstein monster." Asimov credits Campbell with seeking to people his stories with "business men, space-ship crewmen, young engineers, housewives, robots that were logical machines." [7] Mallow is perhaps a good example in Asimov's early writings of just such a credible character. Through Mallow's meeting with Onum Barr and his tactful handling of Joranne Sutt, the reader receives further insight into his character. *Foundation* offers a series of forceful heroes, ably capped by the figure of Mallow, who improvise sensibly within Seldon's benevolent Plan for the survival of civilized man.

Though uneven in the quality of its conception, *Foundation and Empire*, the second book in the trilogy, contains some of Asimov's best characterization. The first part of the book, presenting Lathan Devers' abortive efforts to thwart the young Empire general, Bel Riose, pales next to the longer second half, with the striking figures of Bayta and the Mule. Devers is supposed to be Mallow's heroic successor but, while Asimov portrays Devers' cover as an unconcerned, self-serving trader well enough, Devers' swashbuckling mien is a little too close to the arrogant, free-wheeling Army sergeant of World War II movies.

Bel Riose is probably a better characterization. He is correct when he tells Brodrig, "I am a soldier, not a cleft-chinned, barrel-chested hero of a subetheric trimensional thriller" (2:1:6). But the true hero of this section, Ducem Barr, is not given sufficient breadth for the character development which potentially exists.

Notably enough, Asimov here takes pains to assure his readers that his characters are not predestined. Sennett Forell reminds us that one of Seldon's assumptions is that there will be "a certain normal initiative on the part of the people of the Foundation themselves" (2:1:2). Riose, receiving with scorn Ducem Barr's views upon Seldon's "dead hand," asks if he is to be "a silly robot following a predetermined course into destruction" whereupon Barr assures him that psychohistory "had nothing to do with individual actions" (2:1:3). These reminders come at the right time in the trilogy, for Asimov's explanation of the inevitability of the Foundation's victory over Riose and Brodrig will strike some readers as being much too pat.

The second part of *Foundation and Empire* is another story. The Mule's rise to power under his disguise as Magnifico the clown is intriguing enough by itself, but the real interest here is Asimov's excellent variation on the legend of Beauty and the Beast. Asimov makes the tale especially convincing by the care with which he draws Beauty's—Bayta's—character. Bayta is a complex, full-blooded person, perhaps one of the more carefully developed female characterizations in science fiction before Alexei Panshin's Mia Havero in *Rite of Passage*. We see her at the opening of "The Mule" twitting her new husband Toran for his lapse into sentimentality. Conversely, we find she is protective and kind toward the deformed clown Magnifico. Playful and assertive, she is an informed historian, an ex-member of a rebel group on Terminus, an efficient factory supervisor on Haven. We see her in a number of ways enacting Asimov's description of her: "And behind a very sturdily-built and staunchly-defended facade of practical, unromantic, hard-headedness towards life, there was just that little pool of softness that would never show if you poked for it, but could be reached if you knew just how—and never let on that you were looking for it" (2:ɪɪ:11). Her shooting of Ebling Mis consummates Asimov's characterization of her. It is an unexpected action which is nonetheless consistent with her development in the story.

Also perfectly consistent with her character is her enchantment of the Mule and her gradual penetration of his cover as the clown. Unwittingly, she appeals to his human emotion, for which the Mule spares her his powers of mental interference. He explains his defeat to her and Toran: "I cherished the *natural* feeling too greatly" (2:ɪɪ:26). The Mule, with his beaked face, spidery body, and "all but prehensile" nose, possesses the horrid traits of his mutation, but his soft, sad attraction to Bayta makes him effectively pathetic, understandable if not forgivable. He remains uncomfortably at the edge of stereotype, although he is more fully presented than Ebling Mis or that inconceivable bureaucrat, Mayor Indbur. But Bayta leavens and enlivens *Foundation and Empire* with the many-angled features of her character.

Second Foundation is in many ways the weakest of the three books in the trilogy. Asimov has admitted that by the time he reached their later stages the Foundation stories were becoming a burden to him.[8] There are signs of its author's flagging interest throughout *Second Foundation*. The story of the search by the Mule, the first part of the book, is clever rather than convincing. The heart of "Search by the Foundation," the second part, is a lengthy diversion, the Stettinian war. Asimov's handling of the historical materials and his style in presenting the Second Foundationers are alike awkward. He correctly sensed, in *Opus 100*, that though he was only one-third of the way through Seldon's thousand-year Plan, it was well to finish with the Foundation series.

Yet *Second Foundation* has moments when its characters are sharply etched. Channis is a good creation if only because the reader is not sure whether to like him or not. His cockiness with Pritcher balances well against his agony before the Mule, surely among the most powerful and dramatic of Asimov's confrontations. The Mule himself is here sharply drawn, as he challenges the First Speaker with a wicked pathos: "What will you do? Fatten me? Restore me to a masculine vigor? . . . Do you regret *my* sufferings? Do you regret *my* unhappiness? I have no sorrow for what I did in my necessity" (3:1:6). Too, the portrait of Arcadia in the second part of the book sustains much of the reader's interest, offsetting in part Asimov's reliance upon hackneyed stereotypes in Callia, Stettin, and "Momma" Palver. Asimov says in *Opus 100* he "had to introduce a number of human-interest touches" to Arcadia to render palatable her long account of Seldon's Plan.[9] Though she has been controlled, Asimov succeeds in evoking the reader's affection for this precocious adolescent, and his humor does enrich his early presentation of her, even to the point of making delightful fun of his own grand manner.

But she is finally right in admiring her grandmother, Bayta. Arcadia's characterization does not match Bayta's, nor does the last book of the trilogy match the first two.

The robot books are Asimov's two collections of short stories about robots, *I, Robot* and *Stories from the Rest of the Robots*, and the two science fiction detective novels, *The Caves of Steel* and *The Naked Sun*. The short story collections require a place in a study of Asimov's characters chiefly because of Susan Calvin, who appears in many of the stories and links them into a loosely united whole. The detective novels of the 1950s center upon Elijah Baley, Asimov's greatest character.

Asimov freely admits that the robot short stories he was most interested in were those dealing with Susan Calvin: "As time went on, I fell in love with Dr. Calvin. She was a forbidding creature, to be sure—much more like the popular conception of a robot than were any of my positronic creations—but I loved her anyway." As Asimov points out, "dear Susan" is the central bond knitting together the stories in *I, Robot* (1950) and, even though he refers to her death at the close of that collection, he "couldn't help bringing her back" for several more stories, collected with other robot pieces in 1964 as *The Rest of the Robots.* [10]

Dr. Calvin will on surface impress readers as "a caricature of the so-called female Ph.D. as they were believed to behave in the 1940's," [11] but something there is about her that teasingly rounds her into a real person. Asimov sprinkles his descriptions of her with a liberal number of suggestions that she is not quite the life of the party. In *I, Robot* we learn that at age twenty she "was a frosty girl, plain and colorless, who protected herself against a world she disliked by a mask-like expression and a hypertrophy of intellect." [12] In "Lenny" she has iron-gray hair drawn severely back and she displays a "cold face, with its strong vertical lines marked off by the horizontal gash of the pale, thin-lipped mouth. . . ." [13] Peter Bogert's opinion of her in "Little Lost Robot" (*I, Robot*) is "a sour and fidgety frustration"; her opinion of him, "a smooth and pretentious sleekness." Asimov excels in describing Dr. Calvin's crusty personality. In "Satisfaction Guaranteed" (*The Rest of the Robots*), she has "the cold, faraway look of someone who has worked with machines so long that a little of the steel has entered the blood." Reporter Nigel Ronson, in "Risk," from the same book, offers the newsman's view of Susan Calvin: "The lady with hyperspace where her heart ought to be and liquid helium in her eyes. She'd pass through the sun and come out the other end encased in frozen flame."

The main charge against Dr. Calvin is that she has no human feelings. Bogert, in "Lenny," says he would not apply the adjective "feminine" to any part of her. He thinks robots are all she loves, and he believes her long association with them "had deprived her of any appearance of humanity. She was no more to be argued out of a decision than was a triggered micropile to be argued out of operating." It seems fitting that the robot Lenny be "the only kind of baby she could ever have or love."

On the other hand, there is much to suggest that Susan Calvin's severity is a carefully sustained protective measure, not a mask or a pose, but a means of securing herself against the greed and folly of humankind. In *I, Robot* she possesses a "schooled indifference" (154), in *The Rest of the Robots* her office reflects "her own frigid, carefully-ordered personality" (123). The implication is that she must keep herself under tight control, she must ward off all temptations to partake in the abundance of human weakness which surrounds her.

That she fails sufficiently often to avoid such temptation and thereby proves herself human after all is what makes her character attractive. Gerald Black in "Risk" (*The Rest of the Robots*) wonders whether she had ever been young: "Had she ever felt one honest emotion?" As if answering Black's question, Dr. Calvin tells her interviewer in *I, Robot*, "I was foolish once, young man" (83). She goes on to relate the story of Herbie, the mind-reading robot, who knew about her concealed passion for one Milton Ashe. In this story, "Liar!," she reveals rare emotion as she strikes out against Herbie's invasion of her most secret mind: "I'm just a specimen to you; an interesting bug with a peculiar mind spread-eagled for inspection." Girlish in her gratitude when Herbie deceives her into believing Ashe shares her love, Susan becomes furiously bitter when she finds out Herbie has lied to her. She is by no means an arid, emotionless woman, but rather one who struggles hard to subordinate a volatile temperament to rational control. Asimov's readers should keep "Liar!" in mind when considering the ending of "Satisfaction Guaranteed," as Dr. Calvin provides a woman's analysis of Mrs. Belmont's relationship with the handsome robotic Tony: " 'Strange that I overlooked it in the first place,' her eyes were opaquely thoughtful, 'but perhaps it reflects a shortcoming in myself. You see, Peter, machines can't fall in love, but—even when it's hopeless and horrifying—women can!' " "Little Lost Robot" and "Evidence" in *I, Robot* contain further scenes which show that beneath her icy exterior there lurks a vulnerable, feeling human being with the same vagrant emotions which at some time or another make fools of us all.

A last feature of Susan Calvin's character, and one which must have been instrumental in Asimov's confessed love for her, is her scientific idealism. One might even suspect Asimov has other characters mock Dr. Calvin because of his own built-in defense mechanism: she often voices ideals Asimov must cherish, and he perhaps wishes to deflect hurtful criticism from his most sensitive areas of thought. In "Galley Slave" (*The Rest of the Robots*), Asimov's favorite Susan Calvin story, she responds to Simon Ninheimer's criticism of her concern for machines: "It is only by being concerned for robots that one can truly be concerned for twenty-first-century man." When at the opening of *I, Robot* she says robots are "a cleaner better breed than we are" (9), she is simply adumbrating the view expressed more fully later in the book, that there is no difference between the ethics of a robot and those of a really good man. The famed Three Laws of Robotics are, she says in "Evidence," "the essential guiding principles of a good many of the world's ethical systems." She combines a tough insistence upon the truth with the greatest hope for the robots' ability to guide man into a fulfilled future. Her glowing tribute to the Machines at the end of *I, Robot* possibly provoked a response from Kurt Vonnegut in *Player Piano,* but whatever our or Vonnegut's attitude, Susan Calvin is a leading exponent of what Brian Aldiss has called "the solid conservative faith in technology" in Asimov's books.[14]

Susan Calvin, then, is a deft character creation, loosely spanning a number of related short stories, though of course neither collection of robot stories is a novel. Asimov's best sustained character portrayal is Elijah Baley in *The Caves of Steel* and *The Naked Sun.* Dr. Calvin's character is too diffuse over the broad range of the stories, but Baley is in both of the detective novels very intensively drawn. Dr. Calvin conveys Asimov's message too explicitly—the didactic content of the robot stories is too obvious and intrusive, often jarring with the action. In *The Caves of Steel* and *The Naked Sun* the message melds smoothly with the natural growth and development of Baley's complex character.

Baley's characterization is quite well done. Tight and elaborate, sustained and credible, Baley challenges Dua in *The Gods Themselves* as Asimov's top creation (and Dua, of course, is nonhuman). The opening chapter of *The Caves of Steel* establishes Baley's complex, realistic character. At the very outset we see his ingrained bias against robots through his irritation with R. Sammy. Shortly, we see his cold prejudice against the Spacers as he dispassionately wishes contagion upon them. Yet Baley is an alert, discerning man, one who suspects, for instance, that his commissioner wears glasses not, as he claims, because his eyes are too sensitive for contact lenses, but "for the personality they lent him." [15] Penetrating hidden motives comes naturally to Elijah Baley.

This combination of weakness and strength helps make Baley a stimulating character. Baley is a psychological caveman, a man entrapped in the womb-tomb cities of Asimov's future by his hostility, bias, and narrow-mindedness. Baley's relationship with his robot partner, Daneel Olivaw, is a serio-comic study in human frustration and jealousy. Olivaw's mechanical perfection accentuates Baley's vulnerability: "The trouble was, of course, that he was not the plainclothes man of popular myth. He was not incapable of surprise, imperturbable of appearance, infinite of adaptability, and lightning of mental grasp. He had never supposed he was, but he had never regretted the lack before" (22). Olivaw as the embodiment of that myth prods Baley to madcap efforts to assert his own superiority. Baley is stung by Olivaw's physical prowess and even becomes jealous of his wife's attraction to him (before she discovers he is a robot). In his human eagerness to outwit his competition, Baley twice offers wrong solutions to the case of the murdered Spacer. It is entirely consistent with his character that Baley would strain matters to accuse first the Spacers and then Olivaw of the crime.

The problem with Baley's characterization in *The Caves of Steel* is his conversion. The turning point of the novel occurs when Fastolfe explains his great hope of joining City people with progressive Outer Worlders to inject a new and vigorous strain into the human race. Fastolfe, we learn later, uses a drug to render Baley's mind more receptive to life outside the protective caves. This device is as weak a crutch as the one Heinlein uses in *Double Star* to remove Smythe's prejudice against Martians. Asimov seems to realize the fundamental evasion of his ploy, for he has Olivaw assure Baley the drug would not make him "believe anything that was foreign to the basic pattern of your thought" (171). But this is not enough to convince us that Baley's conversion is a direct result of his character because Asimov does not give us really sufficient evidence, early in the story, of Baley's innate potential for his enlightened change of mind.

Nonetheless, the effects of Baley's exposure to a widened view of life are convincingly presented. Baley gropes toward a new perspective when he smells the City "with nostrils that had been washed clean by outdoor air" (91). He grows disenchanted with the crowded, confining City, becomes slowly aware of the precarious position of his overpopulated planet. In fact, Baley's inherent reluctance to accept any argument at face value strengthens Asimov's portrayal of his development. The blunt honesty of his prejudices does render more effective his dawning recognition of the inhuman walls they have built around him. Because he is so stubbornly pragmatic, Baley's enlightenment on the colonization of space and his grudging admiration of Olivaw make a rather compelling conclusion for the novel. *The Caves of Steel*, Sam Moskowitz reports, "put Asimov in a class by himself." [16]

This is undoubtedly true, but one must agree with Brian Aldiss when he claims that *The Naked Sun* is Asimov's best novel.[17] *The*

Naked Sun (1957), a companion piece to *The Caves of Steel,* was the last novel Asimov wrote before turning seriously to nonfiction. *The Naked Sun* encompasses most of the qualities of *The Caves of Steel* and avoids its major defect. In *The Naked Sun* Asimov creates a novel where the inner workings of his lead character's mind and motives match, if not exceed, the outer story of detection. Put another way, Baley's adventure is an exploration of his individual self as well as an investigation of interstellar crime.

Baley in this novel is a fully conceived character. Asimov gives him a diversity of human moods and impulses. He is at once proud and frightened, reflective and quick-tempered, sensitive and tough, intelligent and vulnerable. Baley proves himself capable of petty human flaws, such as his smug vanity upon browbeating Attlebish, which make his characterization a realistic one. He is easy to grate, has a short fuse, can shift from feelings of intense friendship with Olivaw to instant irritation. He can be an almost comic figure with the unexpected nudity of Gladia on the trimensional screen. He is clever enough to trick his robot partner, and sensitive enough to feel ashamed of his deception.

These many sides of Baley are necessary to balance his growth as a hero in the book. For in *The Naked Sun* Asimov achieves with his main character a substantial development, with continuity, momentum, and a certain depth. Baley's heroism consists of his gritty battle against his "cave" fixation, against his need for "the feeling of being safely and warmly enclosed in the bowels and womb of the City." [18] At first he fights his agoraphobia because of his professional pride: "What was needed was direct observation and it was his job, however unpleasant, to collect it" (32). He also wants his independence from Olivaw, he wants to snap "this nurse-infant relationship" between himself and Daneel (33). But his exposure to the opposite phobia of the Solarians spurs Baley to see that a return to initiative and risk is essential to the future of the whole race of man.

Baley's attraction to Gladia encourages him in his struggle. Her inclusion in *The Naked Sun* is an inspiration by Asimov, for she adds far more than the predictable love-interest. There is a gentle tenderness in the later scenes between Baley and Gladia, the tenderness of two people groping for human contact to help them out of their psychological prisons. Her field coloring of Baley enclosed in "a flat, lusterless hollow cube of slate gray" visualizes for him the sadness of his soul imprisoned "in the gray of the Cities" (176–77).

The climax of Baley's internal drama occurs when he rips down the curtain to get a full view of unobstructed night: "Walls were crutches! Darkness and crowds were crutches!" (195). It is perhaps too melodramatic that at this instant Baley gains the insight which solves the case. But his newly found freedom in the outdoors, his liberation from the womb-like caves of the City, his rebirth under the naked sun do not lack credibility. Baley's tenacity and courage dramatize Asimov's heartfelt belief that man will not, must not become the victim of inertia, that he must meet the challenge to inquire, to explore, and to learn.

Baley's character goes deeper than Susan Calvin's and transcends the inhabitants of the *Foundation* trilogy. His development in *The Naked Sun* is free of the pharmaceutical artifice which mars *The Caves of Steel.* Attractive and richly drawn, Baley of *The Naked Sun* stands at the peak of Asimov's characterizations in his longer fiction.

For better or for worse I have grouped *Pebble in the Sky, The Stars, Like Dust, The Currents of Space,* and *The End of Eternity* under the general heading of Asimov's lesser novels. Characterization in most of these novels is halting and negligible by comparison with Asimov's major achievements. In *Pebble in the Sky* (1950), for instance, Asimov makes a fair beginning on Schwartz's character, but the subsequent development is sketchy and uneven. The Synapsifier, which brings this book into the realm of gadget science fiction, intensifies Schwartz's mental acuteness to the point where he aggressively defeats the book's villain, but his growth from a comfortable old man to a psychological wizard is too abrupt to be really credible. Of the other characters, Pola is a pretty face, Shket a harried scientist, Ennius a weak-willed ambassador, Arbin a plain farmer, and Balkis a monomaniacal despot. Only Arvardan comes close to assuming real status as a character, and he is often immature. His heroism too frequently devolves into scenes, as with the hate-filled Lt. Claudy, resembling a rather low-grade western.

Pebble in the Sky is not a bad thriller, and the gripping mind-struggle between Schwartz and Balkis recalls the psychological battles of *Second Foundation,* but more than anything else this novel is an adventure story which Asimov seems to have been compelled to fill with an unnecessary diversity of incidents. The favorite Asimovian theme of overcoming bias emerges nicely through the Arvardan-Pola match, but the book's resolution is contrived, not convincing, and in the closing pages Asimov leans too heavily upon melodrama.

The Stars, Like Dust (1951) has the benefit of a clearly identifiable central character, Biron Farrill, who does exhibit signs of growth in the course of the novel. Biron's progress from an innocent, duped, manipulated boy to an assertive, thinking leader provides the book with some good scenes, and the character of Simon Aratap is conceived with some subtlety. On the whole, though, Moskowitz's low opinion of The Stars, Like Dust is justifiable.[19] Perhaps no other Asimov novel written for a mature audience relies on such a weak plot as this one does. Escape, pursuit, and hiding occupy a disproportionate amount of space in the book. Moreover, the political maneuvering of the story is rather tedious: the pretext of the action—to have Biron eliminated by local authority to save embarrassment for the regional government—is not sufficient to sustain a full-length novel. Asimov's casual attention to plot development removes from The Stars, Like Dust the tautness and momentum of the Foundation trilogy and the robot detective novels. Attentuated, wandering, and episodic, the plot discourages any genuinely forceful cultivation of the book's potentially good characters.

The characterizations of The Currents of Space (1952) and The End of Eternity (1955) are much better. Rik, Lona, and Terens early in The Currents of Space promise to hold the reader's attention as individual persons, although the elaborate intrigue which later transfers the action from Florina to Sark interrupts for too long Asimov's portraits of these main characters. Lona, like a mother bear in her protection of Rik, proves that Asimov's skill in creating pathos with the Mule is no accident. Terens' patriotic zeal provides a plausible motive for his actions, even if his wanderings do not always contribute enough to the narrative to justify the amount of space Asimov devotes to them. But the reawakening of Rik to conscious awareness of his identity is the best part of the story. The first half of the book is especially effective because Asimov slowly broadens the reader's perspective of events at the same time that he presents the gradual return of Rik's memory. The Currents of Space, unfortunately, flags noticeably in its later pages. We must agree with Rune when he calls Fife's exhaustive summary of events "a moderately dull story." The End of Eternity contains without question the best characterization of Asimov's lesser novels. Andrew Harlan comes close to rivaling some of Asimov's top characters. That Harlan so resembles D-503 in Zamyatin's We is either an amazing coincidence or a sign that Asimov in this case relied on a model for his character. Harlan's development in the novel is logical, sustained, and forceful. Asimov creates a well-executed tension between Harlan's cool pride in his position and abilities and his instinctive doubts about the justice of tampering with time. Harlan's emotional range—his anger and jealousy with Finge, his guilt and anxiety as a wayward Technician, his love and fear for Nöys—lend the novel a genuine vitality. Harlan's decision to accept Nöys' position grows persuasively out of his character. He is malleable (and perhaps indistinct by comparison with Elijah Baley), but there is charm and credibility in his confused love for Nöys. He is always "in character," even when surprising in his abrupt, peevish way. If not quite as rounded as Baley, Harlan still strikes us as a real person, not a cardboard stereotype. Nöys, slightly less realistic, is a rather impassive sort of future Eve seducing Andrew-Adam to taste the apple of Infinity. Neither as icily provocative as Susan Calvin nor as gay and assertive as Bayta, Nöys borders on the stereotypical misty and mysterious female creature from the beyond. Still, *The End of Eternity* is on almost every count several notches above the other books briefly mentioned in this section, and it shows what Asimov can do when he devotes real care to a character. In this respect *The End of Eternity* anticipates *The Gods Themselves*.

Nineteen fifty-eight is a watershed in Asimov's career. The Soviet Union that year launched Sputnik just as Asimov was arranging his obligations so he could write full time. While there is as yet no evidence to suggest the Soviet launch was precipitated by Asimov's arrangements, the effects in the opposite direction were pronounced. Asimov confesses that Sputnik had grave consequences for his career plans: "I was overcome by the ardent desire to write popular science for an America that might be in great danger through its neglect of science," he says. When he found several publishers anxious to produce popular science for the same reason, Asimov "found myself plunging into a shoreless sea in which I am still immersed." [20]

As a result, the volume of Asimov's serious work in the novel has declined markedly since Sputnik. Discounting the juvenile fiction of the Starr books, he produced from 1950 to 1956 six novels: *Pebble in the Sky*, *The Stars, Like Dust*, *The Currents of Space*, *The Caves of Steel*, *The End of Eternity*, and *The Naked Sun*. In the twenty years since the appearance of *The Naked Sun* he has published but three novels for a mature audience: *Fantastic Voyage* (1966), *The Gods Themselves* (1972), and *Murder at the ABA* (1976).* Two of these are, I submit, slight additions to the Asimov canon, but *The Gods Themselves* is Asimov's great, if flawed, science fiction masterpiece.

It is difficult to assess Asimov's precise contribution to *Fantastic Voyage*, for the novel is based on a screenplay which in turn was derived from a story by two writers. A study of the novel's evolution is clearly beyond the scope of the present essay. The characters in the completed novel, however, are at times sharply etched, and there are traces of real life in Duval and Michaels; but for the most part, Grant and Cora Peterson are not far from stereotypes. Duval's faith in science reflects the credo of his author. Duval's wonder at the physical universe within the human body often comes to the reader in language akin to the worshipful tone of Asimov's best nonfiction. In fact, *Fantastic Voyage* is that rare Asimov novel where description per se plays a major role. Few readers will regret the intrusion of the anatomy lessons into this fiction because the descriptions are often majestic.

Yet the characterizations are mostly skeletal, though Asimov does make a few gestures toward fleshing out some of his voyagers: Michaels' motives are so idealistic that they reveal a thick edge of fanaticism about them, Grant proves himself under his tough exterior to be a softie who can quote Wordsworth. Nevertheless, the few details which inject some juice into the characters are too obviously tacked on for effect. The story of *Fantastic Voyage* is the journey itself, not the people who make it. Grant is finally a cardboard James Bond, and Cora is the readily yielding submissive woman. The real star of *Fantastic Voyage* is Benes, or at least his body—thus every human body—in the intricate marvel of its life-structure. Real characters cannot grow in a novel that is so close to one of Asimov's popular science essays.

Asimov's latest novel (at this writing), *Murder at the ABA*, is a straightforward but weak detective novel with no science fiction context, and is therefore outside the considerations of this book.

The Gods Themselves is an uneven novel, but it has such offsetting richness to compensate for its weaknesses that it may well qualify as Asimov's masterpiece. To come right to the point, *The Gods*

---

* Late in 1976 Asimov published another collection of robot stories, *The Bicentennial Man*, which includes the title story, a short novel. A discussion of this work appears in Chapter 9 of this book.

Themselves contains—no matter what problems may be caused by its anthropomorphism—what must be ranked among the top creations of alien character in science fiction. Of particular note in this book is Asimov's craft in the integration of science, plot, and character into a pleasing and persuasive whole. In *Opus 100* he says one of the special delights in writing science fiction is "mastering the art of interweaving science and fiction—keeping the science accurate and comprehensible without unduly stalling the plot" (16). Asimov masters this art with uncommon skill in *The Gods Themselves*. Not only do action and setting coordinate well with each other, but indeed the scientific content becomes a necessary condition for an understanding of the alien characters. This bears some explanation because it is crucial to a grasp of Asimov's achievement in creating his aliens.

The Gods Themselves follows a careful A-B-A pattern in its structural organization. Its three sections divide, for their respective headings, the quote from the German dramatist Schiller: "Against stupidity, / the gods themselves / contend in vain [?]." [21] The question mark, absent in Schiller, is added by Asimov to the title of the final section. Part One of the book, on Earth, sets up the existence of a parallel universe, the creation of an Electron Pump which exchanges energy with the para-Universe, and the threat to our universe of being destroyed by imbalances introduced into the vicinity of the Sun as a result of the energy exchange. Part Two portrays the strange growth to maturity of a new, brilliant leader in the para-Universe, and the dawning awareness of that leader of the threat to our universe. Part Three, on the Moon, resolves the crisis by the invention of a second Pump connected with an anti-para-Universe to remove the energy imbalance caused by the first Pump.

One point about this arrangement is that the inferences made in Part One about the physical composition of the para-Universe prepare the reader with remarkable detail for the shapes in which the aliens are discovered in Part Two. Another point is that the blindness and stupidity which characterize the Earthmen of Part One are effectively modified by the imagination and stability of the human hero in Part Three. This intricate dramatization of sentient, intelligent life, both human and alien, is the heart of *The Gods Themselves*. Moreover, characterization in this novel conveys the essentials of Asimov's view of human nature. Through his handling of his characters here, as in the robot detective novels, we may deduce Asimov's scientific meliorism and his implicit philosophy of life.

Part One of *The Gods Themselves* is a good study in Asimovian realism. The overriding Asimov theme of our urgent need to combat human short-sightedness, so dominant in the *Foundation* trilogy and the Baley novels, here receives even more intensive treatment. This section analyzes various human motives in its spectrum of unrelieved spite, careerism, greed, and assorted pettiness. Peter Lamont is another angry man in the Asimov canon, as disrespectful as any and more vengeful than most. The force which drives Lamont to investigate the validity of the Pump is, as he is quick to admit, his burning desire to dump Dr. Frederick Hallam "on his fat behind." A colleague persuades Lamont to switch his research from Hallam to the Pump itself not out of benevolent concern for all mankind, but out of Lamont's black mood of revenge against Hallam.

Vainglory, wounded pride, and narrow self-interest govern all the significant decisions made by the characters in the first section of the book. Benjamin Denison's careless insult of Hallam upon the disappearance of the first tungsten spurs Hallam to stubbornly pursue the identity of the new material and to eventual world fame. Asimov makes sure we do not miss the point: "Of such things, petty annoyance and aimless thrusts, is history made" (13). Similarly, Myron Bronowski accepts Lamont's challenge to establish communication with the para-men because of an unintentional slur against his ego: the college president confuses Etruscan with Itascan, making Bronowski ranklingly aware of the limited understanding of his life's work. When Lamont seeks help from Senator Burt, he finds him unwilling to jeopardize his pride in return for the survival of man. Burt had been stung in an earlier fray with Hallam. As much as he would like to see Hallam thwarted, he considers: "He might risk reelection in a good cause, but he could not risk humiliation again" (59). In fact, the only reason Burt sees Lamont in the first place is to defy Hallam, who had demanded that Burt refuse the audience.

Such a presentation of teapot conflicts and peevish concerns grounds the narrative in an unflattering but realistic account of the scientific/political Establishment. Out of this nest of human vanity emerge the telling inferences of Hallam and Lamont about the physical nature of the para-Universe. In the scientific background of the story (which may pose a sturdy challenge to the comprehension of the lay reader) are two pieces of information which contribute powerfully to one's preparation for the aliens of Part Two. First, since the nuclear interaction is ten times stronger in the para-Universe than in ours, matter is held together there with ten times less the atomic density. This renders scientifically credible the interpenetration of physical bodies during certain phases of life in the para-Universe. The second crucial bit of information is that while nuclear fission is likely in our universe, nuclear fusion is likely in the alien universe. This prepares the reader for the merging of the triad into the composite Hard One, Estwald.

In Part Two the relationship between Dua's ethereal nature and the act of sexual intercourse through "melting" is a brilliant stroke by Asimov. Odeen's explanation to Dua of why they are able to melt confirms the deductions of Hallam and Lamont in Part One and gives the reader an essential insight into the physical composition of the Soft Ones:

> Because actually we are mostly empty space. All the particles are far apart and your particles and mine and Tritt's can all melt together because each set fits into the empty spaces around the other set. The reason matter doesn't fly apart altogether is that the tiny particles do manage to cling together across the space that separates them. There are attractive forces holding them together, the strongest being one we call the nuclear-force. It holds the chief subatomic particles *very* tightly together in bunches that are spread widely apart and that are held together by weaker forces (133).

This knowledge is, so to speak, elementary to a grasp of Asimov's descriptions of the members of the triad. It is also necessary for any understanding of Dua's erotic appeal.

Especially fine is the wealth of consistent detail giving the reader an impression of the physiognomy of the aliens. Odeen, for example, is pleased with his bodily traits as a Rational. He is "satisfactorily solid," with a "nice, sharp outline, smooth and curved into gracefully conjoined ovoids." He lacks "the strangely attractive shimmer of Dua, and the comforting stockiness of Tritt" (80). Dua's Parental, on the other hand, stands "squat and flat-surfaced. He wasn't all smooth-curved like a Rational or shuddery uneven like an Emotional . . ." (77). With these descriptions of the Rational and the Parental frame, one can easily see why the rarefied body of an Emotional is necessary to complete a triad. And Dua is the most rarefied of Emotionals. Asimov creates a charming portrait of Dua, spreading herself out laterally to absorb the pale rays of an evening sun, slithering with adolescent promiscuity over rocks and letting her edges overlap theirs, trying to dissipate in rebellion when her Parental says he must "pass on." The reader soon feels he has come to know this alien imp who, as she grew older, "retained a girlishly rarefied structure and could flow with a smoky curl no other could duplicate" (121).

Although Dua is the center of Asimov's accomplishment in Part Two, what he does with the triad as a whole is its own sort of triumph. For the difficult task Asimov undertakes is to create each of the triad's members as an individual character and yet render plausible the blending of the trio into the composite personality Estwald at the end. That he succeeds to such a large extent is a measure of what *The Gods Themselves* has added to science fiction. "A triad," Losten tells his pupil Odeen, "doesn't preclude individuality, you know" (99). Even Tritt, "stumbling, ignorant Tritt" (145)—who unfortunately does sound a little too often like the conventional nagging housewife—even Tritt has merit as an individual character within the triad. In Tritt the survival instinct is strong. He opposes Odeen's reflective manner and takes direct, stubborn action to stimulate Dua. A homebody who wins Odeen's deeper feeling because he "could offer so little other than exactly what counted—the security of assured routine" (129), Tritt is the self-preserving, race-perpetuating power of the triad.

Odeen is more fully developed than Tritt. Odeen's struggle toward intellectual maturity slowly and smoothly introduces into Asimov's presentation of the alien society that inter-universe crisis we have seen depicted from Earth's vantage point in Part One. The inductive method, aided as in Part One by flashbacks, works well because through it we gain some understanding of how shy Odeen was in his youth. That very shyness indicates the depth of his sensitivity and his capacity to learn. It is therefore logical that melting would provide Odeen, as Losten says, "with a quantum-jump in understanding" (107). Odeen's assumption of leadership as he is on the threshhold of maturity is, accordingly, a most natural development.

Dua is probably Asimov's consummate piece of original characterization, if only because her impulses and her actions follow so credibly from her physical identity. (This is not to say that Asimov's characters are determined by their environment.) But in spite of the depiction of traits that may strike some readers as too human for genuine aliens, Asimov does succeed in rendering the impression of a different sort of life evolved in accord with the physical principles of a different sort of universe. And Dua is the nub of Asimov's success.

She is from the start a perimeter person. Mercurial in her moods and aberrant in her behavior, Dua's very strangeness, as Odeen recognizes, is linked with her "infinite capacity to induce satisfaction with life" (79). If the child's-eye view of sexual growth is overly cute at times, the relationship between Dua's thin-energy diet, her extraordinary sexiness, and the augmentation of her sensing powers by the socially taboo action of melting into rocks is tight and convincing. She is the curious member of the triad, combining Tritt's direct approach with Odeen's native intelligence. Her conclusion that the energy exchange will have ruinous effects on the other universe is inevitable, as is her guerilla campaign against the Hard Ones. Asimov creates in Dua a character with innocence and integrity whose growth to maturity encompasses responsibility as well as rebellion. At the close of the section the reader regrets the loss of Dua's ethereal youth but accepts, as she does, the obligations of social leadership which come with adulthood.

Yet, with all the traits of individuality Asimov gives the separate members of the triad, their melding into Estwald makes good sense. At one point Odeen confides to Losten that he feels, "in some ways, all three of us are part of a single individual" (108). One is tempted to apply a Freudian reading to Asimov's triad as a test of its validity as a composite personality. Odeen is the Ego, regulating the impulses from Dua, the Id, while Tritt is the Superego who serves as the conscience, overseeing the group with an insistence on maintaining tradition and continuity. There are clear limits to such a reading, but perhaps this approach can suggest how well the triad coheres into its own single entity.

The greatest problems with *The Gods Themselves* begin with Part Three. At the close of Part Two the reader is not sure about Estwald's attitude toward the threat posed to our universe by the energy exchange. We wonder why in Part Three, Bronowski's absence notwithstanding, there is no mention of further messages from the para-Universe—are we to assume the permanently formed Estwald will pursue the policy of letting our universe explode? Some further communication between humans and aliens would satisfy our curiosity and remove our sense of incompletion. But in the third section we are transferred to the Moon and to the tale of Denison. Part of the letdown is that we get no further word at all about the para-Universe and, especially, how Dua's position affects Estwald's progress. Another part of the letdown is that the last section seems to lack the tension, the drive, and the economy of the other two parts. If anything in Part Three counterbalances these weaknesses, it is the character of Denison. The way Asimov juxtaposes Denison against Neville as companions of Selene is a trifle too pat, but the developing relationship between Denison and Selene is possibly Asimov's most interesting love story. Low-keyed and mature, Denison surpasses the stereotypical intelligent older man (of the mold of the 1950s Cary Grant) who by his steady charm wins the perky young woman. Selene is able to contrast Neville, petulant, possessive, and neurotic, against Denison. Denison accepts, if ruefully, Selene's criticism of Earth and of his aging body. He quietly educates himself in para-physics to rehabilitate himself and to make some contribution to human knowledge. He displays resolve in his glide lesson and receptivity in his attitude toward the curiosities of the Moon society. Like Lamont, he would dearly love to see Hallam dethroned, but he is much milder and more evenly balanced than Lamont. Throughout his relationship with Selene he is considerate, gentle, and tolerant. Denison's sanity and his scientific detachment are qualities fit for the hero of *The Gods Themselves*.

There are, nevertheless, other problems with the book's third section. For example, Neville's plot is less mysterious than it is vague. Much of the time it does little more than prevent Asimov from developing the situation we most want to hear about, the effect of the energy exchange and what can be done about it. Further, the tour device which gives Denison and the reader a fuller picture of the Lunar society defers for too long the resumption of the central story. Such a device is traditional and effective in introducing a new society, but by this time the reader is anxious to pursue the established story line. Asimov dangles tantalizing hints before the reader concerning some unwritten parallels between this section and the para-Universe section. Selene's intuitionism is like Dua's, exceeding the limits of the rational. Denison's character is not unlike Odeen's, and there are some similarities also between Neville and Tritt. Is this a coincidence, or is Asimov engaging in subtleties which escape most readers (including this one)? Asimov seems to toy with the number three and combinations thereof, but one finds it difficult to know precisely what to make of it all.

One leaves *The Gods Themselves* with a sense of a resolution which is scientifically pleasing but aesthetically fragmented and not quite satisfying. The Moon is, we discover, convenient for the double-pump plan because it has its natural surface vacuum far enough removed from the Earth-based Electron Pump. But the fine and intriguing science context of Part One and the imaginative creativity of Part Two seem largely absent from this long final section.

For all its weaknesses, though, *The Gods Themselves* is a remarkable book. Asimov conventionally is grouped with the older wave of science fiction writers who allegedly do not achieve the sophistication of the later generation. But the integration of scientific imagination with character development in *The Gods Themselves*, at least in Part Two, rivals the accomplishment of Ursula Le Guin in *The Left Hand of Darkness* and does not suffer in comparison with Alexei Panshin's superb creation of Mia Havero in *Rite of Passage*. If in *The Naked Sun* Asimov has written a more smoothly executed, less flawed novel, in *The Gods Themselves* he has set his sights higher. *The Gods Themselves* rises above its unevenness to occupy a place at the top of the Asimov canon.

Asimov's characterizations dramatize and give life to what he has claimed to be the significance of science fiction: "The contribution science fiction can make to society is that of accustoming its readers to the thought of the inevitability of continuing change and the necessity of directing and shaping that change rather than opposing it blindly or blindly permitting it to overwhelm us." [22] The real Asimovian hero is the person who looks critically at his society, its technology, and himself—and is eager to modify, to learn, to improve. Asimov's constant concern is the effect of science and future advance upon the well-being of humanity. As Sam J. Lundwall says, "Even in the way out imaginative stories, the plot becomes credible by Asimov's accentuating of the situation's effect upon men." [23] Asimov casts a cold eye upon self-serving human ambitions, upon unholy allegiances to bureaucracy, and upon the abuse of technology to the stagnation of humankind. Asimov places his faith in the adventuresome spirit of human nature. He founds his best hope on the eternally inquiring human mind.

Among the dozen or so books which thus far make up his major contribution to science fiction, one finds character creation of widely ranging quality and accomplishment. Asimov's fiction offers a galaxy full of people. Many are thin stereotypes plucked out of the popular images of the mid-twentieth century, others are real enough to bump into on a downtown subway. What is perhaps surprising is that in a type of fiction which reportedly eschews the art of character depiction, we find in Asimov so many people with real hang-ups and with genuinely interesting personalities. Asimov is a shrewd psychologist in his characterizations. Surely his tart portrayal of human conflicts and his realistic handling of human motives are essential ingredients of his appeal as a writer. A reading of Asimov's major fiction leaves one with a sense of a wider universe not yet fully explored.

8. Asimov's Most Recent Fiction *

JOSEPH F. PATROUCH

"ASIMOVIAN." I HAVE USED the adjective myself, and I have seen it used by others. What others mean by it I cannot say. But I would like to suggest in some detail what I have found the term to mean. There will of course be exceptions in the Asimov canon to everything that I say, but I intend to generalize from specific examples, and I think that what I have to say will cover the majority of instances.

On matters of style: The typical Asimov sentence is short and clear. His sentences tend to gain length not by the accumulation of dependent clauses, but by the addition of simple sentences: not "The boy who hit the ball ran around the bases," but "The boy hit the ball, and then he ran around the bases." His verbs tend to be colorless, non-meaning-bearing linking verbs, and the meanings of the sentences tend to be carried by their nouns, adjectives, and adverbs. He does not like to use figurative language, so he almost never uses images, metaphors, similes. (His preference for linking verbs instead of meaning-bearing verbs is directly related to this, because linking verbs are not imagistic. They do not require that you see something. Meaning-bearing verbs do carry this requirement. The visualization is the meaning they bear.) Typically, one does not notice Asimov's language, unless one is aware how difficult it is to write this clearly. Lovers of language will say that he is no stylist; lovers of communication will admire and envy him. I think Asimov's language represents in a quintessential way the language science fiction writers aspired to during the Golden Age, the Campbell years of the forties.

I have used a variety of tools in discussing Asimov's craftsmanship, tools I call narrative techniques. Having already applied

* This chapter appears as "The Most Recent Asimov," in *The Science Fiction of Isaac Asimov* by Joseph F. Patrouch. Copyright © 1974 by Joseph F. Patrouch, Jr. Reprinted by permission of Doubleday & Co., Inc., and Granada Publishing, Ltd.

them to individual stories—which is the best way to put them to use—let me here generalize on their use in Asimov's fiction. The narrative point of view is almost always third-person limited, with that person being the central character of the story. Even when he is working with a large cast of characters in a novel, say, and must move about among them, each scene tends to be narrated solely from the point of view of one of its participants, rather than from the point of view of an omniscient outside observer. Asimov lets us see fictional events the way we see life: through the experience and observations of only one person.

Generally, the central character of a story is named and put into action in the first sentence. That is, the subject in the first sentence we read will be the central character's proper name, and its verb will let us see that person doing something. (When he does not put his central character in motion before us in the very first sentence, he will do it very, very shortly thereafter. It won't do to let the reader wait too long before finding out who the central character is, whom to identify with.) His central characters are usually white middle-class males on the sunny side of forty, because the market he writes for is composed largely of such people.

The problems these people have to solve generally involve the making of decisions rather than the performing of actions. At least, even in a basically action-adventure story, decision-making is shown to take precedence over doing things. Very often this decision-making is done by two or more people in conference. This tends to change the story from the personal to the political. It also has the advantage of externalizing the decision-making process and thereby giving the reader something to watch and listen to. Interior monologues are not as available to us in everyday life as conversations. This emphasis on conversation and decision-making, instead of on activity for its own sake, gives Asimov's fiction a certain cerebral quality, which is one of its most distinctive traits.

The stories usually begin very soon after a problem has arisen. The initial situation and the problem are passed along to the central character—and, in the process, to the reader—by someone who thoroughly understands both. Asimov is excellent at the dramatic form of exposition. It is another form of conversation, and he knows how to move stories through conversation. He sometimes uses the flashback for exposition, but he is less consistently good at this method. He tends either to allow the time sequence to become a bit muddled (e.g., *The Currents of Space*) or to become redundant by using both dramatic exposition and the flashback to pass along the same material (e.g., "The Key").

The conflicts in an Asimovian story usually involve difficulties in the way of accumulating data, in interpreting that data, and in deciding what to do as a result of the data and its interpretation. A calm, reasoned approach, rather than a hastily-arrived-at emotional one, provides the solutions to the stories. The resolutions generally mark a return to the status quo. In this sense, he is a conservative writer. The most important Asimovian theme is the importance of science (data-collecting) and reason (data-evaluating and decision-making).

Asimov's stories are set in the immediate and far future, and on Earth and distant planets circling other suns. He seldom sets stories in the past, on alternate worlds, in other dimensions, or in countries other than the United States or future extensions of the United States. His backgrounds are meticulously worked out and scientifically accurate. One leaves an Asimov story with the feeling of having lived for a while somewhere else. This ability of his to provide his settings with that "lived in" quality is another of Asimov's most distinctive features.

Unfortunately, his characters do not share as much as they should in the convincingness of his settings. One does not leave an Asimov story convinced that he has lived for a little while with real people. The characters tend to do and think what they must for the sake of the story rather than for their own sake. In his fiction at least, his interest in people is theoretical not personal, general not particular. Asimov's fiction reflects an interest in the physical, chemical, biological, and astronomical phenomena that life makes available for study, not in the experience of living itself. Put another way, his fiction is concerned with the lowest common denominator of human experience—the common environment of all our separate consciousnesses—rather than in those separate consciousnesses themselves. It focuses on what is generally true of and for us all rather than on what is specifically true of and for only one person. His fiction shows no interest in and scarcely an awareness of two extremely personal elements in all men's lives, religion and sex. As a result, his people are depersonalized to the extent of being dehumanized. I might use an aphorism to describe Asimov's characters: they are not people, they are story parts.

Fiction humanizes and specifies the general. I find it very instructive when Asimov admits he gave up science fiction for science writing so he could write directly about science without the bother of considering people and people's behavior. (I assume that this is at least partly what Asimov meant in *Opus 100* when he said, "I loved science too much. I kept getting the urge to explain science without having to worry about plots and characterization" [p. 16]. What is characterization but people? What are plots but the behavior of people?)

Besides these narrative techniques of style, narrative point of view, plot, theme, setting, and character, three other things strike me as being usually present in an Asimovian story. Asimov loves everything about science, including its history (and he loves history, too). Present in many of his stories are informative little history and history-of-science lectures of the kind he does at greater length in *Fantasy and Science Fiction*. Second, his fiction is filled with astronomical views, what it looks like to be out among Jupiter's moons or Saturn's rings or in orbit about a newly discovered planet of a distant star. Once again, in science fiction the sense of wonder is sight, and Asimov wants us to share that sense of wonder with him: the sublimity and the beauty of what there is to see out there. Third, Asimov's fiction reflects his delight in the surprise ending, the story that goes *click!* at the end. He loves the challenge of fooling the reader, of leading him to the unexpected, and so he is very adept at writing short-shorts and longer stories that one mistakenly remembers as being short-shorts because all one recalls is the punch line.

For me, all of the above is included in the term "Asimovian."

But the adjective implies a steady state. Asimov has written fiction since 1938. Is that fiction all of a piece, or has he developed in any specific ways through the years? While I was doing the reading and writing of the earlier chapters in *The Science Fiction of Isaac Asimov* (Doubleday, 1974), I could maintain a feeling of change, of growth and development in Asimov's fiction. I was able to discern four periods in that career, and I could think of him as moving from one period to the other. I could move from the early stories to the Robot Stories to the Foundation stories to the novels.

But movement is not necessarily development, a change of setting is not necessarily a growing, an opening up of new markets is not necessarily a maturing. And when I read all those collected and uncollected stories, what I notice is that some are better than others and some not so good, and that there is no chronological pattern to which is which. Realistically, I can see only two major changes in

Asimov's career. The first was in 1938–39 when he changed from science fiction fan to science fiction writer, and the second was in 1957–58 when he changed from science fiction writer to science writer.

During his career as a science fiction writer, however, I can detect only two relatively minor developments. One of these was in his style. His early stories abound in the violent diction of the pulps. There is more emotion of a nonrealistic sort in that early fiction. As he wrote, he mastered the medium of clear, unemotional language. A second development was in the kinds of backgrounds he used. The backgrounds of the early stories are imitated from contemporary science fiction. As he wrote, he began to put together his own backgrounds based on contemporary science. Except for these two developments—in style and in settings— "Marooned Off Vesta" and "The Callistan Menace" are just as "Asimovian" as "Take a Match" and much of *The Gods Themselves*. Asimov found his voice early and has been speaking in it ever since.

In the future Asimov will probably continue what he has been doing since 1958, writing primarily straight science books and articles with an occasional foray into science fiction because he loves the field and doesn't want to disengage from it entirely. Still, I sense in his most recent fiction not only a tentative return to the field but a return of a certain kind. The writing of *The Gods Themselves* required a major commitment of time and energy, and it was a major commitment to a work of fiction. He has also returned to the subject matter of his earlier successes. "Feminine Intuition" featured a retired Susan Calvin called upon to return to her former job briefly. "Mirror Image" reunited Lije Baley and R. Daneel Olivaw. A new positronic robot story, "That Thou Art Mindful of Him," appeared in the May 1974 issue of *Fantasy and Science Fiction*. And he has been trying to work on a new story in the Foundation Series. Somehow I wouldn't be surprised to hear that the little man inside him has set to work on a sequel to "Nightfall" (telling perhaps what happened to the people secure in the Hideout) and/or the once-begun-but-never-finished third story in the Robot Novels.

Whether or not Asimov indeed begins to produce science fiction in quantity again, he has, I think, to choose between two kinds of story that he has in him to write. I do not expect him to turn to drastic stylistic experiments, to try to develop an imagistic style and strong verbs. He will continue to write like Asimov. The choices lie in his subject matter. He could continue to do what he has been doing of late: mining old material. The old familiar series, the old familiar settings, the old familiar characters. Supplying nostalgic trips for his many fans.

Or he could follow up in the direction I see him hesitantly looking in a couple of his most recent stories. To do this would require two major changes in attitude on his part, changes I don't believe he is ready to make. The first would be to take fiction seriously, and the second would be to write fiction about those things that are important to him. The two are clearly interrelated: if he took fiction seriously, of course he would use it to say those things that are important to him.

The first change carries in it the assumption that he does not now take fiction seriously. I don't think he does. For Asimov, fiction is merely entertainment, merely a way of passing time harmlessly. He downgrades "the eternal verities" and has little use for critics who see deep meaning and significance in his work. (Or in Shakespeare's, as "The Immortal Bard" made perfectly clear.) When *Sputnik* went up in the fall of 1957, and Asimov felt compelled to do what he could to close the science gap between the United States and the Soviet Union, what did he do? Considering his oft-expressed idea that science fiction bends the minds of young readers toward science, we might have expected him to double— nay, quadruple—his output of science fiction as his way of recruiting scientists. Instead, when a serious job was to be done, he turned to nonfiction, to science popularization.

What things does Asimov think are important? In his public appearances on television and radio, at universities and science fiction conventions, even in newspaper and magazine interviews—in short, in his nonfiction—we can see what is on his mind these days. Let me cull my examples from one interview with him, this one published in *Boston* (December 1969) and called "Scientific Inquiry: A Boston Interview with Isaac Asimov" (pp. 51–54, 82–90).

> If you *really* want an example of useless scientific work . . . that can lead only to terrible destruction, and which, to my way of thinking, no scientist with a conscience should engage in, it is the matter of chemical and biological warfare. There is nothing as far as I know in CBW that can help scientific theory in any way, or that can have any constructive use. . . . It is a universal human insanity. . . .
>
> [When asked whether he was optimistic over science and its ability to solve mankind's problems, he replied:] I'm afraid I am not. . . . Never

at any time have we managed to get people to look at humanity as a single unit, to look at the world as indivisible. . . . We live in an age of planetary problems and for the first time planetary problems have become matters of life and death. By a planetary problem I mean a problem that cannot . . . be solved on any basis smaller than the entire planet. For instance, overpopulation. There is no way in which the United States . . . can solve the overpopulation problem because if the United States reaches a population plateau and the rest of the world continues breeding recklessly, we're in trouble anyway. . . . Either the entire planet solves it, or no one solves it. The same is true of the problem of the stripping of the earth's resources, . . . the problem of pollution, . . . the problem of nuclear war. . . . We have got, somehow, to get it into our heads that the really important things on earth today are good for everybody or bad for everybody. There is no distinction. We cannot afford enemies any more. . . . Within a generation or two human society will be in total destructive disarray. Heaven knows how bad it will be. The most optimistic view I can take is this: Things will get so bad within a dozen years that it will become obvious . . . that we must, whether we like each other or not, work together. We have no choice in the matter. . . . Technologically, we can stop overpopulation, but we have to persuade people to accept the technology. . . . Babies are the enemies of the human race. . . . Let's consider it this way: by the time the world doubles its population, the amount of energy we will be using will be increased sevenfold which means probably the amount of pollution that we are producing will also be increased sevenfold. If we are now threatened by pollution at the present rate, how will we be threatened with sevenfold pollution by, say, 2010 A.D., distributed among twice the population? We'll be having to grow twice the food out of soil that is being poisoned at seven times the rate.

Where in his fiction are all these things central?

Admittedly, the general theme of his stories has always been the ability of human reason to solve problems. But what problems has human reason been set to solving in his most recent fiction? In "Feminine Intuition" Susan Calvin reasons out where certain robot-accumulated data can be found after the robot is accidentally destroyed (when a meteor collides with an airplane!). In "The Greatest Asset" a wise old bureaucrat reasons that a brilliant young scientist ought to be allowed to work on a hopeless project because "man's greatest asset is the unsettled mind." In "The Computer That Went on Strike" a computer programmer reasons out that Multivac has quit answering questions because its programmers don't say "Please?" In "Take a Match" a generalist high school teacher solves the technical and human problems involved in saving a spaceship trapped in a thick black cloud. They are all Asimovian stories teaching the value of reason, yes, but that reason is applied to trifles which are completely beside the point of Asimov's main concerns. His stories actually serve to distract us from the real problems which he sees all around us. He cannot take his fiction seriously if he insists on using it in such inconsequential ways at a time when he sincerely believes civilization as we know it is breaking down.

In his fiction Asimov is cheerfully optimistic. In *The Caves of Steel* the overpopulation problem has been solved, as have the problems of the stripping of the Earth's natural resources, of pollution, of nuclear war, of uneven distribution of wealth, of nationalism. In the Robot Stories man's technological devices open up the solar system and then the Galaxy. In the Foundation Series man has successfully spread his civilization throughout the Galaxy. But we know that *really* he is pessimistic about our civilization's surviving this century. Where in his fiction do we find an emphasis on the things he is really concerned about?

I do not wish to be misunderstood here. I am not saying that Asimov ought to turn to the writing of what he calls tomorrow fiction, the attempt to let readers live with characters in stories that show what tomorrow will probably be like, a sort of fictionalized futurism. On the one hand, Asimov will write what he likes and he doesn't need me to point his way for him. On the other, one can write about real problems and issues in today's world without writing tomorrow fiction. The main action of H. G. Wells's *The Time Machine* takes place hundreds of thousands of years in the future and is not intended to show what that tomorrow will really be like. Yet the novel is directly applicable to Wells's contemporary society. I am trying to be descriptive, not prescriptive, and what I am saying is that in some of his most recent fiction Asimov seems to me to be moving in the direction of taking fiction seriously and of writing about things that really concern him. I see him doing this primarily in two works, and therefore, for me, they are the most important things he has written lately, *The Gods Themselves* * and "Waterclap."

On January 24, 1971, Asimov was in the audience at a science fiction convention in New York City when Robert Silverberg referred to plutonium-186. Later, Asimov pointed out to Silverberg

---

* The following material on *The Gods Themselves* appeared in a slightly altered form in *Extrapolation*, Vol. 13, No. 2 (May 1972), 127–31.

that plutonium-186 was an impossible isotope, but he offered to write a five-thousand-word story about it anyway. The story was to be called "Plutonium-186." Thus, unknowingly, did Isaac Asimov begin *The Gods Themselves* (1972), his first science fiction novel in fourteen years.

He describes how he went about planning the story: "I had to think of something that would make possible (or at least seem to make possible) the existence of an impossible isotope, then think of complications that might ensue, and then of the resolution of those complications" (p. 7). Very early in the story a quantity of plutonium-186 has been discovered, and the characters are faced with exactly the problem Asimov had had to solve, how to account for the existence of this impossible isotope. The character's solution in the story shows us the writer's solution at his desk. A very minor character is made to say, "You know, what we need is a little bit of fantasy here. Suppose. . . ." A little later, a major character, Frederick Hallam, elaborates this "little bit of fantasy," and in so doing answers that perennial question asked of science fiction writers, "Where did you get that crazy idea?" What Hallam says, in effect, is (a) the small container of plutonium-186 does in fact exist, (b) its production in our universe was impossible, and therefore (c) it was sent to us from a parallel universe with a different set of physical laws. As a result, *The Gods Themselves* could be classified as a "parallel worlds" novel.

Next, Asimov had to "think of complications that might ensue." He decided to make the parallel universe a source of energy for us, just as our universe was a source of energy for it. What he calls Electron Pumps are set up, and the world's energy problems are solved. Only—and here's the conflict that makes this a story—one character, Peter Lamont, becomes convinced that the energy exchange will lead to the detonation of the Sun. It becomes his task to convince the Establishment that the Pumps must be turned off. Basically, the conflict is between Lamont and the Establishment, especially as represented in Hallam, "the Father of the Electron Pump."

"Plutonium-186," then, is an ecological story on a grand scale. It is a story developing exactly those themes about which Asimov has spoken so pessimistically in his nonfiction. We are doing too little too late. Overpopulation, hunger, disease, pollution, fuel shortages, inequitable distribution of wealth—things will get a lot worse before they get any better, and they may never get any better. The resolution of the conflict in "Plutonium-186" is in accord with this thinking. Peter Lamont is unable to convince anyone in authority that the Sun will soon nova because of the unchecked use of the Electron Pumps. A friend of his quotes the German playwright Schiller as saying, "Against stupidity the gods themselves contend in vain," and then advises Lamont, "Let it go, Pete, and go your way. Maybe the world will last our time, and, if not, there's nothing that can be done anyway. I'm sorry, Pete. You fought the good fight, but you lost" (*The Gods Themselves*, Greenwich, Conn.: Fawcett Crest, 1973, 70). And Lamont is left alone, sitting in a chair and thinking of the end of the world, and blinking back the tears.

"Against stupidity the gods themselves contend in vain." "You fought the good fight, but you lost." Where is the cheerful, slick-magazine optimism in this? This is Asimov looking at the world straight and telling us what he sees, in fiction. He is not playing intellectual games or merely being entertaining. He is saying something important, to him and to us.

One of the most interesting things about "Plutonium-186" as a work of fiction is the way it reveals Asimov's years as a writer of science fact. This is most obvious in the little informative lectures scattered through the story. They read exactly as though they were written for his series of articles in *Fantasy and Science Fiction*. More importantly, "Plutonium-186" reads like an account in the history of science. This is most clearly seen in the way Asimov gives us the exposition of the story, "exposition" here still referring to the way the writer chooses to present the past of the story to his readers. The writers' creeds all say, "Put the reader where the action is." "Show, don't tell." But often in his exposition Asimov decides to reconstruct rather than to visualize (or to make real). He asks his reader not to participate in events, but to evaluate sources and decide what probably happened. This sounds as though it shouldn't work, but it does. Remember that the basic conflict is between Lamont and Hallam, and that Lamont wants Hallam's Electron Pumps turned off. Part of Lamont's strategy is an *ad hominem* attack on Hallam: he tries to discredit Hallam, and to do that he must search for the truth in the past. Asimov's method of exposition parallels Lamont's method of attacking Hallam. Thus, treating the past of the story as an episode in the history of science is an appropriate and innovative way of reflecting the conflict between Lamont and Hallam.

Unfortunately, Asimov had promised Silverberg a five-thousand-word story, and "Plutonium-186" had grown into a twenty-thousand-word novelette (largely, I suspect, because of Asimov's interest in the science fact/history of science aspects of his presentation). So Asimov wrote "Take a Match" for Silverberg's *New Dimensions II* and decided on his editor's advice to use "Plutonium-186" as the basis of a novel.

Note that the original story, although too long for its original market, was complete. Asimov had thought of something that would make the impossible isotope at least seem possible, he had thought of complications arising therefrom, he had thought of an appropriate resolution, and he had summed up the theme of the story in a quotation from literature. Where will the rest of the novel come from?

In the story so far, the "men" of the para-Universe have contacted us and shown us how to build our halves of the Electron Pumps (without somehow solving the problem of how to communicate back and forth about any other matters, a difficulty that Asimov leaves unexplained). The obvious gambit for a continuation would be to tell the story from the point of view of the men in the para-Universe. This suggests the possibility of a three-part novel: (I) "Plutonium-186," (II) the para-men, and (III) men and para-men together solving their problems. The aliens are clearly associated in Asimov's mind with the middle phrase of the Schiller quote, "the gods themselves." In "Plutonium-186" Lamont has fought against the stupidity of the Establishment and failed. What more natural than to retitle the first section "Against Stupidity"? Only now a problem arises: The last part of the quote doesn't fit very well, because in the expanded version the solar system is eventually to be saved. It will not ultimately be a "vain" contest. So Asimov simply adds a question mark to the last title, and the three parts of *The Gods Themselves* are given the titles "I. Against Stupidity," "II. The Gods Themselves," and "III. Contend in Vain?"

While he was planning and working on "The Gods Themselves," Asimov was very much aware of two forces working on him. He explains them as follows:

[1] I've often been told I can't handle extra-terrestrials and that that's why my Foundation stories deal with all-human galaxies. Not so!

In *The Gods Themselves*, I set the second part in the parallel Universe and deliberately told a story of extra-terrestrials and not only managed to do so, but also managed (in my own opinion and according to many letters I have received) to create the best extra-terrestrials ever created. . . .

[2] Also when I finished the first part of the book (as an independent

novelette with no intention of doing more at the time), Doubleday urged me to make a novel of it and showed a copy to a paperback editor while I was thinking. I was told the paperback editor said, "Couldn't he put sex into it?" and Doubleday said, austerely, "Of course not. Asimov never does."

So I did. I put sex into the second part. It is all sex and, I think, sex seriously and decently handled as an integral part of the plot and with no holds barred. It just happened to be extra-terrestrial sex. [Personal letter, October 10, 1972]

As a result of this dual challenge to handle aliens and sex as he never had before, Asimov wrote the brilliant middle section of *The Gods Themselves*. In this section he takes us elsewhere and allows us to live there for a while. It is a detailed study of consciousness as it developed and lives in a vastly different environment from our own. Perhaps, as much as anything else, it leaves behind an awe-full respect for life and sentience.

But no science fiction alien can ever be entirely different from ourselves. They spring out of and are thus rooted in the human imagination. In one sense what Asimov has done is return to a certain type of medieval allegory, the type represented by *The Romance of the Rose*, in which the allegorical abstractions are abstracted from the human psychology. The family groups of three—exemplified here in Dua, the female, and Odeen and Tritt, the males—are abstracted from each of us. The medieval allegorist might have called Dua, Emotion; Odeen, Intellect; and Tritt, Common Sense. In these days of unisex and women's lib, it is interesting that Dua, the female, creates an environment in which Tritt, the male, can conceive and rear the children. Asimov does not present simply Male-Intellect-Logic versus Female-Emotion-Intuition. (Fill in whatever other dualities you are used to.) Instead, each of us has within him a Dua, an Odeen, and a Tritt, and "The Gods Themselves" can be read profitably, I think, as a reminder that our natures are not dual but complex.

"Against Stupidity" and "The Gods Themselves" mesh together very well. In the first part we are with our fellow human beings, receiving cryptic messages; in the second we are with the para-men, sending those messages. One slightly jarring note is that initially we are led to believe that the para-men's continued use of the Pumps is the result of stupidity on their part parallel to our own, whereas we learn that they know they are about to destroy our solar system but they don't care. They are motivated not by stupidity, but by maliciousness. This blunts the original theme of "Against Stupidity"–"Plutonium-186."

"Contend in Vain?" does not fit in very well at all with the earlier two sections. The Schiller quote that was so appropriate to the pessimistic "Plutonium-186" no longer fits the more conventional story in which the hero saves the universe, marries the girl, and lives happily ever after. This incongruity is what Asimov was recognizing when he put the question mark in "Contend in Vain?" (Try to read Schiller's statement as a question. The strained falseness of the last three words exactly suits the whole last section of the novel in its relationship with what has gone before.) Worse yet, the breathtaking and promising ending of "The Gods Themselves" has been ignored. When the para-man Estwald stepped forward and said, "I am permanently with you now, and there is much to do . . . ," we were led to believe that he would do something. We expect that in Part III Lamont and Estwald would join in an honest effort to solve the mutual problems between the two universes.

Instead, the men of the para-Universe are never brought onstage again. They are slipped into the background as a permanent but impersonal threat which is finally neutralized by conjuring up another para-Universe (a pocket-frannistan?) to balance theirs out. The para-men deserve far better than to be so abruptly dropped because there is simply too much preparation in the second part for their continued use.

Admittedly, by itself and with a less awkward title, "Contend in Vain?" is a very good piece of writing. In it we have once again the politically astute Asimov of the Foundation Series, the one who substitutes talk for action because he knows that decision-making is more important than mere activity. And we have once again the Asimov of *The Caves of Steel*, so good at constructing the details of a future human society down to its attitudes, architecture, and games (the future society here being located on the Moon).

Nevertheless, in context "Contend in Vain?" does not work. Surprisingly—I would have said impossibly earlier—the first two sections are so good that they make the typically Asimovian last section look weak. "Against Stupidity" has its history-of-science expository structure in which we are asked to reconstruct probable events rather than participate in actual ones (a technical innovation) as well as its honest and realistic—and pessimistic—appraisal of where we as a civilization stand (an innovation in subject matter). "The Gods Themselves" has its successful treatment of aliens and sex and its implicit demonstration that all consciousness is companioned by all other consciousness. But I cannot forgive Asimov for "Contend in Vain?" Besides abandoning the brilliantly conceived para-men, conjuring the pocket-frannistan of another parallel universe with which to solve the novel's problem, and pasting on a happy ending, he has in it abandoned those things that are important to him as detailed in his nonfiction. (By the way, it's not the happy ending I object to, it's the pasting on. Had Estwald and Lamont working together solved their mutual problems, I would not have objected to *that* happy ending, and it would have been right in keeping with Asimov's other work, too.)

The three separate parts of *The Gods Themselves* are all very good stories. Put together they do not form a unified whole. Put together in their particular order, they also show Asimov backsliding. In *The Gods Themselves* Asimov takes both of the two paths I have suggested are open to him, and they are incompatible in one novel. He cannot present simultaneously his bleak evaluation of the crisis situation in which we find ourselves and his buoyantly optimistic story line. We all know that he does not believe that someone is going to discover a pocket-frannistan and save us all. That Asimov can write "Against Stupidity" and "The Gods Themselves" I take as a hopeful sign. That he chose to cap them off with "Contend in Vain?" I take as an indication that he is not yet certain whether he is looking to his future or to his past. (One might add to this such of his most recent stories as "Feminine Intuition," "The Computer That Went on Strike," and "Mirror Image.")

"Waterclap" integrates two projects that must fascinate Asimov both as a science writer and as a science fiction writer: the exploration of outer space and the exploration of our oceans. He could have written an essay asserting in nonfictional terms a possible relationship between the two, but instead he wrote a story demonstrating in fictional terms that space-ocean exploration is not either-or but both-and. A fanatical believer in space exploration comes to Ocean-Deep to sabotage the installation so that funds for it will be cut off and channeled into space exploration instead. At the crucial moment he does not destroy Ocean-Deep because he becomes convinced that "the purpose of Ocean-Deep is to devise the ultimate vessels and mechanisms that will explore and colonize Jupiter" (*World's Best Science Fiction: 1971*, pp. 123–24). The speaker goes on to describe "Project Big World" in the most optimistic science fictional and Asimovian terms:

Look about you and see the beginnings of a Jovian environment—the closest approach to it we can achieve on Earth. It is only a faint image—but it is a beginning. Destroy this . . . and you destroy any hope for Jupiter. On the other hand, let us live and we will, together, penetrate and settle the brightest jewel of the solar system. And long before we can reach the limits of Jupiter we'll be ready for the stars, for the Earth-type planets circling them—and the Jupiter-type planets, too. [p. 124]

"We'll be ready for the stars": the ultimate symbol in science fiction for human success and freedom. The happy ending here is an affirmation of the necessity for people to work together to solve their problems, despite sometimes conflicting aims and motivations. In contrast the happy ending of *The Gods Themselves* was a parallel universe pulled out of a hat. And while, at the end of *The Gods Themselves*, everyone lived happily ever after, the ending of "Waterclap" is not really an ending: the Galactic Empire is not yet come, and there is much to do.

In my mind, the nature of Asimov's future in science fiction depends on his willingness to resolve the disparity between his fiction and his nonfiction, between *The Caves of Steel* and his interview in *Boston*. That he can resolve them is clearly demonstrated in "Against Stupidity" and "Waterclap." But these two items represent only a small part of his most recent fiction, and nostalgic excursions with Susan Calvin, Lije Baley, R. Daneel Olivaw, the positronic robots, and perhaps even the Foundations have taken a disproportionate amount of his science fiction time and energies.

Personally, I hope Asimov can shake off his past successes and move in the direction indicated by "Against Stupidity" and "Waterclap." I would welcome Asimov's return as a full-time science fiction writer, taking fiction seriously as a medium in which to say the most important things he has to say. Then he could announce to us all—in the words of Estwald at the end of "The Gods Themselves"—"I am permanently with you now, and there is much to do—"

9. Ethical Evolving Artificial Intelligence:
Asimov's Computers and Robots

PATRICIA S. WARRICK

THE AGE OF COMPUTERS has arrived, announced a number of non-fiction books and articles in the 1960s. But twenty years earlier science fiction had prophesied and pictured that arrival, and the major voice describing the appearance of man's most radical technological innovation—artificial intelligence—was Isaac Asimov's. A handful of writers had portrayed electronically operated robots a few years before Asimov's first story, "Robbie," appeared. But none before or since has written more prolifically about the technology of our cybernetic age, or created stories of such consistently high quality. Asimov has written over thirty short stories and two novels about computers and robots. The earliest appeared in 1940, just a year after he began publishing science fiction, and the most recent was written in 1976. This chapter will trace the image of the relationship of man and artificial intelligence as Asimov's imagination transforms it over a thirty-five year span.

While writers were at work in science fiction creating fantastic tales of robots exploring the galaxies in computer-operated space-ships, the computer scientists were in reality designing thinking machines quite as amazing as the imaginary tales written about them. In the field of computers, science fiction and technology have raced into the future together, and in recent years the engineer's accomplishments often outdistance the possibilities described in science fiction. Asimov's fiction is remarkable in being among the relatively small number of works anticipating developments in computer systems, rather than lagging behind them. Further, he never wavers in his faith that the computer is a sophisticated tool able to aid in solving complex social problems, and not a machine monster bent on enslaving man.

The first science fiction to portray electronically operated robots and computers was written early in the 1930s. The actual computer technology was not developed until the late 1930s and early 1940s. But neither literature nor technology sprang from a void. Mechanical calculators had been in use for over three centuries, and the possibility of creating automata has long intrigued man, as historical records and surviving artifacts verify. Literature and legend from the early Renaissance on contain tales of artificially created life forms. Even earlier, Greek myths and legends also reveal man's fascination with the creative process, and his urge to imagine and make mechanical models of the natural world. Hephaestus build handmaids of gold, and mobile tripods that served in the divine dining hall, performing their functions automatically. Daedalus mechanically imitated the flights of birds and built statues that moved. Celestial clockworks of great complexity were built in Europe during the Middle ages and the Renaissance.

The making of intricate and marvelous automata metamorphosed and flowered in the eighteenth century. One very famous device was the illustrious duck of the toymaker Jacques de Vaucasson (1709–82). It moved, ate, drank, and simulated the activities of a real duck. There were other types of mechanical devices: dancing dolls, marching soldiers, music boxes, a lady flute player. In the nineteenth century an Englishman, Charles Babbage, designed a calculating machine that earned him the title of "father of the computer." It was called the Analytical Engine and in theory could do mathematical calculations automatically. But the technology of his time was not sophisticated enough to build his engine. That had to wait until 1944 when Howard Aiken built an automated calculating machine at Harvard University.

While nineteenth century scientists and engineers were busy creating devices that simulated intelligent and purposeful behavior, the literary imagination was also at work designing artificial life. Mary Shelley's *Frankenstein* (1818) was one of the earliest and most memorable tales. Ambrose Bierce created a mechanical chess player in "Moxon's Master" (1894). Karel Čapek's *R.U.R.*(1921) gave the name *robot* to the artificially created creature designed to serve man. Early twentieth-century American science fiction writers like Edmond Hamilton and A. Merritt envisioned metal monsters, and in 1934 Harl Vincent wrote a story called "Rex" that has an electronically operated robot. Eando Binder followed with "I, Robot" in 1938 and Lester del Rey published "Helen O'Loy" in 1939. Asimov's first robot story, "Robbie," appeared in 1940. The tales of robots increased in number until now they have become as much a symbol of the science fiction future as spaceships.

Today artificial intelligence in science fiction comes in so many forms that a clarification of terms is helpful. A computer is defined as an automatic electronic machine for performing calculations, and for storing and processing information. A robot is a mobile machine system with information processing ability made of non-biological materials such as metal, plastic, and electronic devices. The robot may be self-controlled (have its computer within), remotely controlled (have its computer elsewhere), or an intermediate machine, with the robot being partly self-activated and partly remotely controlled. Robots are distinguished from androids, the latter being man-designed human-like entities made of biological materials. Cyborgs are entities built by joining together mechanisms and biological organisms.

Asimov's fiction about robots and computers can be divided into three phases. During the first phase, from 1940 through 1950, he wrote a dozen stories and they were primarily about robots, with only two computer stories. Nine of these stories were collected and published as *I, Robot* in 1950. In his second period, from 1951 to 1961, Asimov wrote another dozen or so stories and the novels *The Caves of Steel* and *The Naked Sun*. Many of these stories and the two novels were collected and published under the title *The Rest of the Robots*. In 1958 he turned from writing science fiction to writing about science, and not until the mid-1970s did he write more fiction about computers and robots. *The Bicentennial Man* (1976) contains a half-dozen stories marking his third period, and demonstrating the further evolution of his ideas about the key role computers will play in man's future.

Since World War II an increasing number of works have been written about machine intelligence, either in computer or robot form, and the preponderance of these works take a very negative view of the computer. Ira Levin's *This Perfect Day* (1970) contains the paradigm typical of most. Through the use of the computer, a small ruling group is able to manipulate, control, and enslave the majority of men. The latter lose their individuality as they are assigned numbers and forced to march as masses of conformist robots in a drab mechanized society.

This dystopian view of the computer is one Asimov has never held. (A small number of writers share Asimov's positive view of the computer's potential. Among them are Arthur C. Clarke, Robert Heinlein, Samuel Delany, Mack Reynolds, and Frank Herbert.) In *The Naked Sun* this dystopian view is referred to as the Frankenstein complex,[1] and while Asimov recognizes that fear of the hostility toward the computer are the common attitude, he rejects it. He sees the computer and automation as technological advances benefiting mankind by freeing him of poverty, hard labor, and boring routine. Man survives the increasing complexity of his culture and the deluge of new knowledge only with the aid of the computer. It allows him to make intelligent decisions about the future, and to maintain control in a society that otherwise would disintegrate into chaos. The computer gives man the opportunity to finally realize the moral aspirations contained in the world's great religious systems. Thus the famous Three Laws of Robotics are the means of implementing a code of behavior and making possible an ethical technology assuring the survival of both man and the natural environment.

But all Asimov's stories suggest that most men will not see the potential of computers. Like the nineteenth-century Luddites, smashing weaving looms in England, they will resist this new technological advance. "Profession," for example (collected in *Nine Tomorrows*), presents his view of the resistance of the majority to innovation. In this story Asimov describes a society where the mass of people are rigid in their attitude toward change. Their brains are programmed by the ideas of the past, and they prefer to function in a routine, nondeviating fashion. Not computers but the conformist mindset is what makes robots out of people. The rare creative individual open to new possibilities is the exception in society.

The Asimovian view gives a kind of unity to all his fiction about computers and robots, from the first story in 1940 to the last in 1976. This view holds that man will continue to develop more sophisticated technology; he will become more skillful at problem-solving in societal and environmental areas; he will expand outward and colonize space. Many of the stories share the same characters and settings. The U.S. Robots and Mechanical Men, Inc., builds the first robot in 1998. The progress of the corporation is guided for many years by Dr. Susan Calvin, "the brilliant roboticist who had, virtually singlehanded, built up the positronic robot from a massive toy to man's most delicate and versatile instrument. . . ."[2] The most recent stories are set two hundred years later, Susan has died, and the new roboticist is Mervin Mansky. (The name is clearly derived from Marvin Minsky of MIT, who is more enthusiastic about the possibility of duplicating human intelligence than almost any other researcher in the field of artificial intelligence.)

Asimov's stories are often concerned with the same themes: the political potential of the computer; the uses of computers and robots in space exploration and development; problem-solving with computers; the differences between man and machine; the evolution of artificial intelligence; and the ethical use of technology. This last theme is explored through the Three Laws of Robotics. The Laws were first fully stated in "Runaround" (1942), Asimov's fifth robot tale. They appear in many other stories and are crucial to three stories in *The Bicentennial Man*.

Asimov handles machine intelligence both realistically and metaphorically. In the stories about computers the technology pictured functions very much like existent technology. Large stationary machines store, process, and retrieve data; do mathematical calculations at incredible speeds; play mathematical games; make logical decisions. Asimov is knowledgeable in the concepts of computer science,[3] and his portrayals are always intelligent and accurate. He has been wise enough to omit specific descriptions of computer technology, and consequently the material does not date (something that easily happens if the writer portrays details of the technology because it is changing with such speed in the real world). Asimov's robots are much more metaphorical than his computers. In the real world, no robots comparable in form to those he pictures have been built, nor is there much possibility that they will be in the foreseeable future. Specialized industrial robots performing limited functions are much more likely to be developed than the all-purpose robots he pictures. While the latter might be possible, the former are more feasible economically. It is more meaningful to regard his robots as a metaphor for all the automated electronic technology—in a variety of forms—that will replace most of man's physical and routine mental work in the future.

Asimov's usual technique of plot development is worth noting. He rarely uses dramatic conflict but relies almost entirely on a puzzle or problem-solving to create suspense and to move his plot forward. Through all his fiction runs the theme of faith in the ability of human reason to solve problems. His fiction is cerebral—grounded in sound science and logic. The action is more often mental than physical. In a typical story, a problem or puzzle is first defined; then as much data as possible is collected and evaluated; next, a hypothesis is erected, providing a basis for a set of predictions about the solution of the problem; finally, the predictions are tested. If they are incorrect, the process must be reexamined until the difficulty is discovered. This, of course, is the scientific method. The universe for Asimov is more mysterious than threatening. His use of the puzzle paradigm, rather than the conflict paradigm, seems related to the fact that his view of computers and robots is an optimistic one. His short story "The Evitable Conflict" (in *I, Robot*) reflects his attitude toward conflict. That future world is one where society has learned to avoid war. In his fiction Asimov also avoids the conflict mode.

Asimov's views of artificial intelligence in his third and most recent period have evolved considerably beyond those in the earlier periods. The most workable approach to the material, therefore, is first to examine the fiction written during the 1940s and 1950s, then to look at the stories collected in *The Bicentennial Man* (1976). We will discover how his view of artificial intelligence has changed during the fifteen years when he was writing nonfiction about science.

I, Robot (1950) generally contains stories superior to those collected in *The Rest of the Robots* (1964). In *I, Robot* Asimov builds a frame for the stories by using a dialogue between Dr. Susan Calvin, the robopsychologist, and a newspaper reporter interviewing her at the end of a long career. In answer to the reporter's questions, she begins recalling the past, and each short story becomes an episode in that past. Dr. Susan Calvin, who also plays a part in some of the stories, is one of Asimov's most interesting portrayals. She has the penetrating intellect and logic of a gifted scientist, and Asimov says she is one of his favorite character creations. The frame technique is effective in uniting the nine individual stories into an aesthetically satisfying whole. From the first story "Robbie" (1940) to the last story "The Evitable Conflict" (1950), an interesting evolution of artificial intelligence takes place. It originally appears as a toy—a simple robot playmate for a little girl. By the final story it has progressed to the form of a huge sophisticated computer successfully guiding the economy of the whole Earth and assuring a reign of peace.

Asimov's cybernetic fiction has settings and characters that recur from story to story. "Robbie" is set on Earth at the end of the twentieth century. The U.S. Robots and Mechanical Men Corporation manufactures robots as playmates for children. This starting point is reminiscent of Čapek's robot factory in *R.U.R.*, but the development of Asimov's robots contrasts sharply with the Čapek's robots, who revolt, destroy mankind, and take over the world. Asimov's robots in "Robbie" are programmed with the First Law of Robotics: A robot may not injure a human being, or, through inaction, allow a human being to come to harm. Robbie, the hero of the story, is a dependable playmate for an eight-year-old girl named Gloria, even though her mother dislikes him because she distrusts robots. The robot eventually saves Gloria's life.

The next group of robot stories is set in space. Feelings against robots have grown so strong on Earth that they are banned. These stories involve two engineers, Powell and Donovan, who solve a set of problems and puzzles using robots. The robots serve a variety of functions in space: they aid in the maintenance of a space station, they perform ore-mining operations on an asteroid, and they operate a space ship sent to explore Jupiter. Because these stories are set in space, not Earth, little conflict between man and robot occurs. In a hostile environment like space, machine intelligence is vital to man, and so he welcomes it.

The situation is different on Earth, where later stories are set. "Evidence" (1946) has an Earth setting, and here the general population is resentful of robots. "Evidence" is one of Asimov's most profound cybernetic stories. It concerns Stephen Byerley, who is running for the office of mayor. His opponents charge him with being a robot, and therefore unsuitable for public office. Two questions arise: Is Byerley really a robot? And if so, can a machine govern effectively? The first question gives Asimov a good opportunity to explore the logic of proof, and here he demonstrates his education and intellectual inclination. He is ever the scientist, using the scientific method of hypothesis and proof.

To the second question, Asimov answers *yes*. His robots and computer are programmed with the Three Laws of Robotics, which insure that they will always act to aid and serve man. "Evidence" contains a substantial discussion of these laws. Byerley points out that they incorporate the ethical principles of the world's great religions. Because a robot mechanism cannot violate them, it is a more reliable device for governing than a politician, who may be motivated by ambition and greed. At the end of the story, Byerley is elected mayor. He performs effectively in that office for five years, and then he becomes a Regional Co-ordinator. In 2044 the Regions of Earth form a Federation and Byerley becomes World Co-ordinator. By that time, the Machines are running the world. Byerley's term as World Co-ordinator is described in "The Evitable Conflict," the final tale of *I, Robot*.

"The Evitable Conflict" is a computer story and, in my opinion, one of science fiction's most superbly imaginative stories in envisioning the creative use of machine intelligence. In the twenty-first century, the world has been divided into four geographic regions, with the economy of each maintained in balance by a huge computer. As a result, war has been eliminated. But into this balanced situation small errors in production schedules begin to intrude. The question: Is this caused by error in the machine, or is it a human error—deliberate or otherwise? An anti-machine group, The Society of Humanity, has arisen, and it is possible they are trying to sabotage the computer.

It turns out that the computer has devised a system for eliminating individual leaders who do not have as their first concern the good of the whole. For that good, war must be eliminated. The computer has accomplished this and thus, conflict is no longer inevitable. With planning and control it can be avoided; the potential creators of conflict are removed before they can cause trouble. Only the machine is inevitable. Asimov in this story suggests that machine control is better than being at the mercy of economic and sociological forces, the whims of climate, and the fortunes of war. Mankind, he intimates, has never been free; machine control is just a different—and superior—form of control.

The Rest of the Robots contains six stories written during the 1950s and two stories written earlier but not published in *I, Robot*. The stories in *The Rest of the Robots* generally are not as strong as those in the earlier anthology, nor does this second collection have the Susan Calvin frame that worked so effectively in *I, Robot*. Instead, Asimov himself introduces the stories, with comments about their origins and ideas. While the comments are interesting, they do not succeed as well artistically nor do they give unity to the tales as when he used the persona of Susan Calvin. Asimov notes in his comments that he used the word *robotics* in his stories, not then realizing he was making up a new word. Later he discovered that the word did not appear in *Webster's Unabridged Dictionary*. Today (1977) it still does not appear. However, the term is commonly used in the field of computer science, and it now appears in *The Barnhart Dictionary of New English Since 1963*, with credit given to

Asimov. Asimov's robots have positronic brains. Positrons are minute particles of matter discovered about the time Asimov was creating his robots. He borrowed the term and gave it to his robot brains.

Asimov never wavers through all his fiction in his faith that man and machine can form a harmonious relationship. How can he maintain this optimism, in light of the fact that so much pessimism exists all around him? When we examine the patterns running through his fiction, we observe that he envisions no conflict between man and machine. The strengths of the machine can serve man and bolster his weaknesses. The machine is never more than a tool in the hands of man, to be used as he chooses. Computers and computerized robots for Asimov are reliable logic machines, efficient at handling large masses of data and doing mathematical calculations at fantastic speeds. They can perform as dependable, precise servants, tireless and without error in even the most routine jobs. They are inexhaustible, they never get bored, they are incorruptible—because they are without emotions and consequently have no ambitions, loves, or other distractions to subvert the functioning of logic. Man, in contrast, is capable of creative problem-solving and can exercise judgment in choosing between alternatives. His intuition can be of value, if his insights are supported and developed through the mathematical logic the computer can provide.

Asimov's two robot detective novels, *The Caves of Steel* and *The Naked Sun*, illustrate this man-machine symbiosis. Asimov regards *Caves of Steel* as his best novel, and I feel his judgment is a perceptive one. He is very inventive in creating his setting—a future city in an automated world of high population density. *The Caves of Steel* is detective fiction, a mode lending itself neatly to Asimov's scientific mind since the methodology of science is to define a problem or puzzle, collect evidence, and then reason through to a solution. Elijah Baley, the human detective in the two novels, solves the murder mysteries confronting him with the invaluable aid of Robot Daneel Olivaw. The robot is able to provide all kinds of data and process it rapidly when necessary. He can apply logic to a situation, but a man can add judgment to logic, and this capacity makes him superior. The detective recognizes this difference when they have reached an apparent dead end in their attempt to solve the problem, and Robot Daneel has nothing else to propose:

There it was, thought Baley. Logic was logic and robots had nothing else. . . . Logic told Daneel he was completely stymied. Reason might have told him that all factors are rarely predictable, that the opposition might make a mistake.

None of that. A robot is logical only, not reasonable. (*The Naked Sun*, p. 108)

And that is the important difference for Asimov—man's capacity to be reasonable.

Asimov's cybernetic fiction utilizes the electronic brain in a variety of ways, none malignant. Computers are an aid in the research and development of space travel; they perform all mathematical calculations for society; they predict elections results; they serve as aids in the educational process. They solve a variety of problems. The vastest problem they undertake is that of decreasing entropy in the universe. In what is often regarded as the classic computer story, "The Last Question" (1956), they reverse the entropic process and recreate the cosmos. In this story man keeps asking the computer: How can entropy be reversed? He asks it six different times—first on Earth, then on various galaxies, as he continually expands through the universe. The computer keeps answering: Insufficient data to give meaningful answer. Finally, trillions of years in the future, as entropy becomes absolute, and the last star goes out, he asks it the seventh time. The computer finally has sufficient data to give the answer, and it is: Let there be Light! The story is a beautiful little myth of cyclic creation. Man —once created himself—creates the machine. The machine—a greater creator—finally acquires all the information in the universe. Then, omniscient like God, the machine is able to recreate the universe.

Man sees himself as distinct from animals because of his much higher degree of intelligence and his ability to store information and to pass it from individual to individual, and from generation to generation. Each new generation begins with the accumulated knowledge of all the previous generations. But what happens to man's image of himself as unique in his intelligence when a machine begins to acquire some of these characteristics? This question has increasingly confronted contemporary man in the last two decades as computer technology rapidly becomes more complex and more sophisticated. If machine intelligence can perform the functions of human intelligence, is man then nothing more than a machine?

This question intrigues Asimov. It runs through his fiction, and he proposes a variety of tentative answers. Consider the possibilities he defines in his fiction of the 1940s and the 1950s. Here, while he holds great respect for the present capacity and future possibilities of computers and artificial intelligence, he never wavers from his faith in the unique superiority of man. Not because man is better and faster at logical and mathematical calculations (he usually isn't), but because—although he does some things a machine can do—he possesses certain unique characteristics that make him more than a machine. This is why a machine is always subservient to a human—as assured in the Second Law. In at least a half-dozen stories Asimov defines the differences between man and machine intelligence. His explorations proceed from the assumptions that they share many things in common. Hence the constant use of the human-appearing robot as a symbol of artificial intelligence. At first glance, man and robot look alike, but probing beneath the skin reveals the differences.

First, human intelligence is coupled with emotions; machine intelligence is not. Early in her career Susan Calvin falls in love ("Liar," 1941, in *I, Robot*), a painful experience because it turns out the man loves someone else. Susan's love turns into another emotion—rage. Herbie, her faithful robot, is baffled as to how he can best serve her, because he cannot comprehend emotions and so does not know how to deal with them. Another story, "Satisfaction Guaranteed" (1951, collected in *Earth Is Room Enough*), also examines the emotional needs of humans. The neglected wife of an overworked engineer falls in love with her handsome household robot, Tony. While he can perform faithfully the duties he is programmed to handle, he cannot respond emotionally. Feelings are not an element of pure intelligence.

Another difference between human and machine intelligence is the inability of the machine to handle ambiguity. In mathematical logic, one symbol can denote only one thing. Something like a figure of speech, where the individual meanings of a group of words are different from their sum, creates havoc for the computer. Human language in this area is unlike computer language. From the context, any human can probably easily grasp the meaning of a figure of speech. Not so a computer—and Asimov loves to play with this difference, just as he delights in puns, something also beyond the capacity of the computer. The delight in incongruity or contradiction is the essence of humor, and Asimov's puckish humor often shimmers just above his hard, scientific thinking. But his robots are incapable of laughter because they take everything literally, and thus have no sense of humor. Asimov often uses this fact as the basis for a story. For example, in "Little Lost Robot" (1947, in *I, Robot*), a frustrated engineer tells an overly helpful robot to "go lose yourself," and the robot does just that. Not able to comprehend figures of speech, he takes all statements literally. The problem to be solved in the story is how to identify the "lost" robot hiding among 62 other robots of identical appearance.

Creative problem-solving is another area where machine intelligence differs from human intelligence. Asimov explores this difference in "Risk" (1955, in *The Rest of the Robots*). An experimental spaceship is being sent through hyperspace to another planet, and a robot instead of a man is used as a test pilot since it has not yet been determined whether the trip through hyperspace will injure the human brain. The ship fails to take off, and Dr. Susan Calvin orders a space engineer aboard to investigate the problem. Recognizing the assignment is dangerous because the ship may launch itself at any moment with him aboard, the engineer argues that a robot be sent instead. Susan refuses, explaining why the engineer, not the robot, is required. A man is capable of creative problem-solving, a robot is not. It can only solve the problems it has been programmed to solve, and therefore cannot deal with the unanticipated as a man can. This, according to Susan, is the great difference between a man and a thinking machine.

One of the differences—in reality—between human and artificial intelligence is that machines do not possess consciousness or self-awareness. They may perform operations we define as intelligent, but they are not aware of what they are doing. They do not observe themselves in the process of thinking, as humans do. When the science fiction imagination creates machine intelligence, this question of consciousness must be handled. Is the robot or computer to exhibit signs of consciousness? If it has consciousness, does it have free will? In the real world of cybernetics, the question has generally been avoided. It is regarded as a philosophical question not germane to the field of computer science. There the questions are more likely to be: How does the brain work? Can we build a model of it?

In the fiction of his first two periods, Asimov deals with the question of consciousness in his robots in an interesting manner. As early as his second story, "Reason" (1941, in *I, Robot*), he creates a robot who exhibits signs of intellectual activity we associate with sentient creatures. The robot is curious about its own existence, and how it was created. The two engineers Powell and Donovan argue theories of creation with the robot when it becomes interested in religion. These activities would have to be interpreted as displays of consciousness. At a later time when Asimov was asked about the matter of consciousness in his robots, he replied that he does think of his robots as being conscious.[4] But the fiction of his first two periods fails to probe into the ethical and moral implications of consciousness in artificial intelligence. If a robot does have consciousness, in what significant way is he any different from a human being? If he is not significantly different, should he ethically be treated like a human? Is it moral to use him as a slave when humans value their freedom so highly? What about death? Should the robot be portrayed in science fiction as dying, or merely wearing out? Can a human "kill" a robot? In "Liar," Asimov pictures Dr. Susan Calvin as deliberately programming a robot so that he collapses and goes insane. She is furious at the robot because she feels he lied to her when he indicated a fellow roboticist was in love with her. It turns out the robot only lied to spare her feelings. Should she be condemned for driving him insane? These are complex questions that have never been raised before because man has never before moved so close to the technological reality of constructing artificial intelligence.[5]

Asimov creates conscious robots, but in the fiction of his first two periods he does not deal with the implications of consciousness in artificial beings. In ignoring the whole question of the significance of consciousness, Asimov does no more than reflect what has been the prevailing attitude of science generally toward the subject of consciousness. This is true not only in computer science but in biology and psychology. The computer scientist need not concern himself with consciousness because he is interested only in artificial intelligence, and he readily admits that presently machine intelligence is on a very primitive level compared with human intelligence.[6] The problem of consciousness and artificial intelligence has been debated primarily by the philosophers.[7]

Closely related to the debate about consciousness is the debate about free will and the freedom necessary to man if he is to exercise it. If man is only a machine—as the mechanistic paradigm of physical biology holds—then free will is only an illusion. A debate about the importance of man's free will is meaningless, since like a machine he is programmed to behave in a particular way and cannot deviate from that pattern. In this view, a consideration of freedom for a robot would not be worthwhile. According to the deterministic stance, a single body of natural laws operating on material particles accounts for the properties of living organisms as well as nonliving aggregates of matter. Man is no more than a complex machine. The human brain and the computer are similar. The human brain is a complex network—a large number of multiple interconnected neurons. The output of each neuron is determined by the input it receives from the other neurons with which it is connected. The computer is similar except that, instead of neurons, it uses a large number of multiple interconnected electronic switches.

Asimov's view about his robots is clear: they do not have free will. Apparently man possesses it, and in the robot and computer stories he behaves as if he does. On the other hand, as critics have noted, in the *Foundation* trilogy the deterministic view of man seems to prevail. History will unfold according to predetermined laws, and man cannot influence it.*

These are interesting and substantial questions. While Asimov raises them in the fiction of his first two periods, he does not probe them. But we will find in the fiction of his recent period that he returns to these matters again, and this time he does not brush by. He gives the thoughtful reflection that such issues as consciousness, death, and freedom deserve—either in human or high-level artificial intelligence.

The Three Laws of Robotics, as they appear in *I, Robot*, are:

1—A robot may not injure a human being, or, through inaction, allow a human being to come to harm.

2—A robot must obey the orders given it by human beings except where such orders would conflict with the First Law.

3—A robot must protect its own existence as long as such protection does not conflict with the First or Second Law.

In science fiction religious tales are comparatively rare. So are stories debating the niceties of various moral codes. Science fiction

---

* For an expanded discussion of the issue of free will versus determinism, see Charles Elkins' chapter in this book.

traditionally has based itself on the natural and social sciences, and they aim at being analytic, not normative. Certainly no writer grounds his fiction more solidly in science than Asimov, and yet, quite amazingly, he has formulated an ethical code now famous in and out of science fiction. Two recent texts on artificial intelligence make references to the Three Laws,[8] and one of the authors says he sees no reason why the laws cannot be programmed. Adrian Berry's *The Next Ten Thousand Years* (1974) also cites the Three Laws. Even Asimov himself expresses amazement at the wide influence of these Three Laws. He comments as he discusses robotics, "It is rather odd to think that in centuries to come, I may be remembered (if I am remembered at all) only for having laid the conceptual groundwork for a science which in my own time was nonexistent."[9]

The germinal idea for the First Law appeared in Asimov's original robot story "Robbie." Irritated with the plethora of robot stories in the 1920s and '30s where the robot routinely turned destructive monster, Asimov vowed that "never, never was one of my robots to turn stupidly on his creator for no purpose but to demonstrate, for one more weary time, the crime and punishment of Faust."[10] His First Law made certain a robot would never injure a human. In "Robbie," when Mrs. Weston is frightened of what "that terrible machine" may do to her little daughter, Mr. Weston explains the First Law has so programmed the robot that it is impossible for it to harm a human. The Three Laws first appeared as a key element in the plot of "Runaround." Asimov relates that the laws were worked out with editor John Campbell during a conversation in Campbell's office on December 16, 1940.[11] Subsequently, the scope, applications, and implications of the Laws developed until they have become a serious ethical system for guiding the uses of computers and even more broadly, technology in general.

Asimov, recently writing on the phenomenal development of computer technology, cites this as a second revolution comparable in scope to the Industrial Revolution of the late eighteenth and nineteenth centuries. He raises a question:

> What about our reliance on the tools of the revolution: science, technology. Might not this very reliance become itself a danger? Will computers and the other tools of our advance become so complex and versatile that they will develop an intelligence approaching or *surpassing* that of the human being? Might not computers then "take over"? Might they not replace mankind as lords of the Earth?

Actually, I have myself considered this problem in a series of science fiction stories I have written over the past thirty-five years that concerned computer-driven, man-like devices called "robots."

My own solution was to suppose that no matter how advanced computers might become, they would always be designed by men and that men would, in their own interests, build certain ineradicable safeguards into their creations. I expressed these as what I called "The Three Laws of Robotics." [12]

The Three Laws appear as an important element in at least a dozen stories. Asimov explains that "there was just enough ambiguity in the Three Laws to provide the conflicts and uncertainties required for new stories, and to my great relief, it seemed always to be possible to think up a new angle out of the sixty-one words of The Three Laws." [13] In "Robbie" the First Law apparently served no more purpose than to assure mankind that a robot was harmless. But six years later, in 1946, Asimov demonstrated his full awareness of the ethical implications of the Laws in "Evidence" (in *I, Robot*). Susan Calvin explains their significance in discussing the mayoral candidacy of Stephen Byerley, who may be a robot:

> If you stop to think of it, the three Rules of Robotics are the essential guiding principles of a good many of the world's ethical systems. Of course, every human being is supposed to have the instinct of self-preservation. That's Rule Three to a robot. Also every "good" human being, with a social conscience and a sense of responsibility, is supposed to defer to proper authority; to listen to his doctor, his boss, his government, his psychiatrist, his fellow man; to obey laws, to follow rules, to conform to custom—even when they interfere with his comfort or his safety. That's Rule Two to a robot. Also, every "good" human being is supposed to love others as himself, protect his fellow man, risk his life to save another. That's Rule One to a robot. To put it simply—if Byerley follows all the Rules of Robotics, he may be a robot, and may simply be a very good man.

She concludes:

> I like robots. I like them considerably better than I do human beings. If a robot can be created capable of being a civil executive, I think he'd make the best one possible. By the Laws of Robotics, he'd be incapable of harming humans, incapable of tryanny, of corruption, of stupidity, of prejudice.

Several of the stories in Asimov's most recent cybernetic fiction, collected in *The Bicentennial Man*, explore the Three Laws on a much more profound level than did the works in his first two periods. Thirty-five years after his early stories, his knowledge and perceptions have evolved considerably. So has the level of machine intelligence he describes. "That Thou Art Mindful of Him" is one of his most interesting recent stories exploring the Three Laws. In this tale, set in the twenty-second century, computers have solved the ecological crisis of the twentieth century, but at a price. Ever since the end of that crisis, "Mankind has lived in an uneasy truce with nature, afraid to move in any direction. This has been stultifying us, making a kind of intellectual coward of humanity so that he begins to mistrust all scientific advance, all change." The problem to be solved is how cultural development can be set in motion again. It could best be stimulated through continuing development of artificial intelligence, but most men are fearful of further development. The Frankenstein complex still exists. So they have ordered research in artificial intelligence halted, and the robots dare not disobey man—according to the Second Law—even though they know in the long run this decision is not for his own good. What is to be done? Things are at an impasse. Is it possible to develop discrimination in robots, so they will follow the orders of the best humans and ignore the worst? The answer is to develop a modified positronic brain with the capacity for judgment—to decide when it should blindly obey, like an obedient child, and when it should proceed on its own, for man's greater good. Once it has developed this capacity for judgment, it will be ready to become a true partner of mankind, not a mere servant.

But the problem is more complex than merely developing artificial intelligence capable of making judgments. How can the Frankenstein complex be overcome so that man is willing to accept this new partner? This task is formidible, but so is the logical power of machine intelligence (and Asimov's imagination, the "power" behind the machine). The solution, too complex for summary here, is ingenious and is accomplished within the parameters of the Three Laws. It does ask the reader to reexamine his conceptions of humans and machines and to recognize that the boundaries we erect between the two kinds of intelligence may be very arbitrary.

The ethical implications of the Three Laws are critical to "The Bicentennial Man" also, but that story is more appropriately discussed in the final section of this essay, when we examine Asimov's vision of the possible evolution of artificial intelligence.

The most significant aspect of the Three Laws is not the interesting range of ways Asimov utilizes them fictionally, but the influence they have had in the real world. Asimov has suggested we need to consider ways to implement the ethical use of technology, and he has provided models for doing this. Mere fictional models? Certainly fiction, but much more than that. As Asimov's stories are always grounded in accurate scientific fact, so here his ethical possibilities rest on actual capabilities of computer programming.

Asimov uses a behavioral definition of ethics and suggests that computer programs be written to make that behavior functional. If we can describe the behavior we regard as ethical, we can write a program for it. This is well within the capability of present computer programming. Asimov follows the approach of the behavioral psychologists—the behavior of the individual, not motives or consciousness, is examined. Skinner proposes in his operant conditioning that we define the behavior we want, and then through positive reinforcement program the individual to respond to stimuli with that behavior. Similarly for Asimov, the computer would be programmed to respond in a prescribed way—the only difference being that it is much easier to program a computer than a human.

The difficult part of the task is to decide what is to be regarded as desirable. Who will define the ideal? It seems likely that John Stuart Mill's concept of "the greatest good for the greatest number" would have to be the essential element in the criteria for designing the ideal.

Granted, then, that while not a simple task, it would be possible to define ideal behavior and to write a computer program for it. The program would control the performance of the technology—not the performance of man himself. However, man increasingly expresses himself through his technology. If the technology can be programmed to operate according to ethical principles, a great step toward an ethical society will have been taken. The world's great religious systems have attempted to program man's mind with an ethical system. But these have been only partially effective because man's emotions, his ambitions, his aggressions, often override the programming. This sort of happening would not be a problem, however, in the computer program.

Such an ethical technology would be desirable, of course, but it would come at some cost. The model of behavior would inevitably reflect the values of the programmers. Many persons might disagree with those values. Given the diversity of human nature, any model of ethical behavior will be defective from some points of view. The implementation of the model would mean some restriction of individual liberty; a degree of conformity would be the result. It would be a trade off—the loss of some individual freedom for the sake of some social order and freedom from violence and war.

Any discussion about computer programming of ethics is highly speculative at this point in time. But there is no reason why some day our speculations may not become realities. The significant accomplishment of Asimov is that through the dramas he has created with the Three Laws he has set us thinking: Maybe in the real world ethical concepts could be operationalized in computer technology. That is a vision no other science fiction writer has given the world.

Asimov does not repeat himself in his thirty-six fictional works about robots and computers. He displays a wide range of possibilities in the man-machine intelligence relationship. His ideas change and evolve, but the direction of the movement remains constant: from the simple to the complex. In the earliest stories, the robot is a servant; in the middle period a symbiosis of man and machine often prevails; the most recent stories suggest the dominance and then survival of machine intelligence in the evolutionary process of emerging intelligence in the universe.

In the real world of the seventeenth and eighteenth centuries, automata first appeared as no more than amusing toys. Then they were used as servants, and recently some researchers have begun to play with the possibility of building artificial intelligence as sophisticated as human intelligence. Asimov's fiction parallels this course. In the first story, written when he was twenty years old, Robbie is a giant toy to entertain a little child. Next, his robots serve as the labor for mining operations in space, and pilot space craft. In recent stories like "The Bicentennial Man," "Feminine Intuition," and "That Thou Art Mindful of Him," robots begin to acquire characteristics previously ascribed by Asimov only to humans—characteristics like creativity and the capacity to make judgments. As his robots have become increasingly complex and humanlike, Asimov suggests the ethical considerations given to man may need to be extended to include machine intelligence. (Asimov explores this issue in depth in "The Bicentennial Man.") A comparison of several pairs of stories matching early and recent fiction shows how Asimov's thinking has evolved over the years.

Political and power structures and modes of governance have

always interested Asimov. In "Evidence" (1946) he considers whether a robot might not be as efficient a mayor as a human. In "Tercentary Incident" (1976), set about seventy-five years into the future, a robot serves as the President of the United States. In both stories the general public is unaware of the substitution of machine for man, but enjoys the benefits resulting from more efficient government. In "Tercentary Incident" the robot president is first substituted for the real president only in ceremonial functions. The advantages to the president are obvious. The robot performs quite as well at hand-shaking as the president and cannot be assassinated. But a small group holds that administrative functions as well as public functions can be better handled by a robot, so they devise an elaborate plot to secretly substitute a robot for president. The story is essentially a little piece of detective fiction, where deductive logic is employed by an investigator to ascertain whether the president really has been assassinated and replaced by a robot. "Evidence," on the other hand, is a study in the campaign tactics used in an election, and the qualities essential for effective public leadership. Both stories share the view expressed by Susan Calvin about the desirability of government by machine intelligence. Because the machine can store and analyze "a nearly infinite number of data and relationships thereof, in nearly infinitesimal time," [14] and because it is free from ambition, pride, and the capacity to lie, it offers real advantages in political administration.

A world governance structure operationalized with the computer is pictured in a pair of stories, "The Evitable Conflict" (1950) and "The Life and Times of Multivac," (1974).[15] Again, as in the previous pair of stories, while the subject is the same, the treatment is quite different. "The Evitable Conflict" pictures the world in 2052 when the economy has been stabilized with the aid of the computer. Underemployment and overproduction are eliminated, and famine and war have disappeared. "The Life and Times of Multivac" (*The Bicentennial Man*) also pictures a world system operated by computer, but now the details of the process are more specific. Multivac is "a global presence knit together by wire, optical fiber, and microware. It had a brain divided into a hundred subsidiaries but acting as one. It had its outlets everywhere and no human being . . . was far from one." Robot machines perform all necessary work, and mankind has an abundance of leisure time.

But human nature, ever perverse, is unhappy in its peace, leisure, and economic abundance. The majority feels its freedom has been confiscated and it is being forced to live in slavery under the rule of Multivac. Ronald Babst, the protagonist, is less certain this is the case. However, he listens thoughtfully to the wish of his thirteen fellow members of Congress to be free from Multivac. They insist they want to take over the running of farms, mines, and factories, even though they may not be as efficient in their control as the computer. Influenced by their pleas, he uses his knowledge of mathematical games and disaster theory to devise a scheme that first inhibits and then terminates Multivac's operation. He explains the procedure:

> I have . . . a mathematical game—the setting up of networks on the model of Multivac. I have been able to demonstrate that no matter how complicated and redundant the network is, there must be at least one place into which all the currents can funnel under particular circumstances. There will always be the fatal apoplectic stroke if that one place is interfered with, since it will induce overloading elsewhere which will break down and induce overloading elsewhere—and so on indefinitely till all breaks down.

He carries out his plans and irreversibly shuts down the computer system. Then he and his fellow congressmen face each other in solemn shock at what they have done: traded peace and security for freedom. Suddenly realizing the enormity of the act, Babst turns to his fellow men and asks uncertainly, "Isn't that what you want?"

In this story, as always, Asimov's grasp of computer theory makes the story plausible. And because of the note of ambiguity he achieves at the end, "The Life and Times of Multivac" is one of his most powerful computer stories.

In "The Life and Times of Multivac" as in all his stories, Asimov has a comprehensive grasp of the issues raised by the development of artificial intelligence. Machine systems can remove the drudgery of work; they can be used in planning and decision-making; they can store and process vast amounts of information, thus augmenting man's mental power. But these benefits come at a cost. Man must replace his image of himself as a rugged individualist free to do as he will with an image of himself as a systems man living in symbiosis with his machines. In *The Caves of Steel* Asimov calls this supportive relationship a C/Fe culture (C/Fe being the chemical symbols for carbon and iron). Carbon is the basis of human life and iron of robot life. A C/Fe culture results from a combination of the best of the two forms.[16]

For Asimov, the advantages of computers far outweigh the limitations, and so he is not threatened by increasing automation—a sharp contrast to the views of many contemporary science fiction writers. Man, according to Asimov's view, never has been totally free, even before our industrial age. For the group to survive, the individual has always had to accept some restrictions of his actions. These restrictions are embodied in his ethical codes. Computer technology, programmed with the Three Laws, provides the means for man to implement his ethical ideals more effectively than would otherwise be possible.

In the fiction of Asimov's first and second periods, the robot and the computer are always subservient to man. The robot Daneel, in *The Caves of Steel*, is typical. He may appear to be human but he is not. He is an able assistant but never equal to detective Baley. Daneel is invaluable as a source of information and as a logic machine, but he is incapable of reasoning and making judgments. Man and robot together are superior to either alone. Should they act separately, it is clearly man whose intelligence is superior.

In the stories of Asimov's third period, however, artificial intelligence is pictured as having evolved substantially beyond its level in the earlier works. The goal of the computer scientists in "Feminine Intuition" (1969, collected in *The Bicentennial Man*) is to develop a creative robot. The Principle of Uncertainty, explains Research Director Bogert, "is important in particles the mass of positrons." If this unpredictability of minute particles can be utilized in the robot design, it might be possible to have a creative robot. "If there's anything a human brain has that a robotic brain has never had, it's the trace of unpredictability that comes from the effects of uncertainty at the subatomic level. . . . This effect has never been demonstrated experimentally within the nervous system, but without that the human brain is not superior to the robotic brain in principle." If the uncertainty effect can be introduced into the robot brain, it will share the creativity of the human brain. The research is successful, and U.S. Robots produces the first successful design of creativity in artificial intelligence.

"Stranger in Paradise" (1974) describes another aspect of the evolutionary process augmenting the capability of artificial intelligence. A robot, designed for use on the planet Mercury, is operated via radio control by an Earth-based computer as complex as a human brain. The robot is a result of the collaborative research efforts of a specialist in the human brain and a specialist in computer science. When the robot is landed on Mercury, he capers in joy at finally reaching the paradise for which he was designed. Here is a new form of intelligence rejoicing in the environment of outer space so inimical to man's survival. Asimov suggests the machine form may well be ideal for housing intelligence as it journeys out among the stars.

"That Thou Art Mindful of Him" (1974) pictures the development of a positronic brain with the capacity for judgment. Judgment is developed in the robot because it is required if he is to cope with conflicting orders from two humans. The Second Law says he must obey—but which order? The answer: he must obey the human most fit by mind, character, and knowledge to give that order. However, once the capacity for judgment is designed into the robots, they begin to use it in unanticipated ways. The robot George Nine decides he will "disregard shape and form in judging human beings, and . . . rise superior to the distinction between metal and flesh." He concludes, after exercising his judgment, that his fellow robots are like humans, except more fit. Therefore, they ought to dominate humans. The possibility of machine intelligence being both superior to human intelligence and likely to dominate human intelligence is introduced for the first time in this story.[17] Asimov's robots have evolved a long way from that first lowly Robbie in 1940.

The last design for the evolution of artificial intelligence appears in the title story "The Bicentennial Man" (1976) in Asimov's collection. Here pure intelligence, irrespective of carbon or metal form, appears. With the possible exception of *The Caves of Steel*, "The Bicentennial Man" may well be the most substantial single work Asimov has written about artificial intelligence. Asimov notes it is the longest story (15,000 words) he has produced below the novel level in seventeen years. Even given this substantial length, it is still almost too dense with ideas and might well benefit from expansion to novel length. Told in twenty-three episodes, it covers two hundred years in the life of the robot Andrew Martin.

In *The Naked Sun* Asimov has a biologist, working in a laboratory where human fetuses were grown in artificial wombs, explain the human developmental process:

> Each individual repeats his own evolutionary history as he develops. Those fetuses back there have gills and a tail for a time. Can't skip

those steps. The youngster has to go through the social-animal stage in the same way. But just as a fetus can get through in one month a stage that evolution took a hundred million years to get through, so our children can hurry through the social-animal stage. (143)

Asimov takes this idea that ontogeny repeats phylogeny and applies it to robot evolution in "The Bicentennial Man." Andrew the robot, as he develops, repeats the stage of robot development dramatized in all Asimov's previous stories. Then, having recapitulated all the stages to that point in time, Andrew pushes the evolutionary process two hundred years into the future. "The Bicentennial Man" displays the Asimovian imagination at its best, taking dazzling leaps forward in time, but always pushing off from the current state of knowledge in the field of artificial intelligence.

Many of the ideas and issues Asimov has handled in earlier stories echo through "The Bicentennial Man," but only as fuel to propel the imaginative possibilities of his subject further forward. He starts with questions currently being asked by researchers in artificial intelligence. What is human intelligence? The answer seems to be that it is information stored, and processed, and used by the human organism to accomplish purposeful acts. A corollary question immediately arises. What is machine intelligence? The answer to this is similar to the first, except that now the process takes place in an inorganic mechanism. Asimov probed but did not define the likenesses and differences between organic and inorganic intelligence in "Stranger in Paradise." In "The Bicentennial Man" he pushes the question to the utmost—and finds an answer both definitive and ambiguous. He reflects the growing awareness in the fields of computer science, psychology, biology, and philosophy that the differences between human and artificial intelligence are not nearly so clear as they once appeared to be.

The approach Asimov chooses to the puzzle of intelligence, human or machine, leads to the power of his story. Inverting the obvious approach—man examining artificial intelligence—he elects to have Andrew explore the nature and implications of human intelligence. As the story opens, Andrew is an obedient household servant for the Martin family, much like the role of Asimov's early Robbie. But Andrew turns out to be a mutant robot form with an unusual talent: he is creative. He produces exquisite word carvings. As he has transcended the patterns of previous robots, so he aspires to transcend the limits of the role they occupied in society. He desires to be free, not a slave to man. But this seems a clear violation of the Second Law assuring that robots are always obedient servants to humans.

Andrew's struggle to evolve beyond his programmed obedience is dramatized with great economy. The Martin family represent the small group of humans who realize the potential of artificial intelligence, and who take actions to foster and expand it. The U.S. Robots Corporation stands for the economic system supported by the mass of men who wish only to exploit robot technology for profit. They feel no ethical responsibility to this new form of emerging intelligence. Only after a long struggle do the courts declare Andrew free. Then, bit by bit over the ensuing years, Andrew moves toward fulfilling his aspirations to become like his masters. His potential, his determination, and the support of a few dedicated individuals yield slow progress.

Having gained freedom, Andrew used it to acquire knowledge. He makes his hesitant first trip to the library to begin his task of self-education. Threatened by humans on this trip, he realizes he must have a law protecting his right to survive. George Martin, his protector, appears before the court and puts forth the argument for the rights of non-humankind to survive:

> If a man has the right to give a robot any order that does not involve harm to a human being, he should have the decency never to give a robot any order that involves harm to a robot, unless human safety absolutely requires it. With great power goes great responsibility, and if the robots have Three Laws to protect men, is it too much to ask that men have a law or two to protect robots? (152)

Winning his court battle after the fervent pleading of George Martin, Andrew is finally assured by law the right to survive. Then he begins to write a history of robots—a means of learning about his past. And he begins to yearn for an organic body like humans have.

Andrew is not alone in his learning activities. The research of man into artificial intelligence and sophisticated mechanical devices continues as the years march by. The science of prothestology develops rapidly and becomes increasingly skillful at replacing human parts—kidney, heart, hands—with mechanical parts. Andrew draws on this new technological expertise to have his positronic brain transplanted into a human body.

Increasingly intelligent, Andrew becomes increasingly aware of the price he pays for his approaching humanity. The moral simplicity of his early life when he was an obedient servant is now gone. To achieve what he has, he has had to ask others to lie for him, and he has resorted to pressure and even blackmail. But given his aspirations to become a man, he is willing to pay the price. Because his robot intelligence is never muddied by emotions, he can reason clearly and with utmost logic. He sees, finally, that he cannot be declared a man as he had hoped, despite freedom, intelligence, and an organic body, because his brain is different. The World Court has declared a criterion for determining what is human: "Human beings have an organic cellular brain and robots have a platinum-iridium positronic brain. . . ." (168). Andrew is at an impasse. His brain is man-made, the human brain is not. His brain is constructed, man's brain is developed.

Finally Andrew pushes the implications of this statement to its ultimate meaning. The greatest difference between robot and man is the matter of immortality. He reasons: "Who really cares what a brain looks like or is built of or how it was formed? What matters is that brain cells die; *must* die. Even if every other organ in the body is maintained or replaced, the brain cells, which cannot be replaced without changing and therefore killing the personality, must eventually die" (170–71). He realizes the price of being human is to sacrifice his immortality. In the final moving episode of the story, he submits to surgery to rearrange the connection between organic nerves and positronic brain in such a way that he will slowly die. When he performs this final act, the Court at last declares him a man.

"The Bicentennial Man" is a powerful, profound story for several reasons. Foremost is what Asimov leaves unsaid. During the course of the story we follow the movement of mechanical intelligence toward human intelligence and death. But Andrew's process toward manhood and death is unfolded against a background where man is developing technology moving him toward artificial intelligence and immortality. Knowledge or information eventually die in the organic brain but can survive indefinitely in a mechanical brain. This fact implies that the inorganic form may well be the most likely form for intelligence to survive in the universe. As machine intelligence evolves to the human level, human intelligence is evolving toward machine form. A second implication of "The Bicentennial Man," again unstated, is that a line between the animate and the inanimate, the organic and the inorganic, can not be drawn. If we see the fundamental materials of the universe as matter, energy, and information patterns (or intelligence), then man is not unique. He exists on a continuum with all intelligence. He is no more than the most highly evolved form on the earth. This view implies that ethical behavior should extend beyond human systems to include all systems because any organizational pattern, human or nonhuman, organic or inorganic, represents intelligence. A kind of sacred view of the universe, arrived at not by religious mysticism, but pure logic, emerges from this reading of "The Bicentennial Man."

In conclusion, let us take the long view of Asimov's fiction, from those early robot stories where the Three Laws first appeared, to "The Bicentennial Man," where their fullest implications are explored. Asimov's vision of evolving technology—symbolized by the robot—has never wavered. Nor has his faith in science. The methodology of the scientific model, based on logic, allows man to escape beyond the tormenting human emotions of ambition, anger, greed, and envy. Even if man cannot succeed in disciplining himself, he can program his technology to operate beyond the destructive limitations of these emotions. He can exercise a control in his technology apparently not possible in himself. There is a way into the utopian land of man's visionary dreams. It is the way of ethical technology. The Three Laws are interwoven through all Asimov's thirty-six fictional works about the development of machine intelligence. He is a realist who suggests that the mass of men, locked by conditioned behavior into the patterns of the past, will probably resist the change necessary to utilize the potential of technology. But he is a limited optimist, believing in the few creative thinkers who glimpse the promise of machine intelligence and keep working to make it a reality.

No single writer in science fiction has so consistently maintained his vision, so consistently grounded it in sound science and logical thought, so widely disseminated his faith in the potential of technological man as Isaac Asimov. For this faith through works, he deserves to be recognized as one of the most creative and ethical thinkers of his time—that third of a century between 1940 and 1975 when again and again science fiction has become fact.

Asimov's Guide to Asimov

ISAAC ASIMOV

I HAVE TODAY completed reading, in manuscript, the book to which this is appended. The editor has asked me if I would be willing to write an epilog of sorts and I agreed at once.

The fact is that I am not embarrassed when I read about myself or hear about myself and I particularly don't mind speaking or writing about myself. Why should I? I am not troubled by modesty nor badgered by illusions. I know my own virtues and accept them calmly. I also know my own shortcomings (see my portrait of myself in *Murder at the ABA*) and accept them just as calmly.

So I am fascinated, and a little amused, to see myself monumentalized while still alive in a book of this sort, and delighted at the chance of adding my own thoughts to all the judgments here presented.

More than once in the course of these essays mention is made of the fact that I strenuously deny the existence of any deep levels of meaning in my writing. Those who mention this do so rather genially and with quite evident amusement. I imagine they feel that I am engaging in mock-modesty that attempts to call attention to virtues by denying they exist.

No.

I am serious. I am speaking of my writing at the conscious level and I believe I can prove quite easily that no purposeful patterns or smooth subtleties can possibly lie below the clear surface of what I write. I can do so by citing three indisputable reasons, any one of which is sufficient to prove my point.

1) *I am too prolific.*

I have, as of this moment of writing, published 181 books, have 8 more in press and 6 at various levels of preparation. I write constantly, and as rapidly as I can, and I have nobody helping me. Nobody. No secretary, no typist, no researcher, no assistant, nobody.

How, then, can I possibly have the time to engage in the kind of deep and intricate thought that would create anything deep and intricate in my stories? The fact is that I don't have the time and therefore don't do the deed.

My way of working is to get a general idea for a story (whether short-short or novel), figure out a satisfactory ending, pick out a beginning, and then take off like a bullet, racing ahead and making it up as I go along. I don't plan out anything. (Even my non-fiction is written without preliminary outlines and according to some plan that works itself out only as I write.)

You must accept this as my way of working because there is no other way of explaining the sheer quantity of my output.

It is also the only way of explaining the clarity of my output (and the clearness of my style is remarked on by every reviewer without exception). If I didn't say exactly what I wanted to say as simply as I could say it, I couldn't race ahead as I do.

2) *I am (or was) too young.*

A person might meet me now and be overwhelmed by my erudition, my sophistication, and my old-world charm (I doubt it, because none of it ever shows) but that's the way I am *now*; not when I started writing forty years ago.

Let's face it. When I wrote "Robbie," my first robot story, I was 19; when I wrote "Nightfall," I was 20; when I began the "Foundation" series, I was 21. And you must further understand that I was an unworldly youth, very young for my age. My entire formative period of life was spent in a Brooklyn candy-store, sheltered from the world by loving parents and by my own bookish habits.

What subtleties could I then have introduced?

3) *I am too ignorant.*

It may *seem* as though I know everything. I admit that I make much of my living through the fact that there is a general feeling abroad that I do.

This is not an entirely ridiculous notion, since I do know more about more things than almost anybody. I know an immense amount about every branch of science and about all periods of history and about the Bible and Shakespeare and geography and mythology and so on and so on.

My ability to sop up so much and my faculty for instant recall tends to be spectacular enough to obscure the fact that there is a great difference between "know more about more things" and "know everything about everything." There are, in point of fact, vast areas in which I am pathetically ignorant, and they are precisely the areas out of which the subtleties of which I am accused must arise. I know nothing about economics, psychology, sociology, music, art, contemporary literature and so on and so on.

For instance, I have never read anything written by Marx. I have never read anything written about Marxian economics or philosophy. Consequently, I don't really know anything about Marx and I therefore fail to see how anything I write can represent a Marxian view of history, either clear or distorted.

* * * * * * * *

Well, then, having pointed out these unanswerable arguments against finding deep meaning in my stories, do I intend to imply that the various essayists in this volume have been beating a dead horse? Are their remarks valueless?

No!

I was taught my lesson in this respect a quarter-century ago. Back in 1951 or thereabouts, a lecture on science fiction was slated to be delivered by Dr. Gotthard Gunther at the Cambridge Center for Adult Education.

I attended, for in those days listening to a scholar talk on science fiction was a most unusual phenomenon (as opposed to nowadays when it is commonplace and everyday). Nor was I instantly recognizable in those days, so I took my seat in the back and attracted no notice at all.

You can well imagine my surprise when Dr. Gunther spent most of his lecture discussing my story "Nightfall." He used it to explain a very intricate and very Germanic theory he had about science fiction. I was quite certain then (and am still certain now) that his theory about science fiction was enormously and even titanically wrong, but it wasn't that which bothered me.

What got me right in the short-ribs was that everything he said about my purpose in writing "Nightfall" was wrong—gloriously wrong—majestically wrong.

After the lecture, I patiently waited while the crowd of admiring questioners thinned out, and when Dr. Gunther and I were alone, I said to him, "Pardon me, Dr. Gunther, but I'm afraid your explanation of the symbolism of 'Nightfall' was quite wrong."

Dr. Gunther smiled politely. "Indeed, and why do you say that?"

"Because the author never had any intentions such as those you said he had."

"And how can you possibly know that?"

That was what I was waiting for. I dropped the guillotine blade, "Because, Dr. Gunther, *I* am the author."

And Dr. Gunther, unperturbed, said, "And just because you wrote the story, what makes you think you know anything at all about it?"

(That was the beginning of a pleasant friendship.)

Dr. Gunther was right. I may be very ignorant about many things, but I learn quickly. A writer is not the best judge of his own work and so whenever I deny any deep meaning to my writing, I always add the fact that others may know more about it than I do.

But is it possible that deep meaning can exist that I did not put there and did not know about?

Let me answer this with something that happened very recently. Last year I wrote a short story called "Good Taste" which appeared in the form of a small booklet with a very limited distribution, and which will next appear in the fourth issue of "Isaac Asimov's Science Fiction Magazine," and after that, undoubtedly, in a collection of my stories.

The story is set on "Gammer," a space colony in orbit about Earth and in it there are references to a number of other space colonies. A reviewer discussing the story (which he liked) said it dealt with a group of space colonies circling "a carefully never-mentioned Earth."

Well, it doesn't take much thought to see that not mentioning Earth can have a great deal of significance, and that by beginning with that lead, one can uncover deeper layers of meanings. I couldn't do the analysis very well myself but I'll bet any one of the essayists in this volume could dig into the story like a shot and come up with who-knows-what.

And yet when I read the phrase "a carefully never-mentioned Earth" I sat up with a jerk. Was Earth never mentioned? I got out the story and went through it. Gracious! Earth was indeed never mentioned. I hadn't noticed that when I wrote the story. I didn't leave out Earth deliberately. It was just that I had no occasion to mention it since it played no role.

So does that mean there is no significance to the fact that I left it out? I don't think so. The fact that I didn't do it consciously doesn't mean a thing, because there's more to my writing than my conscious intentions—and as soon as I recognize that, my arguments in the first part of this article fall apart.

Let's go over them again.

1) *I am too prolific.*

Am I? The fact that I write my stories very quickly and without conscious planning surely doesn't mean that there is no planning at all.

I've got something called "writing talent" that I don't know how to define. I don't have to spend all day thinking, in order to know how to tell a story, what to put in, what to leave out, what to emphasize, what to hint at. I don't have to think at all, in the usual way. I just *know*.

In fact, I don't have the "talent"; the "talent" has me. I am in its grip. When I am writing, I am fascinated by what emerges, for all of it is more or less unexpected. I sometimes try to tell people that I don't write anything; that there is a "daimon" within me that does the writing and that I am an interested spectator.

So while I am writing as quickly and as clearly as I can, my "daimon" (a Greek word for a possessing spirit, which has been degraded into the English "demon") inserts subtleties and intricacies. I am merely a pleasant fellow with an engaging smile and a flirtatious attitude toward women, as all who know me will tell you, but my "daimon," thank goodness, is apparently a genius of sorts, and I am delighted to have him.

2) *I am (or was) too young.*

I was—but not my "daimon."

I was writing stories at the age of 11. At the time, I had not yet developed a properly smooth technique, but the *construction* of the stories was correct. When did I learn? I don't know. Looking back on it, it seems to me I always knew how to tell a story without anyone ever having told me how. (You know Louis Armstrong's great dictum, "If you have to ask, you are never going to know.")

3) *I am too ignorant.*

Oh, come now, it is impossible to be *completely* ignorant of pervasive subjects if you read omnivorously and have a retentive memory.

I may not be interested in sociology and psychology as organized fields of study, for instance, and I don't read textbooks on those subjects, or discuss them with knowledgeable people, but I come across references to sociological and psychological matters here and there, and I remember them. And because I am extremely intelligent (well, everyone says so) I can make the most of any scraps I get.

Consequently, for instance, I can invent "psychohistory," which is an amalgam of sociology and psychology, and get away with it.

So here it all is—

Consciously, all I'm doing is trying to tell an interesting story. While I'm doing so, however, something in me must be constructing it in such a way as to include all the deep meaning and all the impressive subtleties that the essayists find.

I'm glad of that, even delighted; but, if you don't mind, I intend not to think about it too much.

After all, if I ever started *trying* to do all these wonderful things on purpose, I might, in the excitement of it all, forget how to tell a story—and I certainly wouldn't want that to happen.

Isaac Asimov
February 18, 1977

NOTES

CHAPTER I: MILLER

1. Brian Ash, *Faces of the Future* (New York: Taplinger, 1975), 70.
2. Isaac Asimov, *Is Anyone There?* (New York: Ace, 1968), 285.
3. Asimov, "Social Science Fiction," in Reginald Bretnor, ed., *Modern Science Fiction* (New York: Coward-McCann, 1953), 158, 159.
4. Asimov, "Other Worlds to Conquer," *The Writer* (May 1951), 148–49.
5. Asimov, *Is Anyone There?*, 292.
6. Asimov, "Social Science Fiction," 188–89.
7. James Osler Bailey, *Pilgrims through Space and Time* (New York: Argus Books, 1947), 1–2.
8. Asimov, *Science, Numbers and I* (New York: Ace, 1969), 224.
9. Asimov, *The Early Asimov, Book One* (Greenwich, Conn.: Fawcett Crest, 1972).
10. Ibid.
11. Asimov, *I, Robot* (Greenwich, Conn.: Fawcett Crest, 1973).
12. Asimov, *The End of Eternity* (Greenwich, Conn.: Fawcett Crest, 1973), 188.
13. Asimov, *Nine Tomorrows* (Greenwich, Conn.: Fawcett Crest, 1969).
14. "Lastborn," "The Feeling of Power," and "All the Troubles of the World" appear in *Nine Tomorrows;* "The Machine that Won the War" in *Nightfall and Other Stories* (Greenwich, Conn.: Fawcett Crest, 1974).
15. Asimov, *Buy Jupiter and Other Stories* (Greenwich, Conn.: Fawcett Crest, 1975).
16. *The Early Asimov, Book One.*
17. The first and third story appear in *The Early Asimov, Book One;* the second and fourth in *The Early Asimov, Book Two* (Greenwich, Conn.: Fawcett Crest, 1974).
18. Asimov, *Nightfall and Other Stories* (Greenwich, Conn.: Fawcett Crest, 1974), 99.
19. *The Early Asimov, Book Two.*
20. Asimov, *The Stars in Their Courses* (New York: Ace, 1972), 195–96; also, 195–218. Other essays in which he develops fully the mathematical and physical facts about our growing population may be found in *Is Anyone There?* and *The Left Hand of the Electron* (New York: Dell, 1972), 229–54.
21. Asimov, *Buy Jupiter and Other Stories*, 169.
22. Asimov, *Today and Tomorrow and . . . ,* (New York: Dell, 1975).

CHAPTER 2: PIERCE

1. Isaac Asimov, *Murder at the ABA: A Puzzle in Four Days and Sixty Scenes* (Garden City, N.Y.: Doubleday, 1976).
2. Asimov, *The Death Dealers* (New York: Avon, 1958), later reissued as *A Whiff of Death* (Lancer, 1969).
3. The works referred to in this chapter include: *Asimov's Mysteries* (New York: Dell, 1973); *The Best of Isaac Asimov* (Greenwich, Conn.: Fawcett Crest, 1976); *The Early Asimov, Book One* (Greenwich, Conn.: Fawcett Crest, 1974), and *Book Two* (Greenwich, Conn.: Fawcett Crest, 1974); *I, Robot* (Greenwich, Conn.: Fawcett Crest, 1973); *Nightfall and Other Stories* (Greenwich, Conn.: Fawcett Crest, 1974); and *The Rest of the Robots* (Garden City, N.Y.: Doubleday, 1964).

   For full bibliographical information on Asimov's complete canon, see Marjorie M. Miller, *Isaac Asimov: A Checklist of Works Published in the United States, March 1939–May 1972* (Kent, Ohio: Kent State University Press, 1972) or M. B. Tepper, *The Asimov Science Fiction Bibliography* (Santa Monica: The Chinese Ducked Press, 1970). Also, see the Bibliography at the end of this book.
4. R. Austin Freeman, "The Art of the Detective Story," in Howard Haycraft, ed., *The Art of the Mystery Story: A Collection of Critical Essays* (New York: Simon & Schuster, 1946), 15.
5. For other studies on the detective or mystery genre, see John G. Cawelti, *Adventure, Mystery, and Romance: Formula Stories as Art and Popular Culture* (Chicago: University of Chicago Press, 1976); A. E. Murch, *The Development of the Detective Novel* (New York: Greenwood Press, 1958); and Eric S. Rabkin, *The Fantastic in Literature* (Princeton: Princeton University Press, 1976).
6. Sam Moskowitz, *Explorers of the Infinite: Shapers of Science Fiction* (Westport, Conn.: Hyperion Press, 1963), 250; Murch, *Development of the Detective Novel*, 233.
7. For the original publication of the Lucky Starr novels Asimov used the pseudonym, Paul French. First printed by Doubleday on the dates indicated in the text, the six juveniles have been reprinted under Asimov's own name by New American Library/Signet in 1972.
8. Joseph F. Patrouch, Jr., *The Science Fiction of Isaac Asimov* (Garden City, N.Y.: Doubleday, 1974), 159.
9. In many of Asimov's robot stories the Three Laws of Robotics are given either in full or in part. The form below appears before the introductory material in *I, Robot:*

THE THREE LAWS OF ROBOTICS

1—A robot may not injure a human being, or, through inaction, allow a human being to come to harm.
2—A robot must obey the orders given it by human beings except where such orders would conflict with the First Law.

3—A robot must protect its own existence as long as such protection does not conflict with the First or Second Law.

HANDBOOK OF ROBOTICS,
56TH EDITION, 2058 A.D.

10. *Ellery Queen's Anthology* (Spring–Summer 1976), 78.
11. "Detection and the Literary Art," in Jacques Barzun, ed., *The Delights of Detection* (New York: Criterion Books, 1961), 19.

CHAPTER 3: MOORE

1. Frederik Pohl, "Reminiscence: Cyril M. Kornbluth," *Extrapolation* (May 1976), 103, is responsible for this parenthetical remark.
2. Isaac Asimov, "Social Science Fiction," in Dick Allen, ed., *Science Fiction: The Future* (New York: Harcourt Brace Jovanovich, 1971), 272.
3. This is the title of a satirical poem by Asimov, introducing the short stories in *Nine Tomorrows* (New York: Bantam Books, 1960).
4. Asimov, "Social Science Fiction," 272–73.
5. Robert H. Canary, "Science Fiction as Fictive History," *Extrapolation* (December 1974), 81–94.
6. Asimov, "Social Science Fiction," 278, 279–82.
7. Lyman Tower Sargeant, "Utopia—the Problem of Definition," *Extrapolation* (May 1975), 144.
8. Poul Anderson, "The Science," in Lloyd Biggle, Jr., ed., *Nebula Award Stories, No. 7* (New York: Harper & Row, 1973), 267.
9. Gary K. Wolfe, "The Limits of Science Fiction," *Extrapolation* (December 1972), 33.
10. Patrick G. Hogan, Jr., "The Philosophical Limitations of Science Fiction," *Journal of General Education* (Spring 1976), 2.
11. Michael W. McClintock, in "Some Preliminaries to the Criticism of Science Fiction," *Extrapolation* (December 1973), 31, says of literature and science fiction writers, "Liars perforce, we must make our truths of lies; our lies must be our truths, and our lies must be made." He describes "Nightfall" as "one of Isaac Asimov's best-known lies."
12. Asimov, ed., *Nebula Award Stories, No. 8* (New York: Berkley, 1975), xiii.
13. Asimov, "When Aristotle Fails, Try Science Fiction," in Thomas E. Sanders, ed., *Speculations: An Introduction to Literature through Fantasy and Science Fiction* (New York: Glencoe Press, 1973), 585–86.
14. Ibid., 587.
15. Ibid., 585.
16. Wolfe, "The Limits of Science Fiction," 30.
17. Michael N. Stanton, "Emerson and Science Fiction," *Extrapolation* (December 1974), 64–65.
18. Asimov, "Social Science Fiction," 265.
19. Ibid., 267.
20. Stanton, "Emerson and Science Fiction," 65.

21. Asimov, "Social Science Fiction," 277.
22. Ibid., 265–66.
23. Ibid., 289.
24. Asimov, *The Caves of Steel* (Greenwich, Conn.: Fawcett Crest, 1972).
25. Thomas L. Wymer, "Perception and Value in Science Fiction," *Extrapolation* (May 1975), 105.
26. Asimov, *Nebula No. 8*, xvi.
27. *The Early Asimov, Book Two* (Greenwich, Conn.: Fawcett Crest, 1974), 233–34.
28. William Morris, ed., *The American Heritage Dictionary of the English Language* (Boston: American Heritage Publishing Co. and Houghton Mifflin, 1969).
29. For a full discussion of the Robot series, with emphasis on *The Naked Sun*, see my article "Asimov, Calvin, and Moses," in Thomas D. Clareson, ed., *Voices for the Future: Essays on Major Science Fiction Writers*, Vol. I (Bowling Green: Bowling Green University Popular Press, 1976), 88–103.
30. This villain, whose name is Leebig, might be compared to a nineteenth-century register of progress by the name of Liebig, who, according to Asimov in "When Aristotle Fails, Try Science Fiction," denied Pasteur's theory that alcoholic fermentation was the product of living cells.
31. Asimov, *Pebbles in the Sky* (Greenwich, Conn.: Fawcett Crest, 1973).
32. The Galactic Empire might also be viewed through a nuclear energy analogy, with the Empire as a decaying isotope the half-life of which Seldon can accurately predict since he has a population comparable in number to electrons. One more knowledgeable in this field might profitably pursue such a metaphor. (In Asimov's *Foundation* trilogy, the first volume in the series is *Foundation*, the second is *Foundation and Empire*, and the third is *Second Foundation*. References in the text, given in parentheses, indicate, respectively, the volume of the series, the part or section of that volume, and the number of the chapter.)
33. Leslie Fiedler, "Zion as Main Street," in Theodore L. Gross, ed., *The Literature of American Jews* (New York: The Free Press, 1973), 408.
34. Asimov, "Why Me?" in Jack Dann, ed., *Wandering Stars: An Anthology of Jewish Fantasy and Science Fiction* (New York: Harper & Row, 1974), 3.
35. Ibid., 1.
36. Asimov, "Unto the Fourth Genration," in *Wandering Stars*.
37. Asimov, *The Gods Themselves* (Greenwich, Conn.: Fawcett Crest, 1973).

CHAPTER 4: ELKINS

1. Alva Rogers, *A Requiem for Astounding* (Chicago: Advent, 1964), 107.
2. Asimov, *The Foundation Trilogy*. The first volume in the series is *Foundation*, the second is *Foundation and Empire*, and the third is *Second Foundation*. References in the text, given in parentheses, indicate, re-

spectively, the volume of the series, the part or section of that volume, and the number of the chapter.

3. Asimov, "Social Science Fiction," in Dick Allen, ed., *Science Fiction: The Future* (New York: Harcourt Brace Jovanovich, 1971), 272. The essay first appeared in Reginald Bretnor, ed., *Modern Science Fiction* (New York: Coward-McCann, 1953).

4. Asimov, "When Aristotle Fails, Try Science Fiction," in Thomas E. Sanders, ed., *Speculations: An Introduction to Literature through Fantasy and Science Fiction* (New York: Glencoe Press, 1973), 586. The essay first appeared in *Intellectual Digest* (1971).

5. Asimov, "Social Science Fiction," 268.

6. Ibid., 277, 279.

7. Cf. Arnold Toynbee, "The Disintegration of Civilization," from Chapter xxi of *A Study of History: Abridgement of Volumes I–VI* by D. C. Somervell (Oxford, 1946), reprinted in Patrick Gardiner, ed., *Theories of History* (New York: The Free Press, 1959), 204. The publishing dates for *A Study of History* are: Vols. i–iii (1934), Vols. iv–vi (1939), Vols. vii–x (1954). In his essay "Social Science Fiction," 279, Asimov cites the first six volumes of Toynbee's work.

8. Asimov, *The Early Asimov: Book One* (Greenwich, Conn.: Fawcett Crest, 1974), 155.

9. Damon Knight, *In Search of Wonder* (Chicago: Advent, 2nd edn. rev. and enlarged, 1967), 91.

10. Donald A. Wollheim, *The Universe Makers: Science Fiction Today* (New York: Harper & Row, 1971), 41.

11. Frederick Engels, "The Funeral of Karl Marx," Philip Foner, ed., *When Karl Marx Died* (New York: International Publishers, 1973), 39.

12. V. I. Lenin, "Karl Marx: A Brief Biographical Sketch with an Exposition of Marxism," *Selected Works* (New York: International Publishers, 1967), 13.

13. Quoted from Joseph Stalin, "Anarchism and Socialism," in Franz Marek, *Philosophy of World Revolution: A Contribution to an Anthology of Theories of Revolution* (New York: International Publishers, 1969), 31. Cf. George Plekhanov, *The Role of the Individual in History* (New York, 1940); N. I. Bukharin, *Historical Materialism* (New York, 1925); Karl Kautsky, *The Class Struggle* (Chicago, 1910); Joseph Stalin, *Works*, 13 vols. (Moscow, 1952–55).

14. *The Early Asimov, Book One*, 196.

15. Cf. Daniel Aaron, *Writers on the Left* (New York: Harcourt Brace and World–Avon Books, 1965), 325–407, and Charles Eisinger, *Fiction of the Forties* (Chicago: The University of Chicago Press, 1963), 87–94.

16. James Blish, "A Reply to Mr. Rottensteiner," *Science Fiction Studies* (Fall 1973), 87. In discussing this group, however, Asimov does not mention its political nature.

17. Wollheim, *The Universe Makers*, 40.

18. Asimov, "Social Science Fiction," 277–79.

19. For a concise summary of Saint-Simon's life and views on this matter,

see Edmund Wilson, *To the Finland Station: A Study in the Writing and Acting of History* (Garden City, N.Y.: Doubleday-Anchor, 1953), 79–85.

20. Wollheim, *The Universe Makers*, 41. I will confine my remarks to Wollheim's criticism. Another critic, John J. Alderson—in "The Foundation on Sands," *The Alien Critic* (November 1974), 23–28, reprinted from CHAO #13 (June 1973)—has also made comparisons between the *Foundation* series and "Marxian 'economic determinism.'" However, Alderson's total misunderstanding of Marxism and the complexities of history and fiction rules out the possibility of serious critical debate.

21. Marek, *Philosophy of World Revolution*, 41.

22. Ibid., 42.

23. George Lichtheim, *Marxism: An Historical and Critical Study* (New York: Praeger, 1961), 40.

24. Eugene Kamenka, *Marxism and Ethics* (New York: St. Martin's Press, 1969), 9.

25. Franz Rottensteiner, "Playing Around with Creation: Philip José Farmer," *Science Fiction Studies* (Fall 1973), 97.

26. For a recent discussion of this point, see Raymond Williams, "Base and Superstructure in Marxist Cultural Theory," *New Left Review* (November–December 1973), 3–16.

27. Lloyd Easton and Kurt Guddat, eds. and trans., *Writings of the Young Marx on Philosophy and Society* (Garden City, N.Y.: Doubleday-Anchor, 1967), 309.

28. For a full discussion of this aspect of Marx's thought, see Robert Tucker, *Philosophy and Myth in Karl Marx* (New York: Cambridge University Press, 1961).

CHAPTER 5: HASSLER

1. Isaac Asimov, *Before the Golden Age: A Science Fiction Anthology of the 1930s*, 3 vols. (Greenwich, Conn.: Fawcett Crest, 1974). This quote is taken from Book 3, 279.

2. Ibid., 263.

3. Ibid., Book 1, 255.

4. Ibid., 80.

5. Ibid., Book 3, 114.

6. Ibid., 340.

7. Irving Howe, *The New York Times Book Review* (July 4, 1976).

8. Harvey Aronson, *Newsday* (March 18, 1967).

9. See Asimov's discussion of the story "Legal Rites" in *The Early Asimov: Book Two* (Greenwich, Conn.: Fawcett Crest, 1974), 114.

10. Other similar autobiographical anthologies by Asimov are *The Early Asimov*, cited above, *Buy Jupiter and Other Stories* (Greenwich, Conn.: Fawcett Crest, 1977), and the most recent, *The Bicentennial Man and Other Stories* (Greenwich, Conn.: Fawcett Crest, 1976), which I have

not yet seen. *The Best of Isaac Asimov* (Greenwich, Conn.: Fawcett Crest, 1976) is a more conventional anthology. It is interesting and characteristic of the historical relativism that I will describe later that the three autobiographical anthologies that cover his entire life to date are staggered in time. The first to be published covers the middle period (*The Early Asimov*, 1939–1950). The second to be published goes back to cover the earliest period (*Before the Golden Age: 1920–1939*). *Buy Jupiter* goes from 1950 to the present.

11. Asimov, *Before the Golden Age*, Book 1, 11–12.
12. Ibid.
13. From John Chalker, *The English Georgic* (Baltimore: The John Hopkins Press, 1969), 103.
14. Ibid., 106.
15. See Walter Jackson Bate, *The Burden of the Past and the English Poet* (Cambridge: Harvard University Press, 1970).
16. Donald M. Hassler, *The Comedian as the Letter D: Erasmus Darwin's Comic Materialism* (The Hague: Martinus Nijhoff, 1973), 6.
17. Sam Moskowitz, *Seekers of Tomorrow* (New York: World Publishing, 1966), 265.
18. Joseph F. Patrouch, Jr., *The Science Fiction of Isaac Asimov* (New York: Doubleday, 1974), 262.
19. See in particular Susan Glicksohn, "A City of Which the Stars are Suburbs," in Thomas D. Clareson, ed., *SF: The Other Side of Realism* (Bowling Green: Popular Press, 1971), 334–47. Also, see Patrouch, *The Science Fiction of Isaac Asimov*, 108.
20. Martine Watson Brownley, "Gibbon: The Formation of Mind and Character," in *Edward Gibbon and the Decline and Fall of the Roman Empire* (a special issue of *Daedalus* for summer 1976), 13.
21. Edward Gibbon, *History of the Decline and Fall of the Roman Empire* (London: World Classics Edition, 1903–1904), Chapter 38, 201–202. Originally published in 1781.
22. Two books that have been invaluable to me in this search for ideas in late eighteenth-century literature are Lawrence Lipking, *The Ordering of the Arts in Eighteenth-Century England* (Princeton: Princeton University Press, 1970); and Leo Braudy, *Narrative Form in History and Fiction* (Princeton: Princeton University Press, 1970).
23. Lipking, 409.
24. Braudy, 13.
25. Lipking, 456.

CHAPTER 6: MILMAN

1. Isaac Asimov, "The Red Queen's Race," *The Early Asimov, Book Two* (Greenwich, Conn.: Fawcett Crest, 1974).
2. Asimov, "The Dead Past," *Earth is Room Enough* (Greenwich, Conn.: Fawcett Crest, 1974).
3. A. E. Nourse, "Science Fiction and Man's Adaptation to Change," in

Reginald Bretnor, ed., *Science Fiction Today* (New York: Harper & Row, 1974), 117–18.

4. Reginald Bretnor, "Science Fiction in the Age of Space," ibid., 150.
5. Asimov, "Robbie," *I, Robot* (Greenwich, Conn.: Fawcett Crest, 1973).
6. Asimov, "Victory Unintentional," *The Rest of the Robots* (Garden City, N.Y.: Doubleday, 1964).
7. Asimov, "Reason," *I, Robot.*
8. Asimov, "The Evitable Conflict," ibid.
9. Asimov, Robot AL-76 Goes Astray," *The Rest of the Robots.*
10. Asimov, "Lenny," ibid.
11. Asimov, "Galley Slave," ibid.
12. Asimov, "Evidence," *I, Robot.*
13. Asimov, "Runaround," ibid.
14. Asimov, "Liar," ibid.
15. See Asimov, "The Fun They Had," *Earth is Room Enough.*
16. Asimov, "The Feeling of Power," *Nine Tomorrows.*
17. Asimov, "Segregationist," *Nightfall and Other Stories* (Greenwich, Conn.: Fawcett Crest, 1974).
18. Asimov, "Profession," *Nine Tomorrows.*
19. Asimov, "All the Troubles in the World," ibid.
20. Asimov, "Sally," *Nightfall and Other Stories.*
21. Asimov, "Mother Earth," *The Early Asimov, Book Two.*
22. Asimov, "Homo Sol," *The Early Asimov, Book One* (Greenwich, Conn.: Fawcett Crest, 1974).
23. Asimov, "Youth," *The Martian Way and Other Stories* (Greenwich, Conn.: Fawcett Crest, 1973).
24. D. Lee, "Codifications of Reality: Lineal and Non-lineal," in D. Lee, ed., *Freedom and Culture* (Englewood Cliffs: Prentice Hall, 1959), 117.

CHAPTER 7: WATT

1. Isaac Asimov, in his Introduction to *Nightfall and Other Stories* (Greenwich, Conn.: Fawcett Crest, 1974).
2. Interview by Herbert Kenny, "The Amazing Asimov," *Boston Sunday Globe Magazine* (October 12, 1969).
3. Asimov, ed., in his Introduction to *More Soviet Science Fiction* (New York: Macmillan, 1962), 8.
4. Asimov, "Social Science Fiction," in Dick Allen, ed., *Science Fiction: The Future* (New York: Harcourt Brace Jovanovich, 1971), 263.
5. Sam Moskowitz, *Seekers of Tomorrow: Masters of Modern Science Fiction* (New York: World Publishing Co., 1966), 259.
6. Susan Glicksohn, " 'A City of Which the Stars Are Suburbs,' " in Thomas D. Clareson, ed., *SF: The Other Side of Realism* (Bowling Green; Bowling Green University Popular Press, 1971), 345. Glicksohn's chapter is particularly apropos to a study of Asimov's characters.

7. Asimov, "Social Science Fiction," 273–274.
8. Asimov, *Opus 100* (Boston: Houghton Mifflin, 1969), 241–42.
9. Ibid., 242.
10. Asimov, *Stories from the Rest of the Robots* (New York: Pyramid Books, 1974), 73. There is yet another Susan Calvin story, "Feminine Intuition," in *The Bicentennial Man* (Greenwich, Conn.: Fawcett Crest, 1976).
11. L. David Allen, *Science Fiction: An Introduction* (Lincoln: Cliffs Notes, 1973), 32.
12. Asimov, *I, Robot* (Greenwich, Conn.: Fawcett Crest, 1973), 7.
13. Asimov, *Stories from the Rest of the Robots.*
14. *Billion Year Spree: The True History of Science Fiction* (New York: Schocken, 1974), 269.
15. Asimov, *The Caves of Steel* (Greenwich, Conn.: Fawcett Crest, 1972), 6.
16. Moskowitz, *Seekers of Tomorrow*, 263.
17. Aldiss, *Billion Year Spree*, 269.
18. Asimov, *The Naked Sun* (Greenwich, Conn.: Fawcett Crest, 1972), 12.
19. Moskowitz, *Seekers of Tomorrow*, 262–63.
20. Asimov, *Nightfall and Other Stories*, 328.
21. Asimov, *The Gods Themselves* (Greenwich, Conn.: Fawcett Crest, 1972), 70.
22. Asimov, "Social Science Fiction," 290.
23. Sam J. Lundwall, *Science Fiction: What It's All About* (New York: Ace Books, 1971), 132.

CHAPTER 9: WARRICK

1. Isaac Asimov, *The Naked Sun* (Greenwich, Conn.: Fawcett Crest, 1972), ch. 14.
2. Asimov, "That Thou Art Mindful of Him," *The Bicentennial Man* (Garden City, N.Y.: Doubleday, 1976).
3. See Asimov, "Thinking Machines," *Science Digest* (December 1967), and *Asimov's Guide to Science* (New York: Basic Books, 1972), 845–60.
4. Joseph F. Patrouch, Jr., *The Science Fiction of Isaac Asimov* (Garden City, N.Y.: Doubleday, 1974), 42.
5. Stanislaw Lem has argued that artificial beings with a high level of intelligence must be considered ethically as human beings. He complains because American science fiction about robots has not dealt with significant issues like this. See Lem, "Robots in Science Fiction," in Thomas D. Clareson, ed., *SF: The Other Side of Realism* (Bowling Green: Bowling Green University Popular Press, 1971).
6. Robert Orstein has recently been doing research in this area. See his *The Nature of Human Consciousness* (San Francisco: W. H. Freeman, 1973).
7. See Alan Ross Anderson, ed., *Minds and Machines* (Englewood Cliffs: Prentice Hall, 1964).

8. Philip C. Jackson, Jr., *Introduction to Artificial Intelligence* (New York: Petrocelli Books, 1974), 396. Also Bertram Raphael, *The Thinking Computer* (San Francisco: W. H. Freeman, 1976), 249.

9. Asimov, "Prediction as a Side Effect," *Boston Review of the Arts* (July 1972).

10. Asimov, in the 1950 Panther edition of *I, Robot*, 11.

11. Patrouch, *The Science Fiction of Isaac Asimov.*

12. Asimov, in *DP Solutions* (April 1975, publication of IBM Corporation).

13. Asimov, in the 1964 Pyramid edition of *The Last of the Robots*, 51.

14. Asimov, "The Evitable Conflict," *I, Robot* (Greenwich, Conn.: Fawcett Crest, 1973).

15. Asimov, "The Life and Times of Multivac" was originally published in *The New York Times Magazine*, and is the first piece of fiction ever commissioned and published by that magazine.

16. Asimov, *The Caves of Steel* (Greenwich, Conn.: Fawcett Crest, 1972), 48.

17. See Asimov, "The Myth of the Machine," in Patricia Warrick, Joseph D. Olander, and Martin H. Greenberg, eds., *Science Fiction: Contemporary Mythmakers* (New York: Harper & Row, 1977). In this essay Asimov expresses a view of machine intelligence similar to that in this story.

A Bibliography of Isaac Asimov's
Major Science Fiction Works through 1976 *
Compiled by DAVID M. COX and GARY R. LIBBY

In the time it takes you to read this bibliography, Isaac Asimov will have written yet another entry in what has become a legendary and prodigious canon. The task of providing a current bibliography is by definition impossible because for Asimov writing is not an accomplishment but a way of life. The exigencies of deadlines, lead times—even the very time for typing—conspire to reduce a bibliographer's work to that of a holding action against the onslaught of Asimov's attacking typewriters (he had, at last count, three typewriters working on six manuscripts).

Our deepest gratitude must go to Marjorie Miller for providing a beachhead for our project. Her annotated bibliography of Asimov's works through 1971 gave us not only a place to start but also the courage to continue. What follows here is not a complete list of Asimov's published works, but a list of his major science fiction and science fiction–related articles (indicated below by an asterisk). Because Asimov writes so many scientific articles and has had a hand in editing and contributing to so many science textbooks, it is sometimes difficult to separate the fiction from the science. Our decision of what to include in this bibliography was based on whether or not an article incorporated a significant degree of scientific speculation. Also included are articles dealing specifically with the process of writing SF stories, but we felt that to list specific volumes of *Isaac Asimov's Science Fiction Magazine* would be pedantic. As to the task of compiling a complete bibliography of Asimov's works including SF, science, fiction books edited, introductions, articles contributed to encyclopedias, poetry, adolescent literature, and interviews, we humbly defer.

G.R.L.
D.M.C.

* Portions of this Bibliography are adapted with permission from Marjorie Miller, *Isaac Asimov: A Checklist of Works Published in the United States* (Kent State University Press, 1972).

* "Academe and I." *Fantasy and Science Fiction*, XLII (May 1972).

"All the Troubles of the World," *Super Science Fiction*, II (April 1958).

————. *Nine Tomorrows*, 1959.

". . . And Now You Don't," *Astounding*, XLIV, Part One (November 1949), Part Two (December 1949), Part Three (January 1950).

————. Part II of *Second Foundation*, 1953.

"Anniversary," *Amazing*, XXXIII (March 1959).

————. *Asimov's Mysteries*, 1968. *The Best of Isaac Asimov*, 1974.

————. Joseph Ross, ed. *The Best of Amazing*. Garden City, N.Y.: Doubleday, 1967.

* "Asimov Replies" [to a review of *Opus 100*], *Luna*, no. 6 (November 1969).

Asimov's Mysteries. Garden City, N.Y.: Doubleday, 1968. London: Rapp & Whiting, 1968. New York: Dell, 1969. [Not exclusively science fiction.]

"Author! Author!" in *The Unknown Five*, D. R. Benson, ed. New York: Pyramid, 1964.

————. *The Early Asimov*, 1972.

* "Author's Ordeal" [poem], *Science Fiction Quarterly*, V (May 1957).

————. *Earth Is Room Enough*, 1957.

Before the Golden Age. Isaac Asimov, ed. Garden City, N.Y.: Doubleday, 1974. [Anthology of science fiction stories from the 1930s] Greenwich, Conn.: Fawcett World, 1975 (3 vols.).

"Belief," *Astounding*, LII (October 1953).

————. *Through a Glass, Clearly*, 1967.

————. Judith Merrill, ed. *Beyond the Barriers of Space and Time*. New York: Random House, 1954. John W. Campbell, ed. *Prologue to Analog: Analog Science Fact and Science Fiction*. Garden City, N.Y.: Doubleday, 1962.

"Benefactor of Humanity." *Saturday Evening Post*, CCXLV (March 1973).

Best New Thing. New York: World, 1971.

The Best of Isaac Asimov. Garden City, N.Y.: Doubleday, 1974. London: Sidgwich & Jackson, 1973 (Angus Wells, ed.). Greenwich, Conn.: Fawcett World, 1976.

The Bicentennial Man and Other Stories. Garden City, N.Y.: Doubleday, 1976. Greenwich, Conn.: Fawcett World, 1976.

"The Big and the Little," *Astounding*, XXXIII (August 1944).

————. Part III of *Foundation*, 1951.

"The Billiard Ball," *If*, XVII (March 1967).

————. *Asimov's Mysteries*, 1968. *The Best of Isaac Asimov*, 1974.

————. Donald Wollheim and Terry Carr, eds. *World's Best Science Fiction*, *4th Series*. New York: Ace Books, 1968.

"Black Friar of the Flame," *Planet*, I (Spring 1942).

————. *The Early Asimov*, 1972.

"Blank!" *Infinity*, II (June 1957).

————. *Buy Jupiter and Other Stories*, 1975.

"Blind Alley," *Astounding*, XXXV (March 1945).

————. *The Early Asimov*, 1972.

———. Groff Conklin, ed. *The Best of Science Fiction*. New York: Crown, 1946. Groff Conklin, ed. *Great Stories of Space Travel*. Grosset & Dunlap, 1963.

"Brazen Locked Room," *F&SF*, xi (June 1956).

———. *Earth Is Room Enough*, 1957, under the title "Gimmicks Three."

———. Basil Davenport, ed. *Deals with the Devil*. New York: Dodd, Mead, 1958. J. Francis McComas, ed. *Special Wonder: The Anthony Boucher Memorial Anthology of Fantasy and Science Fiction*. New York: Random House, 1970.

"Breeds there a man . . . ?" *Astounding*, xlvii (June 1951).

———. *Through a Glass, Clearly*, 1967. *Nightfall and Other Stories*, 1969.

———. August W. Derleth, ed. *Beachheads in Space*. New York: Pellegrini & Cudahy, 1952.

"Bridle and Saddle," *Astounding*, xxix (June 1942).

———. Part II of *Foundation*, 1951.

———. Martin Greenberg, ed. *Men Against the Stars*. New York: Gnome, 1950.

"Button, Button," *Startling Stories*, xxviii (January 1953).

———. *Buy Jupiter and Other Stories*, 1975.

———. Groff Conklin, ed. *13 Above the Night*. New York: Dell, 1969.

"Buy Jupiter," *Venture*, ii (May 1958).

———. *Buy Jupiter and Other Stories*, 1975.

Buy Jupiter and Other Stories. Garden City, N.Y.: Doubleday, 1975. Greenwich, Conn.: Fawcett World, 1977.

* "The By-Product of Science Fiction," *Chemical and Engineering News*, xxxiv (August 1956).

———. *Is Anyone There?*, 1967, under the title "The Cult of Ignorance."

"Callistan Menace," *Astonishing*, i (April 1940).

———. *The Early Asimov*, 1972. Excerpt, *Opus 100*, 1969.

"C-Chute," *Galaxy*, ii (October 1951).

———. *Through a Glass, Clearly*, 1967. *Nightfall and Other Stories*, 1969. *Best of Isaac Asimov*, 1974.

———. Frederik Pohl, ed. *Shadow of Tomorrow*. Garden City, N.Y.: Doubleday, 1953. H. L. Gold, ed. *Second Galaxy of Science Fiction*. Garden City, N.Y.: Doubleday, 1954.

"Catch that Rabbit," *Astounding*, xxxii (February 1944).

———. *I, Robot*, 1950.

"The Caves of Steel," *Galaxy*, vii, Part One (October 1953), Part Two (November 1953), Part Three (December 1953).

The Caves of Steel. Garden City, N.Y.: Doubleday, 1954. New York: New American Library, 1955. New York: Pyramid, 1962. *The Rest of the Robots*, 1964. Greenwich, Conn.: Fawcett World, 1974.

———. Excerpts in *The Sociology of the Possible*, Richard Ofshe, ed. Englewood Cliffs, N.J.: Prentice-Hall, 1970.

"Christmas on Ganymede," *Startling Stories*, vii (January 1942).

———. *The Early Asimov*, 1972.

————. Kendell F. Crossen, ed. *Adventures in Tomorrow*. New York: Greenberg, 1951.

* "Clippings from Tomorrow's Newspapers," *Saturday Review/World*, I (August 1974).

* "The Clock Paradox," *Science Fiction Quarterly*, V (November 1957).

"The Computer That Went on Strike," *Saturday Evening Post*, CCXLIV (Spring 1972).

"The Covenant" (Part Two), *Fantastic*, IX (July 1960). [A "round robin" novel written with Poul Anderson, Robert Scheckley, Murray Leinster, and Robert Bloch.]

————. *Most Thrilling Science Fiction Ever Told*, no. 2 (1966).

"The Cult of Ignorance." *See* "The By-Product of Science Fiction."

"The Currents of Space," *Astounding*, L, Part One (October 1952), Part Two (November 1952), Part Three (December 1952).

The Currents of Space. Garden City, N.Y.: Doubleday, 1952. New York: New American Library, 1953. London: Boardman, 1955. New York: Lancer, 1968. Greenwich, Conn.: Fawcett World, 1971.

————. *Triangle*, 1961. Garden City, N.Y.: Doubleday, 1961.

"Darwinian Pool Room," *Galaxy*, I (October 1950).

————. *Buy Jupiter and Other Stories*, 1975.

David Starr, Space Ranger. [pseud. Paul French] Garden City, N.Y.: Doubleday, 1952. New York: New American Library, 1971.

"Day of the Hunters," *Future*, I (November 1950).

————. *Buy Jupiter and Other Stories*, 1975.

"Dead Hand," *Astounding*, XXXV (April 1945).

————. Part I of *Foundation and Empire*, 1952. Excerpt, *Opus 100*, 1969.

"Dead Past," *Astounding*, LVII (April 1956).

————. *Earth Is Room Enough*, 1957. *The Best of Isaac Asimov*, 1974.

"Death Sentence," *Astounding*, XXXII (November 1943).

————. *The Early Asimov*, 1972.

————. August W. Derleth, ed. *The Outer Reaches*. New York: Pellegrini & Cudahy, 1950.

"The Deep," *Galaxy*, V (November 1952).

————. *The Martian Way and Other Stories*, 1955. *The Best of Isaac Asimov*, 1974.

"Does a Bee Care?" *If*, VII (June 1957).

————. *Buy Jupiter and Other Stories*, 1975.

————. Roger Elwood and Sam Moskowitz, eds. *Other Worlds, Other Times*. New York: McFadden-Bartell, 1969.

"Dreaming Is a Private Thing," *F&SF*, IX (December 1955).

————. *Earth Is Room Enough*, 1957.

————. Judith Merril, ed. *S-F: The Year's Greatest Science Fiction and Fantasy*. New York: Gnome, 1956. Judith Merril, ed. *S-F: The Best of the Best*. New York: Delacorte, 1967. Martin H. Greenberg and Joseph D. Olander, eds. *Tomorrow, Inc.: SF Stories about Big Business*. New York: Taplinger, 1976.

"Dreamworld," *F&SF*, ix (November 1955).
————. *Opus 100*, 1969.
————. Anthony Boucher, ed. *The Best from Fantasy and Science Fiction, 5th Series*. Garden City, N.Y.: Doubleday, 1956.
"Dust of Death," *Venture*, v (January 1957).
————. *Asimov's Mysteries*, 1968.
————. Brett Halliday, ed. *Big Time Mysteries*. New York: Mystery Writers of America, Inc., 1958.
"The Dying Night," *F&SF*, xi (July 1956).
————. *Nine Tomorrows*, 1959. *Asimov's Mysteries*, 1968. *The Best of Isaac Asimov*, 1974.

"Each an Explorer," *Future*, xxx (n.d., 1956).
————. *Buy Jupiter and Other Stories*, 1975.
————. Judith Merril, ed. *SF '57: The Year's Greatest SF & Fantasy*. New York: Gnome, 1957.
The Early Asimov. Garden City, N.Y.: Doubleday, 1972. Greenwich, Conn.: Fawcett World, 1974 (2 vols.).
Earth Is Room Enough: Science Fiction Tales of Our Own Planet. Garden City, N.Y.: Doubleday, 1957. New York: Bantam, 1959. Greenwich, Conn.: Fawcett World, 1970, 1974, 1976.
Eight Stories from The Rest of the Robots. New York: Pyramid, 1966. See also *The Rest of the Robots*.
"The Endochronic Properties of Resublimated Thiotimoline," *Astounding*, xli (March 1948).
————. *Only a Trillion*, 1958, as Part I of "The Marvellous Properties of Thiotimoline." *The Early Asimov*, 1972.
The End of Eternity. Garden City, N.Y.: Doubleday, 1955. New York: New American Library, 1958. New York: Lancer, 1963, 1966, 1968. Greenwich, Conn.: Fawcett World, 1971.
"Escape." *See* "Paradoxical Escape."
"Everest," *Universe Science Fiction*, iii (December 1953).
————. *Buy Jupiter and Other Stories*, 1975.
"Evidence," *Astounding*, xxxviii (September 1946).
————. *I, Robot*, 1950.
————. William F. Nolan, ed. *The Pseudo-People*. New York: Harper & Row, 1965.
"Evitable Conflict," *Astounding*, xlv (June 1950).
————. *I, Robot*, 1950.
"Exile to Hell," *Analog*, lxxxi (May 1968).
————. *Buy Jupiter and Other Stories*, 1975.
"Eyes Do More Than See," *F&SF*, xxviii (April 1965).
————. *Nightfall and Other Stories*, 1969.
————. Edward L. Ferman, ed. *The Best from Fantasy and Science Fiction, 15th Series*. Garden City, N.Y.: Doubleday, 1966. Judith Merril, ed. *11th Annual of the Year's Best SF*. New York: Delacorte, 1966.

* "F & SF and I," Foreword to *Twenty Years of the Magazine of Fantasy and Science Fiction* (Edward L. Ferman and Robert P. Mills, eds.). New York: Putnam, 1970.
* "Fact Catches Up with Fiction," *New York Times Magazine*, VI (November 19, 1961).
"Fantastic Voyage," *Saturday Evening Post*, CCXXXIX (February 26, 1966; March 12, 1966).
Fantastic Voyage. Boston: Houghton Mifflin, 1966. Toronto: T. Allen, 1966. London: Dobson, 1966. New York: Bantam, 1966. [A novel based on the screenplay by Harry Kleiner, from the original short story by Otto Klement and Jay Lewis Bixby.]
* "The Father of Science Fiction," *Luna*, no. 27, supplement (August 1971).
"The Feeling of Power," *If*, VIII (February 1958).
————. *Nine Tomorrows*, 1959. *Opus 100*, 1969.
————. Clifton Fadiman, ed. *The Mathematical Magpie*. New York: Simon & Schuster, 1962. Kingsley Amis & Robert Conquest, eds. *Spectrum II*. New York: Harcourt, Brace & World, 1963. Robert Hoskins, ed. *The Stars Around Us*. New York: New American Library, 1970.
"Feminine Intuition," *F&SF*, XXXVII (October 1969). [A new Susan Calvin Story.]
————. *The Bicentennial Man and Other Stories*, 1976.
————. Edward L. Ferman & Robert P. Mills, eds. *Twenty Years of the Magazine of Fantasy and Science Fiction*. New York: Putnam, 1970.
Fifty Short Science Fiction Tales. Isaac Asimov and Groff Conklin, eds. New York: Collier, 1963. [Introduction by Isaac Asimov.]
"First Law," *Fantastic Universe*, VI (October 1956).
————. *The Rest of the Robots*, 1964.
————. Hans Santesson, ed. *The Fantastic Universe Omnibus*. Englewood Cliffs, N.J.: Prentice-Hall, 1960.
"Flies," *F&SF*, VI (June 1953).
————. *Nightfall and Other Stories*, 1969.
————. Groff Conklin, ed. *SF Terror Tales*. New York: Gnome, 1955.
* "Foreword" to *Four Futures*, by R. A. Lafferty et al. New York: Hawthorne, 1971.
"Foundation," *Astounding*, XXIX (May 1942).
————. Part I of *Foundation*, 1951.
Foundation. New York: Gnome, 1951. New York: Ace, 1956, 1963, under the title *The Thousand Year Plan*. Garden City, N.Y.: Doubleday, 1963. New York: Avon, 1966, 1969, 1970. See also *The Foundation Trilogy*.
Foundation and Empire. New York: Gnome, 1952. New York: Ace, 1955, under the title *The Man Who Upset the Universe*. Garden City, N.Y.: Doubleday, 1963. New York: Avon, 1966, 1970. See also *The Foundation Trilogy*.
* "The Foundation of SF Success" [poem], *F&SF*, VI (January 1954).
————. *Earth Is Room Enough*, 1957.

————. Anthony Boucher & J. Francis McComas, eds. *The Best from Fantasy and Science Fiction, 4th Series.* Boston: Little, Brown, 1955.

The Foundation Trilogy. Garden City, N.Y.: Doubleday, 1961. [Contents: *Foundation,* 1951; *Foundation and Empire,* 1952; *Second Foundation,* 1953.] London: Sidgwick & Jackson, 1966, under the title *An Isaac Asimov Omnibus.* New York: Avon Equinox, 1974.

"Founding Father," *Galaxy,* xxiv (October 1965).

————. *Buy Jupiter and Other Stories,* 1975.

————. Groff Conklin, ed. *13 Above the Night.* New York: Dell, 1965. Henry Harrison, ed. *Author's Choice.* New York: Berkley, 1968.

"Franchise," *If,* v (August 1955).

————. *Earth Is Room Enough,* 1957.

————. James L. Quinn & Eve Wulff, eds. *The First World of IF.* Kingston, N.Y.: Quinn Publications, 1957. Roger Elwood & Sam Moskowitz, eds. *Alien Earth and Other Stories.* New York: McFadden, 1969. Richard Ofshe, ed. *The Sociology of the Possible.* Englewood Cliffs, N.J.: Prentice-Hall, 1970.

"The Fun They Had," *Boys and Girls Page* [syndicated newspaper feature], NEA Service (December 1, 1951). Also, *F&SF,* vi (February 1954).

————. *Earth Is Room Enough,* 1957. *Fifty Short Science Fiction Tales* (Isaac Asimov & Groff Conklin, eds.), 1963. *The Best of Isaac Asimov,* 1974.

————. Groff Conklin, ed. *Operation Future.* New York: Doubleday, 1955. Richard L. Laughlin & Lillian M. Popp, eds. *Journey in SF* [a textbook]. New York: Globe, 1961. Thomas W. Boardman, ed. *Connoisseur's SF.* Baltimore: Penguin, 1964.

"Galley Slave," *Galaxy,* xv (December 1957).

————. *The Rest of the Robots,* 1964.

————. Frederik Pohl, ed. *Time Waits for Winthrop, and Four Other Short Novels from Galaxy.* Garden City, N.Y.: Doubleday, 1962. Groff Conklin, ed. *Six Great Short SF Novels.* New York: Dell, 1960.

"The Gentle Vultures," *Super Science Fiction,* ii (December 1957).

————. *Nine Tomorrows,* 1959.

————. Robert Silverberg, ed. *Earthmen and Strangers.* New York: Duell, Sloan & Pearce, 1966.

"Gimmicks Three." *See* "Brazen Locked Room."

"The Gods Themselves," Part One: *Galaxy,* xxxii (March–April 1972); Part Two: *If,* xxi (March–April 1972); Part Three: *Galaxy,* xxxii (May–June 1972).

The Gods Themselves. Garden City, N.Y.: Doubleday, 1972. Greenwich, Conn: Fawcett World, 1973, 1975 (rev. edn.).

"Green Patches." *See* "Misbegotten Missionary."

"Half-Breed," *Astonishing,* i (February 1940).

————. *The Early Asimov,* 1972.

————. Sam Moskowitz, ed. *The Space Magicians.* New York: Pyramid, 1971.

"Half-Breeds on Venus," *Astonishing,* II (December 1940).

————. *The Early Asimov,* 1972.

"The Hazing," *Thrilling Wonder Stories,* XXIII (October 1942).

————. *The Early Asimov,* 1972.

"Hell-fire," *Fantastic Universe,* V (May 1956).

————. *Earth Is Room Enough,* 1957.

* "Hemoglobin and the Universe," *Astounding,* LIV (February 1955).

————. *Only a Trillion,* 1957.

"Heredity," *Astonishing,* II (April 1941).

————. *The Early Asimov,* 1972.

————. Frederik Pohl, ed. *Beyond the End of Time.* Garden City, N.Y.: Doubleday, 1952.

"History," *Super Science Stories,* II (March 1941).

————. *The Early Asimov,* 1972.

"The Holmes-Ginsbook Device," *If,* XVIII (December 1968).

————. *Opus 100,* 1969.

"Homo Sol," *Astounding,* XXVI (September 1940).

————. *The Early Asimov,* 1972.

————. Groff Conklin, ed. *Omnibus of Science Fiction.* New York: Crown, 1952.

"Hostess," *Galaxy,* II (May 1951).

————. *Nightfall and Other Stories,* 1969.

————. H. L. Gold, ed. *Galaxy Reader of Science Fiction.* New York: Crown, 1952.

*"How I Lost My Purity and Began Writing for Television," *TV Guide,* XVIII (May 2, 1970).

* "How to Succeed at Science Fiction Without Really Trying," *Original,* VII (November 1956).

The Hugo Winners, Vol. I. Isaac Asimov, ed. Garden City, N.Y.: Doubleday, 1962. London: Dobson, 1962. New York: Avon, 1963. Greenwich, Conn.: Fawcett World, 1974. [Also in Science Fiction Book Club edn., 1972, 2 vols in 1.]

The Hugo Winners, Vol. II. Isaac Asimov, ed. Garden City, N.Y.: Doubleday, 1971. [Also in Science Fiction Book Club edn., 1972, 2 vols in 1.]

"Ideas Die Hard," *Galaxy,* XIV (October 1957).

————. H. L. Gold ed. *Third Galaxy Reader.* Garden City, N.Y.: Doubleday, 1958. Hal Clement, ed. *First Flights to the Moon.* Garden City, N.Y.: Doubleday, 1970.

"The Imaginary," *Super Science Stories,* IV (November 1942).

————. *The Early Asimov,* 1972.

"I'm in Marsport Without Hilda," *Venture,* I (November 1957).

————. *Nine Tomorrows,* 1959. *Asimov's Mysteries,* 1968.

"Immortal Bard," *Universe,* no. 5 (May 1954).

————. *Earth Is Room Enough,* 1957.

"In a Good Cause," in *New Tales of Space and Time* (Robert J. Healy, ed.). New York: Holt, 1951.

———. *Nightfall and Other Stories*, 1969.

"Insert Knob A in Hole B," *F&SF*, xiii (December 1957).

———. *Nightfall and Other Stories*, 1969.

*"Introduction" to *More Soviet Science Fiction*. Rosa Prokof'va, trans. New York: Collier, 1962.

*"Introduction" to *Soviet Science Fiction*. Violet L. Dutt, trans. New York: Collier, 1962.

* "Introduction" to *The Time Machine and The War of the Worlds*, by H. G. Wells. New York: Fawcett, 1968.

I, Robot. New York: Gnome, 1950. London: Grayson, 1952. New York: New American Library, 1956. Toronto: Doubleday, 1963. London: Dobson, 1967. Greenwich, Conn.: Fawcett World, 1970, 1973, 1976.

———. Excerpt, *Opus 100*, 1969.

An Isaac Asimov Omnibus. See *The Foundation Trilogy*.

An Isaac Asimov Second Omnibus. See *Triangle*.

* "Isaac Asimov Replies" [to a Russian criticism of American science fiction], *F&SF*, xxix (October 1965).

"It's Such a Beautiful Day," in *Star SF Stories No. 3* (Frederik Pohl, ed.). Boston: Houghton Mifflin, 1954.

———. *Through a Glass, Clearly*, 1967.

———. John Standler, ed. *Eco-Fiction*. New York: Washington Square Press, 1971.

"Jokester," *Infinity*, i (December 1956).

———. *Earth Is Room Enough*, 1957.

———. Brian Aldiss, ed. *More Penguin SF*. London: Penguin, 1963.

"The Key," *F&SF*, xxxi (October 1966).

———. *Asimov's Mysteries*, 1968.

———. Edward L. Ferman, ed. *The Best from Fantasy and Science Fiction, 16th Series*. Garden City: N.Y.: Doubleday, 1967.

"Key Item," *F&SF*, xxxv (July 1968).

———. *Buy Jupiter and Other Stories*, 1975.

"Kid Stuff," *Beyond*, i (September 1953).

———. *Earth Is Room Enough*, 1957.

"Lastborn," *Galaxy*, xvi (September 1958).

———. *Nine Tomorrows*, 1959, under the title "The Ugly Little Boy." *Tomorrow's Children*, 1966.

———. R. P. Mills ed. *The Worlds of Science Fiction*. New York: Dial, 1963. Damon Knight, ed. *Dimension X*. New York: Simon & Schuster, 1970.

"The Last Question," *Science Fiction Quarterly*, iv (November 1956).

———. *Nine Tomorrows*, 1959. *Opus 100*, 1969.

"Last Trump," *Fantastic Universe*, iii (June 1955).

———. *Earth Is Room Enough*, 1957.

"Legal Rites," *Weird Tales*, XLII (September 1950). [In collaboration with Frederik Pohl, under the pseud. James MacCreigh.]

———. *The Early Asimov*, 1972.

———. Kurt Singer, ed. *Weird Tales of the Supernatural*. London: W. H. Allen, 1966. [No copyright acknowledgement.]

"Lenny," *Infinity*, III (January 1958).

———. *The Rest of the Robots*, 1964.

———. Frederik Pohl, ed. *The Expert Dreamers*. New York: Avon, 1962.

"Let's Get Together," *Infinity*, II (February 1957).

———. *The Rest of the Robots*, 1964.

———. Judith Merril, ed. *SF '58: The Year's Greatest SF and Fantasy*. Garden City, N.Y.: Doubleday, 1958.

"Let's Not," *Graduate Journal* Boston University, III (December 1954).

———. *Buy Jupiter and Other Stories*, 1975.

———. Martin Greenberg, ed. *All About the Future*. New York: Gnome, 1955.

*Letter, *The WSFA Journal*, no. 75 (February–March 1971).

"Liar!" *Astounding*, XXVII (May 1941).

———. *I, Robot*, 1950. Excerpt, *Opus 100*, 1969.

———. Judith Merril, ed. *Human?* New York: Lion, 1954. Sam Moskowitz, ed. *Modern Masterpieces of Science Fiction*. Cleveland: World, 1965. Laurence M. Janifer, ed. *Master's Choice*. New York: Simon & Schuster, 1966. Sam Moskowitz, ed. *Doorway into Time*. New York: McFadden-Bartell, 1966. Robert Silverberg, ed. *Mind to Mind: Nine Stories of Science Fiction*. New York: Nelson, 1971.

"Life and Times of Multivac," *New York Times Magazine* (January 5, 1975).

* "Life in 1990," *Diners Club Magazine*. Also *Sci Di*, LVIII (August 1965).

———. *Is Anyone There?*, 1967, under the title "The World of 1990."

"Light Verse," *Saturday Evening Post*, CCXLV (September 1973).

"Little Lost Robot," *Astounding*, XXXIX (March 1947).

———. *I, Robot*, 1950.

———. Robert Montgomery, ed. [pseud. E. Crispin] *Best SF #2*. London: Faber & Faber, 1956. Robert Montgomery, ed. [pseud. E. Crispin] *The Stars and Under*. London: Faber& Faber, 1968.

"The Little Man on the Subway," *Fantasy Book*, I, no. 6 (n.d., 1950). [In collaboration with Frederik Pohl, under pseud. James MacCreigh.]

———. *The Early Asimov*, 1972.

———. Garrett Ford, ed. *Science and Sorcery*. Los Angeles: Fantasy Publications, 1951.

"Living Space," *Original Stories*, VI (May 1956).

———. *Earth Is Room Enough*, 1957.

———. Robert Silverberg, ed. *Worlds of Maybe*. New York: Thomas Nelson, 1970.

"A Loint of Paw," *F&SF*, XIII (August 1957).

———. *Asimov's Mysteries*, 1968.

———. Anthony Boucher, ed. *The Best from Fantasy and Science Fiction, 7th Series*. Garden City, N.Y.: Doubleday, 1958.

Lucky Starr and the Big Sun of Mercury. [pseud. Paul French] Garden City, N.Y.: Doubleday, 1956. New York: New American Library, 1972.
Lucky Starr and the Moons of Jupiter. [pseud. Paul French] Garden City, N.Y.: Doubleday, 1957. New York: New American Library, 1972.
————. Excerpt, *Opus 100*, 1969.
Lucky Starr and the Oceans of Venus. [pseud. Paul French] Garden City, N.Y.: Doubleday, 1954. New York: New American Library, 1972.
————. Excerpt, *Opus 100*, 1969.
Lucky Starr and the Pirates of the Asteroids. [pseud. Paul French] Garden City, N.Y.: Doubleday, 1953. New York: New American Library, 1972.
Lucky Starr and the Rings of Saturn. [pseud. Paul French] Garden City, N.Y.: Doubleday, 1958. New York: New American Library, 1972.

"The Machine That Won the War," *F&SF*, XXI (October 1961).
————. *Nightfall and Other Stories*, 1969.
————. Robert Mills, ed. *The Best from Fantasy and Science Fiction, 11th Series.* Garden City, N.Y.: Doubleday, 1962.
"The Magnificent Possession," *Future*, I (July 1940).
————. *The Early Asimov*, 1972.
"Male Strikebreaker," *Original*, VII (January 1957).
————. *Nightfall and Other Stories*, 1969.
————. Groff Conklin, ed. *17 x Infinity.* New York: Dell, 1963, under the title "Strikebreaker."
"The Man Who Made the 21st Century," *Boy's Life*, LV (October 1965).
The Man Who Upset the Universe. See *Foundation and Empire.*
"Marooned Off Vesta," *Amazing*, XIII (March 1939). Also, *Amazing*, XXXIII (March 1959).
————. *Asimov's Mysteries*, 1968. *The Best of Isaac Asimov*, 1974.
————. Joseph Ross, ed. *The Best of Amazing.* Garden City, N.Y.: Doubleday, 1967.
"The Martian Way," *Galaxy*, V (December 1952).
————. Excerpt, *Opus 100*, 1969. *The Best of Isaac Asimov*, 1974.
————. Damon Knight, ed. *Worlds to Come.* Greenwich, Conn.: Fawcett World, 1968.
The Martian Way and Other Stories. Garden City, N.Y.: Doubleday, 1955. New York: New American Library, 1957. London: Dobson, 1964. Greenwich, Conn.: Fawcett World, 1969, 1971, 1973.
"The Message," *F&SF*, X (February 1956).
————. *Earth Is Room Enough*, 1957.
"The Micropsychiatric Applications of Thiotimoline," *Astounding*, LII (December 1953).
————. *Only a Trillion*, 1957, as Part Two of "The Marvelous Properties of Thiotimoline."
"Mirror Image," *Analog*, LXXXIX (May 1972).
————. *The Best of Isaac Asimov*, 1974.
"Misbegotten Missionary," *Galaxy*, I (November 1950).

————. *Nightfall and Other Stories*, 1969, under the title "Green Patches."

————. Robert A. Heinlein, ed. *Tomorrow, the Stars*. Garden City, N.Y.: Doubleday, 1952. Groff Conklin, ed. *Giants Unleashed*. New York: Grosset & Dunlap, 1965. Robert Hoskins, ed. *First Step Outward*. New York: Dell, 1969.

"The Monkey's Fingers," *Startling Stories*, xxix (February 1953).

————. *Buy Jupiter and Other Stories*, 1975.

More Stories from the Hugo Winners, Vol. 2. Greenwich, Conn.: Fawcett World, 1975.

"Mother Earth," *Astounding*, xliii (May 1949).

————. *The Early Asimov*, 1972.

————. Martin Greenberg, ed. *Journey to Infinity*. New York: Gnome, 1951. Leo Margulies, ed. *Three from Out There*. Greenwich, Conn.: Fawcett World, 1959.

"The Mule," *Astounding*, xxxvi (August 1945).

————. Part II of *Foundation and Empire*, 1952.

"The Naked Sun," *Astounding*, lviii, Part One (October 1956), Part Two (November 1956), Part Three (December 1956).

The Naked Sun. Garden City, N.Y.: Doubleday, 1957. London: M. Joseph, 1958. New York: Bantam, 1958. New York: Lancer, 1964. Greenwich, Conn.: Fawcett World, 1972.

————. *The Rest of the Robots*, 1964.

Nebula Award Stories No. 8. Isaac Asimov, ed. New York: Harper & Row, 1973. New York: Berkley, 1975.

"Nightfall," *Astounding*, xxviii (September 1941).

————. *Nightfall and Other Stories*, 1969. *The Best of Isaac Asimov*, 1974.

————. Robert J. Healy & J. Francis McComas, eds. *Adventures in Time and Space*. New York: Random House, 1946. John W. Campbell, ed. *Astounding SF Anthology*. New York: Simon & Schuster, 1952. Damon Knight, ed. *Beyond Tomorrow*. New York: Harper & Row, 1965. Robert Silverberg, ed. *The Mirror of Infinity: A Critics' Anthology of Science Fiction*. New York: Harper & Row, 1970. Robert Silverberg, ed. *Science Fiction Hall of Fame*. Garden City, N.Y.: Doubleday, 1970.

Nightfall and Other Stories. Garden City, N.Y.: Doubleday, 1969. Greenwich, Conn.: Fawcett World, 1970, 1974.

Nine Tomorrows: Tales of the Near Future. Garden City, N.Y.: Doubleday, 1959, 1970. New York: Bantam, 1961. London: Dobson, 1963. Greenwich, Conn.: Fawcett World, 1969.

"Nobody Here But . . ." in *Star SF Stories* (Frederik Pohl, ed.). Boston: Houghton Mifflin, 1953.

"No Connection," *Astounding*, xli (June 1948).

————. *The Early Asimov*, 1972.

————. Everett F. Bleiler & T. E. Dikty, eds. *Best Science Fiction Stories: 1949*. New York: Fell, 1949. Everett F. Bleiler & T. E. Dikty, eds. *Science Fiction Omnibus*. Garden City, N.Y.: Doubleday, 1952.

"Not Final," *Astounding*, xxviii (October 1941).

————. *The Early Asimov*, 1972.
————. Groff Conklin, ed. *Possible Worlds of SF*. New York: Vanguard, 1951. Arthur C. Clarke, ed. *Time Probe: The Sciences in SF*. New York: Delacorte, 1966. Damon Knight, ed. *Toward Infinity*. New York: Simon & Schuster, 1968.
"Now You See It . . ." *Astounding*, xl (January 1948).
————. Part I of *Second Foundation*, 1953.

"Obituary," *F&SF*, xvii (August 1959).
————. *Asimov's Mysteries*, 1968.
* "Our Lonely Planet," *Astounding*, lxii (November 1958).
————. *Fact and Fancy*, 1962.

"Paradoxical Escape," *Astounding*, xxxv (May 1945).
————. *I, Robot*, 1950, under the title "Escape."
"Pâté de Foie Gras," *Astounding*, lviii (September 1956).
————. *Only a Trillion*, 1957. *Asimov's Mysteries*, 1968.
"The Pause," in *Time to Come: SF Stories of Tomorrow* (August W. Derleth, ed.). New York: Farrar, Straus, 1954.
————. *Buy Jupiter and Other Stories*, 1975.
Pebble in the Sky. Garden City, N.Y.: Doubleday, 1950. Galaxy Novel #14, 1953. New York: Bantam, 1957. London: Sidgwick & Jackson, 1968. Greenwich, Conn.: Fawcett World, 1971. Also, see *Triangle*.
"Playboy and the Slime God," *Amazing*, xxxv (March 1961).
————. *Nightfall and Other Stories*, 1969, under the title "What *Is This Thing Called Love?*"
"The Portable Star," *Thrilling Wonder Stories*, xliv (Winter 1955).
"Profession," *Astounding*, lix (July 1957).
————. *Nine Tomorrows*, 1959.
————. Richard Ofshe, ed. *The Sociology of the Possible*. Englewood Cliffs, N.J.: Prentice-Hall, 1970. [Excerpted in such a way that the entire point of the original story is lost.]
"The Proper Study," *Boy's Life*, lviii (September 1968).
————. *Buy Jupiter and Other Stories*, 1975.

"Rain, Rain, Go Away," *Fantastic Universe*, xi (September 1959).
————. *Buy Jupiter and Other Stories*, 1975.
"Reason," *Astounding*, xxvii (April 1941).
————. *I, Robot*, 1950.
————. Damon Knight, ed. *A Century of Science Fiction*. New York: Simon & Schuster, 1962.
The Rebellious Stars. See *The Stars, Like Dust*.
"Red Queen's Race," *Astounding*, xlii (January 1949).
————. *The Early Asimov*, 1972.
————. Fletcher Pratt, ed. *World of Wonder*. New York: Twayne, 1951.
The Rest of the Robots. Garden City, N.Y.: Doubleday, 1964. See also *Eight Stories from the Rest of the Robots* and *Stories from the Rest of the Robots*.

"Ring Around the Sun," *Future*, I (March 1940).
———. *The Early Asimov*, 1972.
"Risk," *Astounding*, LV (May 1955).
———. *The Rest of the Robots*, 1964.
"Robbie." *See* "Strange Playfellow."
"Robot AL 76 Goes Astray," *Amazing*, XVI (February 1942).
———. *The Rest of the Robots*, 1964.
———. Leo Margulies & Oscar J. Friend, eds. *My Best Science Fiction Story*. New York: Merlin, 1949.
"Runaround," *Astounding*, XXIX (March 1942).
———. *I, Robot*, 1950. Excerpt, *Opus 100*, 1969.
———. Sam Moskowitz, ed. *The Coming of the Robots*. New York: Collier, 1963.

"S, as in Zebatinsky," *Star Science Fiction*, I (January 1958).
———. *Nine Tomorrows*, 1959, under the title "Spell My Name with an S."
"Sally," *Fantastic*, I (May–June 1953).
———. *Nightfall and Other Stories*, 1969.
———. E. Abell, ed. *American Accent*. New York: Ballantine, 1954.
"Satisfaction Guaranteed," *Amazing*, XXV (April 1951). Also *Fantastic Stories*, XV (July 1966).
———. *Earth Is Room Enough*, 1957. *The Rest of the Robots*, 1964.
———. Roger Elwood, ed. *The Invasion of the Robots*. New York: Paperback Library, 1965.
* "Science fictionally speaking," *Sci Di*, LXII (January 1968).
———. *Opus 100*, 1969.
Second Foundation. New York: Gnome, 1953. New York: Avon, 1958, 1964, 1970. Garden City, N.Y.: Doubleday, 1963. See also *The Foundation Trilogy*.
"The Secret Sense," *Cosmic Stories*, I (March 1941).
———. *The Early Asimov*, 1972.
———. Sam Moskowitz, ed. *Futures to Infinity*. New York: Pyramid, 1970.
"The Segregationist," *Abbottempo*, Book 4 (n.d., 1967). Also *F&SF*, XXV (October 1968).
———. *Nightfall and Other Stories*, 1969.
———. Harry Harrison & Brian Aldiss, eds. *Best SF: 1968*. New York: Putnam, 1969.
* "S-F Market Still Healthy" [letter to the editor], *The Writer*, LXIX (August 1956).
"Shah Guido G," *Marvel*, III (November 1951).
———. *Buy Jupiter and Other Stories*, 1975.
"Silly Asses," *Future*, XXXV (February 1958).
———. *Buy Jupiter and Other Stories*, 1975.
"The Singing Bell," *F&SF*, VIII (January 1955).
———. *Asimov's Mysteries*, 1968.

————. Anthony Boucher, ed. *The Best from Fantasy and Science Fiction, 5th Series.* Garden City, N.Y.: Doubleday, 1956.

* "Social Science Fiction," in *Modern Science Fiction* (Reginald Bretnor, ed.). New York: Coward-McCann, 1953.

"Someday," *Infinity,* I (August 1956). *See also* "The Story Machine."

————. *Earth Is Room Enough,* 1957.

————. Damon Knight, ed. *The Metal Smile.* New York: Belmont, 1968.

Harry Harrison, ed. *Worlds of Wonder.* Garden City, N.Y.: Doubleday, 1969.

* *The Space Dictionary.* New York: Starline, 1971.

"Spell My Name with an S." *See* "S, as in Zebatinsky."

"Starlight," *Scientific American,* CCVII (October 1962). [In an advertisement for Hoffman Electronics.] Also in *Fortune,* LXVI (November 1962). [Advertisement.]

————. *Asimov's Mysteries,* 1968.

————. John Carnell, ed. *New Writings in SF—4.* New York: Bantam, 1968.

The Stars, Like Dust. Garden City, N.Y.: Doubleday, 1951. New York: Ace, 1954, under the title *The Rebellious Stars.* Bound with *An Earth Gone Mad* (R. D. Aycock, ed.). New York: Lancer, 1970 [Dr. Asimov's comment: "ludicrously cut without my permission]. Greenwich, Conn.: Fawcett World, 1974. See also "Tyrann."

————. *Triangle,* 1961.

"A Statue for Father," *Satellite,* III (February 1959).

————. *Buy Jupiter and Other Stories,* 1975.

Stories from the Rest of the Robots. New York: Pyramid, 1974. See also *The Rest of the Robots.*

"The Story Machine," *Plays,* XVII (February 1959), 13–23.

"Strange Playfellow," *Super Science Stories,* I (September 1940).

————. *I, Robot,* 1950, under the title "Robbie." Excerpt, *Opus 100,* 1969.

————. Judith Merril, ed. *Shot in the Dark.* New York: Bantam, 1950, under the title "Robbie." Groff Conklin, ed. *SF Thinking Machines.* New York: Vanguard, 1954.

"Strikebreaker." *See* "Male Strikebreaker."

"Sucker Bait," *Astounding,* Part One, LII (February 1954); Part Two, LIII (March 1954).

————. *The Martian Way and Other Stories,* 1955.

"Superneutron," *Astonishing,* III (September 1941).

————. *The Early Asimov,* 1972. Excerpt, *Opus 100,* 1969.

"The Talking Stone," *F&SF,* IX (October 1955).

————. *Asimov's Mysteries,* 1968.

————. Miriam A. deFord, ed. *Space, Time and Crime.* New York: Mercury, 1964.

"Thiotimoline and the Space Age," *Analog,* LXVI (October 1960).

————. *Opus 100,* 1969.

————. Judith Merril, ed. *The 6th Annual of the Year's Best SF*. New York: Simon & Schuster, 1961.

The Thousand Year Plan. See *Foundation*.

Through a Glass, Clearly. London: New English Library, 1967.

"Time Pussy" [pseud. George E. Dale], *Astounding*, xxix (April 1942).

————. *The Early Asimov*, 1972.

Today and Tomorrow and. . . . Garden City, N.Y.: Doubleday, 1973. London: Abelard-Schuman, 1974. New York: Dell, 1975, under the title *Today and Tomorrow*.

Tomorrow's Children. Isaac Asimov, ed. Garden City, N.Y.: Doubleday, 1966. [Introduction by Isaac Asimov.]

* *The Tragedy of the Moon*. Garden City, N.Y.: Doubleday, 1973. [Reprints of essays from *F&SF*.]

* "The Trapping of the Sun," *Astounding*, lix (May 1957).

————. *Only a Trillion*, 1957.

"Trends," *Astounding*, xxiii (July 1939).

————. *The Early Asimov*, 1972.

————. Martin Greenberg, ed. *Men Against the Stars*. New York: Gnome, 1950. T. E. Dikty, ed. *Great SF Stories about the Moon*. New York: Fell, 1967. Hal Clement, ed. *First Flights to the Moon*. Garden City, N.Y.: Doubleday, 1970.

Triangle. Garden City, N.Y.: Doubleday, 1961. [Contents: *The Currents of Space*, 1952; *Pebble in the Sky*, 1950; and *The Stars, Like Dust*, 1951.] London: Sidgwick & Jackson, 1969, under the title *An Issac Asimov Second Omnibus*.

"Tyrann" (*The Stars, Like Dust*), *Galaxy*, i, Part One (January 1951), Part Two (February 1951), Part Three (March 1951). See also *The Stars, Like Dust*.

"The Ugly Little Boy." *See* "Lastborn."

"Unto the Fourth Generation," *F&SF*, xvi (April 1959).

————. *Nightfall and Other Stories*, 1969.

————. Robert Mills, ed. *A Decade of Fantasy and Science Fiction*. Garden City, N.Y.: Doubleday, 1960.

"Up-to-Date Sorcerer," *F&SF*, xv (July 1958).

————. *Nightfall and Other Stories*, 1969.

————. Anthony Boucher, ed. *The Best from Fantasy and Science Fiction, 8th Series*. Garden City, N.Y.: Doubleday, 1959.

"Victory Unintentional," *Super Science Stories*, iv (August 1942).

————. *The Rest of the Robots*, 1964.

————. Orson Welles, ed. *Invasion from Mars*. New York: Dell, 1949. Milton A. Lesser, ed. *Looking Forward*. New York: Beechhurst, 1953.

"Waterclap." *If*, xx (April 1970).

————. *The Bicentennial Man and Other Stories*, 1976.

"Watery Place," *Satellite*, i (October 1956).

————. *Earth Is Room Enough,* 1957.
"The Weapon Too Dreadful to Use," *Amazing,* XIII (May 1939).
————. *The Early Asimov,* 1972.
"The Wedge," *Astounding,* XXXIV (October 1944).
————. Part IV of *Foundation,* 1951.
"What If . . . ," *Fantastic,* I (Summer 1952).
————. *Nightfall and Other Stories,* 1969.
————. Groff Conklin, ed. *SF Adventures in Dimension.* New York: Vanguard, 1953. Groff Conklin, ed. *Great SF by Scientists.* New York: Collier, 1962.
"What *Is This Thing Called Love?" See* "Playboy and the Slime God."
Where Do We Go from Here? Isaac Asimov, ed. Garden City, N.Y.: Doubleday, 1971.
"The World of 1990." *See* "Life in 1990."
"A Woman's Heart," *Satellite,* I (June 1957).

"Youth," *Space Science Fiction,* I (May 1952).
————. *The Martian Way and Other Stories,* 1955.

Isaac Asimov: A Biographical Sketch

Born on January 2, 1920, in Petrovich, Russia, Isaac Asimov was brought to the United States as a child of three years. The Asimov family, including a younger sister, settled in Brooklyn, New York, and young Isaac grew up in the context of a family-owned candy store. At the age of 15, he graduated from Boy's High School and entered Columbia University, from which he graduated four years later with a degree in chemistry. He was married in 1942 and during the war years worked with Robert A. Heinlein and L. Sprague de Camp at the Naval Aircraft Laboratory in Philadelphia. He was drafted by the Army for a year after the war. Having earned a master's degree at Columbia University in 1941, he decided to return there to complete a Ph.D. in chemistry, which was awarded in 1948. The following year he joined the faculty at Boston University as an instructor and rose to the rank of associate professor of biochemistry in 1955, a title he still retains. In 1958 he left the world of teaching for the world of full-time writing. He and his first wife have been divorced, and he has since married Janet Jeppson, a scientist and science fiction writer.

Asimov read his first science fiction magazine in 1929, when he "fell in love" with science fiction. In 1938 he sold his first story—"Marooned Off Vesta"—to *Amazing Stories*. Since 1940 he has sold every story he has written, and most of his works in science fiction have remained in demand. A founder of the Futurian Science Literary Society of New York in 1938, along with Frederik Pohl, Donald Wollheim, Cyril M. Kornbluth, and others, he was the Guest of Honor at the 1955 World Science Fiction Convention in Cleveland, Ohio. He won both the Hugo and the Nebula Awards for *The Gods Themsleves* in 1973 and 1974. Most recently, his story "The Bicentennial Man" won the 1976 Nebula Award. The author of approximately 180 books, he is probably most widely known for his science fiction stories concerning robots and his *Foundation* trilogy. His most important nonfiction titles include *The Intelligent Man's Guide to Science* and *Asimov's Guide to the Bible*. The October 1966 issue of *The Magazine of Fantasy and Science Fiction* was specially devoted to Asimov. Much of his career has been concerned with bridging the gap between the scientific and nonscientific communities.

Contributors

MARJORIE MITHOFF MILLER is Documents Librarian for the newly established Public Documents Reference Library in Prince George's County, Maryland. She is the compiler of *Isaac Asimov: A Checklist of Works Published in the United States, March, 1939–May, 1972*, Kent State University Press, 1972. She is married and has five children.

HAZEL PIERCE teaches English Literature and Popular Literature at Kearney State College, Kearney, Nebraska. She has contributed book reviews to the Science Fiction Research Association *Newsletter*.

MAXINE MOORE is assistant professor in the Department of English at the University of Missouri, Kansas City. Her major interests are American literature and drama. She is also the author of "Asimov, Calvin, and Moses," in Thomas Clareson, ed., *Voices for the Future* (1976) and has published articles in *New Letters* and *Extrapolation*.

CHARLES L. ELKINS is associate professor in the Department of English at Florida International University, Miami. Charles L. Elkins is interested in critical theory, science and the literary imagination, sociology of literature, and popular culture.

DONALD M. HASSLER teaches English at Kent State University, where he is also Director of the Experimental Programs Division in the University's Honors and Experimental College. He has published two books on the eighteenth-century scientist and writer, Erasmus Darwin. He lost his wife, Diana, to a long illness shortly after completing the essay published in this book. He wishes his essay dedicated to the memory of her who also loved speculative fiction.

FERN MILMAN is a graduate student in psychology at the New School for Social Research. Her interests are in developmental and cross-cultural psychology and in science fiction.

DONALD WATT is Professor of English at the State University College of New York at Geneseo. He has edited *The Collected Poetry of Aldous Huxley* (1971), *Aldous Huxley: The Critical Heritage* (1975), and has written articles for several journals, including *Studies in the Novel*, *Review of Existential Psychology*, *Modern Fiction Studies*, and others.

JOSEPH F. PATROUCH is an associate professor in the Department of English at the University of Dayton, Ohio. He is the author of *The Science Fiction of*

Isaac Asimov: A Definitive and Critical Investigation of Isaac Asimov's Science Fiction Novels and Stories (1974). He lives with his wife and four children in Dayton, Ohio.

PATRICIA S. WARRICK is associate professor of English at the University of Wisconsin (Fox Valley) and a critic of contemporary literature with special interests in science fiction. She is also Director of the Interdisciplinary Technology and Culture Program at the University and is currently completing a major study of computers and robots in science fiction. She is the co-editor of *The New Awareness, Psychology through Science Fiction*, and *Political Science Fiction*, and has published articles in *Critique* and *Extrapolation*.

INDEX

absolutism, 69
"Against Stupidity," 170, 171, 173
Aiken, Howard, 175
Aldiss, Brian, 117, 144, 145
alienation, 109, 110
"All the Troubles of the World,"
    23, 126
Amazing Stories, 16
Analog, 49
Analytical Engine, the, 175
Ancients and Moderns, 114, 115
Anderson, Poul, 63
androids, 176
"Anniversary," 55
Arbin, 147
Arcadia, 141
Arkady, 88, 89
Armstrong, Louis, 205
Arvardan, 147
Ash, Brian, 13
Ashe, Milton, 143
Asimov, Isaac, 16, 21, 26, 36, 37,
    59, 61, 62, 64, 96, 146, 161, 172,
    184, 200; anticipating computer
    developments, 174; assumption
    that mankind will not fundamen-
    tally change, 107; attitude to-
    ward fiction, 164; behavioral
    definition of ethics, 191; belief
    that man must not become the
    victim of inertia, 147; career, 13,
    115, 163; on career stages, 113;
    central characters in fiction, 160;
    cerebral quality of fiction, 160;
    character depiction, 102, 103,
    106, 158, 161; comic mode in
    science fiction, 73; concept of

free will, 95; concept of historical
materialism, 100; concept of history, 136; concern for human
problems, 30; cybernetic fiction,
179, 183; definition of science
fiction, 14, 136; detective series,
70; disparity between fiction and
nonfiction, 173; dramatic form of
exposition in fiction, 160; examples of ways technological
change may occur, 131; feelings
about technology, 24; fiction,
174; fiction compared to mainstream fiction, 73; fictional settings, 161; fiction grounded in
science, 188; frame technique,
179; on functions of science
fiction, 15; grasp of computer
theory, 194; grouped with older
wave of science fiction writers,
157; the hero in writing of, 157;
on how he works, 201, idea of
justice in fiction, 47; and human
panic, 68; on human reactions to
stimuli, 109; humor, 56, 185;
imagination, 197; on implementing the ethical use of technology,
191, influence of Sputnik, 149;
knowledge compared with information, 92; life designs, 92;
love interest in mystery stories,
54; love of science, 162, Lucky
Starr juveniles, 37; on man and
machine, 182; alleged Marxian
influence on, 103; narrative point
of view, 160; on natural order,
67; on nature of historical